essential

CAR CARE

essential

CAR CARE

Everything You Need to Keep Your Car on the Road and Running Well

Mike Florence & Rob Blumer

Adams Media
Avon, Massachusetts

Published by Adams Media, an F+W Publications Company
57 Littlefield Street, Avon, MA 02322 U.S.A.
www.adamsmedia.com

ISBN: 1-59869-070-1

Printed by KHL Printing Co Pte Ltd, in Singapore.

J I H G F E D C B A

Technical illustrations by Eric Andrews.

Previously published as The Everything® Car Care Book
Copyright ©2002, F+W Publications, Inc.

Contents

Dedication

To Pat and to Mary Ann for love and encouragement.

Acknowledgments

This book would not have been possible without the help of Cole Blumer, Jerry Dixon, Ron Litton, Rick Lowe, Dan Thompson, and our agent, Mary Sue Seymour.

Introduction

GIVEN THE CHEAP COST OF FUEL, an incredible primary and secondary road system, and the vast expanse comprising the good ol' U.S. of A., it's no wonder that Americans love their cars. Vehicles of all types and dimensions are within the financial reach of most Americans, and we love to get out and go.

There was a time when every red-blooded American boy took pride in keeping his car up, changing belts and hoses, giving the engine an annual tune-up, even tweaking his car's performance to impress the guys. It was a time when every father imparted to his son a bit of auto maintenance knowledge as sort of a rite of passage. But a lot has changed.

Today, most men in their forties and older remember when they actually knew something about the engines of automobiles, when they could look under the hood and tell in an instant the difference between a slant-six and a V-8. They find it embarrassing to be unable to explain to a mechanic what's wrong with their car. Meanwhile, most men and women in their thirties think that any era in which normal people understood their cars must have happened before Columbus discovered the drive-through window.

These days, men and women share a common lack of understanding about their cars. Just what is a dual overhead cam or a multiport injection? Gone are the days of hemishifters, carburetors, and timing guns. Today, onboard computers make minute adjustments to engine performance in an instant, adjustments that a home mechanic couldn't accomplish with a loaded toolbox and a weekend with nothing else to do.

Today's cars don't just frustrate their owners with their complexity. Mechanics get frustrated, too—not by the complicated systems that make up the modern automobile, but by owners who know less than ever about the very machines that give them so much freedom and pleasure. Many owners lack even a rudimentary understanding of basic maintenance.

It doesn't have to be that way. You can be a good mechanic's best assistant, and learn to avoid getting ripped off with unnecessary expenses should a mechanical problem find you in a strange city, uncertain about the character naming a problem and quoting a price, then gleaming at you with steely, shifty eyes.

Neither this book nor the most comprehensive service manual made just for your make and model will give you the power to diagnose and repair everything that could go wrong with your car. But this book will help prevent some things from going wrong, allowing you to troubleshoot potential rusting problems, braking problems, and start-up problems before there is even any trouble.

This book will help you avoid costly repairs. It will teach you which maintenance tasks you should do on your own, which tasks you could do if so inclined, and which you should leave to a pro. Most importantly, this book will help you reduce your fear of your car by helping you give it the treatment it deserves, and helping you converse with your mechanic when the treatment your car deserves exceeds your abilities.

CHAPTER 1

Getting to Know Your Car

Automobiles have evolved from easy fixes to technological marvels. Some drivers remember that in a pinch for gasoline, kerosene and mothballs could fuel a hand-me-down Model T. No more. Now there are computer chips and self-adjusting belt tensioners. Most owners—even those who grew up tinkering with and tuning up their first cars—barely recognize their cars today.

Understanding the Internal Combustion Engine

There are two givens at work in the internal combustion engine:

- Gasoline burns. An internal combustion engine means just that: an engine with something burning—combusting—inside.
- The greater the amount of gasoline surface area, the greater the explosion when air and sparks are added. Gasoline is broken into small particles (sprayed) to increase the power of the explosion, and the more particles there are, the more surface exposure of the gasoline to air occurs in the engine.

> Early gasoline was a by-product of the refining process for kerosene. At first, gasoline was thought to be useless. Nikolaus Otto developed a gasoline motor in the mid-1860s. But it was Otto's chief engineer who later harnessed gasoline power for a vehicle. His name? Gottlieb Daimler, as in Daimler-Chrysler.

Containing the Explosion

Since the engine is an "internal" combustion engine, a container must be found to keep the explosion on the inside. Here's an idea. Put the gasoline in a sturdy metal can and press down a tight-fitting lid. Find a way to introduce a lighted match inside that can, and bam! a contained explosion. Well, nearly contained. The lid will blow off.

So the engine isn't perfect just yet, but the "metal can" idea is an example of how an automobile cylinder works. Instead of a can with the lid sealing the opening from the outside, the cylinder is a "can" constructed of thick and sturdy alloys, with the lid sealing the mouth of the cylinder from the inside, like the lid on a soup can. That way, when the gasoline explodes (the spark plug provides the match-like spark), the lid moves straight up in the identical line of motion every time.

Solving Two Problems

Two problems must be solved to make our engine work. After the explosion, the exhaust must be siphoned off and a new supply of fuel must be introduced. After all, one explosion won't propel a car very far. And there is a second problem, a problem of a different sort: The explosion sends energy in a linear motion, but tires spin around. To restate the tire problem the way Henry Ford, or Ransom Olds, or Walter Chrysler might have said it: The reciprocating (up and down motion) energy produced by the gasoline explosion has to be converted into rotary (round and round motion) energy.

Here's the whole description in car talk: The lid of the can is the piston, the container itself is the engine block, and the hole into which the piston fits is the cylinder. And the energy generated by the explosion must be converted over and over from the reciprocating motion of the piston into the rotary motion of the crankshaft.

FACT

Should your mechanic ever say, "You've got a worn piston," or "Your block is cracked," now you'll know what he means. A worn piston means the "lid" that converts the explosion into usable energy is allowing some of the energy to slip by. A cracked block means the "can" is no longer containing the energy.

Problems Solved: The Auto's Four-Stroke Cycle

At the top of the cylinder are a pair of valves. (Okay, so many modern engines have tweaked this basic arrangement by adding additional valves, but the principle is still the same.) The valve that lets the fuel in is called the "intake" valve. The one that lets out the exhaust, the by-product of the explosion, is called the "exhaust" valve.

A cylinder and its valves manipulate pressure in two ways that are no more sophisticated than what a small child at play might do.

Remember sucking on the end of a Coke bottle until all the air inside was gone and your lips were pulled into the opening? All at once, a small leak developed and a tiny stream of air would rush in, making a squeaky noise and tickling your lips. What you did by drawing all the air out of the bottle was to create a vacuum. When the small leak around your lips inevitably developed, it wasn't the empty bottle drawing air back in, it was the normal pressure of the air around us (15 pounds per square inch) pushing its way back in. And every child at some time discovers the joys of blowing up a balloon and releasing it with the end untied.

The compressed air forces its way out of the opening, the area of least resistance. Part of the genius of the four-stroke engine is its use of pressure and vacuum. Pressure and vacuum are keys to the success of the engine's four strokes: intake, compression, firing (power), and exhaust. See **FIGURE 1-1**.

FIGURE 1-1: Four-stroke engine

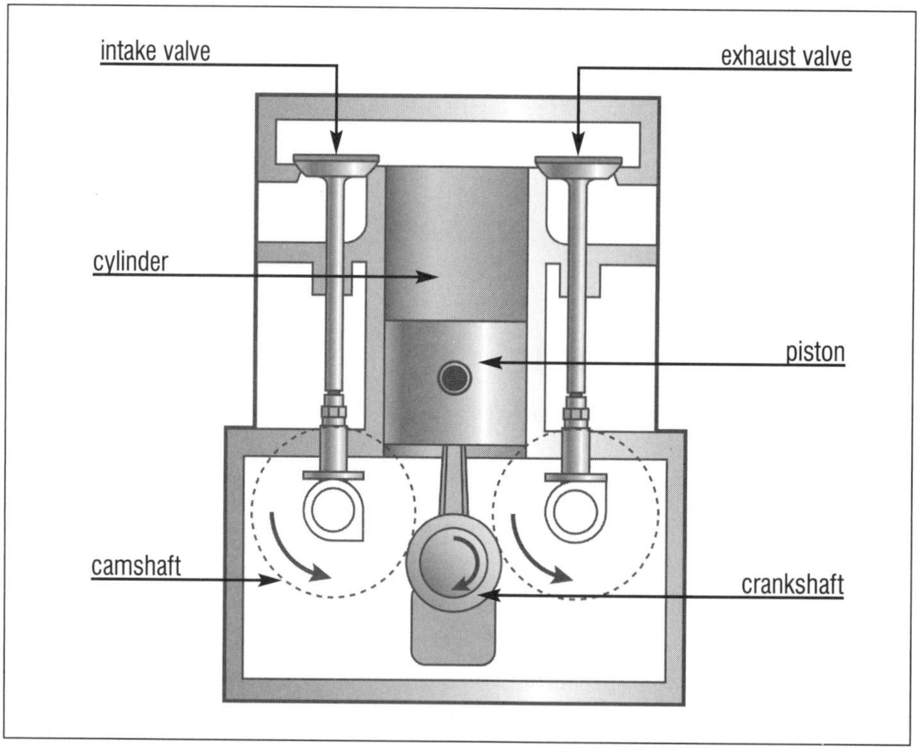

The First Stroke: The Intake Stroke

The first stroke of the cycle is the intake stroke. The crankshaft, located directly below the cylinders on some cars and below and between the cylinders on others, turns and begins to pull the piston down the length of the cylinder. As the piston begins traveling down the cylinder, it forms a vacuum. The intake valve opens when the piston begins its downward movement, and air and fuel are drawn into the void. The engine is designed to time the intake with the downward travel of the piston so that the whole time the piston moves downward, the air/fuel mixture is filling the vacuum in the cylinder. The intake valve shuts when the piston is at the bottom of the cylinder. This is called the intake stroke.

The Second Stroke: The Compression Stroke

The crankshaft continues to spin, forcing the piston to rise, compressing the particles of gasoline and air now in the cylinder from the intake stroke. This compression of the air and fuel mixture will create a more forceful explosion. This is called the compression stroke. The compression stroke ends when the piston has returned to its position at the top of the cylinder.

The Third Stroke: The Firing Stroke

At the finish of the compression stroke, a spark from the spark plug, located near the top of the cylinder where the fuel and air are mixed and compressed, ignites the fuel and air mixture. The fuel explodes and the hot gases expand, forcing the piston down the cylinder (the path of least resistance). This turns the crankshaft and gives the car the power to move forward.

The Fourth Stroke: The Exhaust Stroke

When the piston reaches the bottom of the firing stroke, the exhaust valve opens. And as the crankshaft forces the piston to move back up the cylinder, the exhaust gas is pushed out of the opening covered during the other three strokes by the exhaust valve.

Making the Four Strokes Efficient

If you are not mechanically minded, the preceding four-stroke description probably makes sense to you. But if you like to think about how a thing works, you've probably got a few questions, such as: What opens the valves? And what happens if the valves don't open at exactly the right time?

Simply put, at the end of the crankshaft is a gear. That gear meshes with a gear on another shaft called a camshaft. On the camshaft and beneath each valve is a teardrop-shaped cam lobe. The piston turns (powers) the crankshaft with every firing stroke, and the crankshaft not only powers the car, it also powers the camshaft. And the cam lobes, positioned above each valve, push the valves open each time the camshaft rotates and the cam lobe touches the valve stem. The proper alignment of the gears keeps the engine firing to provide maximum power.

As simple as it all is, it still seems mind-boggling. All that power, all that speed from something as simple as an explosion in a can.

> Most cars built before the 1990s need to have their "timing"—the rhythm of the cams and crankshafts—adjusted once in a while. On some cars you need only a timing light (less than $50) and a screwdriver. Newer cars are computer-controlled and need no adjustments.

The Evolution of Fuel Injection

One feat of the internal combustion engine that hasn't been explained is how it attains and delivers the proper mixture of air and fuel to the cylinder. Until twenty years ago, this procedure was carried out by the carburetors, which had changed very little through the decades. All engines used the same principles. As fuel regulations tightened, requiring greater fuel efficiency and cleaner burning fuel, new ways had to be found to meet the more stringent standards.

FACT

Starting in the late 1970s, a few cars used fuel-injection systems. And all were making the move to computer control. Around the mid-1980s, the last of the computer–controlled carburetors were fazed out, and manufacturers shifted to electronic fuel injection on all vehicles.

These early fuel-injection systems provided an air/fuel mixture much the way a carburetor did. It was a similar system in that fuel was atomized into one carburetor-like opening and was called a "central fuel-injection system" (or a "throttle-body system"). One significant difference between these early fuel-injection systems and a carburetor system was that the fuel injector no longer relied on engine vacuum to pull fuel into the air stream and suck it into the engine.

Fuel injectors inject fuel under pressure. And in the process a finer atomization (mist) is produced, hence better fuel burn, more complete combustion, reduced emissions, and greater economy. Coupled with catalytic converters, early electronic fuel injectors were efficient enough to meet EPA emissions regulations during the 1980s.

As emissions standards tightened again in the 1990s, newer, superior fuel-delivery systems were required, and in the process cars took another step forward in engine efficiency. The newer systems were called multiport injection systems. These systems place an injector on each cylinder, meaning fuel is directly injected into the cylinder, yielding a finer spray of fuel, more complete combustion, reduced emissions, and greater economy.

Recall what you now know about the internal combustion engine. With the carburetor system, when the air intake valve opens, the downward moving piston draws in the air/fuel mixture from the carburetor. The same held true with throttle-body injection. But with multiport injection, a fuel injector sits next to the intake valve of each cylinder. On the downward movement of the piston, only air enters through the intake valve. The atomized fuel is injected separately into the space created by the piston's downward motion.

ALERT!

Government regulations—and the resulting tighter EPA regulations—are one of three prime causes of automotive changes. The other two primary causes are the demands of the buying public and the constant competition among auto manufacturers to produce superior vehicles. The buying public is the clear winner.

Harnessing the Piston's Power: The Transmission

There is more to making a car go than an explosion in the cylinder pushing a piston turning a crankshaft. Some of the earliest backyard mechanics probably learned this lesson the hard way. If there were a direct connection all the way between the explosion in the cylinder to the rolling tires, the engine might never start. The heavy car would already have to be in motion, or there wouldn't be enough energy to get the pistons moving in the first place. Or if an early pioneer parked on a hill and let his horseless carriage roll as he fired it up, it would have stopped dead as soon as he applied the brakes, assuming he had powerful enough brakes to bring it to a halt. Yes, the car needs brakes, but it also needs a way to handle its rotary energy efficiently. It needs a way to transmit the power the engine generates, and to transmit it effectively. A car needs a transmission.

Types of Transmissions

There are two types of transmissions: the manual transmission and the automatic transmission. If you're mashing a clutch with your left foot and changing gears with your right hand, you have a manual transmission. If all your car requires of your feet is that your right foot alternate between the gas pedal and the brake pedal, your car is equipped with an automatic transmission.

Every car company develops its own transmissions. For that reason it is impossible to offer one diagram that shows all the parts of every transmission. But every model of transmission uses the same basic principles to do its job.

E FACT

From time to time a car's transmission becomes an advertised selling feature. In 1931 Chrysler introduced "free-wheeling," a device that allowed drivers to change gears without pressing a clutch pedal. It was a forerunner of the automatic transmission that's used today.

A Transmission Converts Torque

Torque is the power of the twisting action that is sent to the wheels once the reciprocal (up and down motion) energy of the pistons is converted to rotary energy. What the transmission does is increase and decrease the torque according to the demand that the driver places on the automobile. With a manual transmission, the driver selects the amount of torque. With an automatic transmission, the transmission automatically shifts according to demand.

If the car is moving up a steep hill, it requires more torque. If the car is moving on a flat interstate at highway speeds, it requires much less torque. The greater the torque, the greater the pulling power of the engine. Torque, along with engine RPM (revolutions per minute), is how horsepower is measured.

A Transmission Is a Torque Multiplier

The transmission delivers multiplied torque to the propeller shaft. The shaft sends the power to the axle, and the axle to the tires. In low gear and in second gear, an auto transmission is a torque multiplier. Low gear, the gear used when climbing a steep hill, or sometimes when pulling a very heavy load, has a torque multiple of around 3 to 1. Second gear has a torque multiple of about 2 to 1. High gear, used at highway speeds, is a direct drive gear, meaning that there is no torque multiplier. And if you have a car equipped with "overdrive," the torque ratio is in the neighborhood of 0.8 to 1. Every auto transmission establishes its multiples with slight differences, depending on what the designers determine to be the most efficient torque multipliers for a given engine in a specific car.

ALERT!

Highway speeds require less torque conversion from the transmission. If your car is equipped with overdrive, use it on the highway. Properly used, overdrive will reduce engine wear, increase gas mileage, and promote longer engine and transmission life.

Understanding Torque Multiples

Imagine riding a ten-speed bicycle. Your legs are the pistons pumping up and down, the sprocket converts the energy to rotary power, the bicycle chain and the derailleur (the gadget that moves the chain through the gears) are the transmission. If the bike is in first gear—the chain is connected to the smallest front sprocket and to the largest rear sprocket—you may be able to climb even a steep hill and stay seated. Your legs pump rapidly but without a lot of effort, and the bike moves slowly up the hill: high torque, low speed. It is practically impossible to start off in tenth gear and climb the hill. Tenth gear generates low torque but much higher speed for the same amount of leg effort.

The transmission of a car does the same work, but other gears replace the chain. The gears themselves are made of much stronger and heavier metals, and designed to withstand the strains of the automobile's weight and speed.

What happens when pulling a heavy load in too high a gear? Think about peddling a bike up a hill in the wrong gear. If the gear is too high (too little torque), a heavy load strains the engine, causes it to heat up, and over time will reduce engine life.

Steering in the Right Direction

What's left is a means to steer the rolling wheels. There are a variety of steering designs used to control the direction of travel. Among the types are the worm and roller gearbox, and the one most people are apt to have heard of, a rack and pinion gearbox. And just as with the gears of a transmission, steering gearboxes link the amount of turn applied to the steering wheel with the amount of turn taken by the tires in a ratio. Race cars are more direct with steering ratios of 1 to 1, passenger cars less direct, as much as 17 to 1.

Some basic car models come with standard, or manual, steering. That is, all of the power required to turn the steering wheel and aim the car's direction comes from the driver. When the car is at rest with the engine running, the steering can be difficult for a slightly built driver. At highway speeds a driver will probably not notice any difference.

Today most models come with power steering either standard or as an option. With power steering, some of the power from those cylinders and pistons, our original explosions, is converted to make turning the tires easier, especially at low speeds.

> If you're not certain whether your car has manual or power steering, here's an easy way to find out. Turn the car on and leave it in park. If you can place a single finger on the steering wheel and turn that wheel without strain all the way in either direction, you have power steering.

Reviewing the Other Parts of a Car

The idea of an automobile engine is simple, but the demands of car owners make cars complex. Power brakes, power steering, air conditioning, fans to blow cool air in the summer and hot in the winter, lights, power windows, power seats, the CD player. Every system adds strain to the engine directly or indirectly. Making every system work effectively keeps auto engineers in business. Every new system or added convenience keeps the auto buyer begging for more, yet feeling more helpless when repair work becomes necessary.

The following chapters focus on particular areas within the car that you (or someone you hire) can maintain and repair.

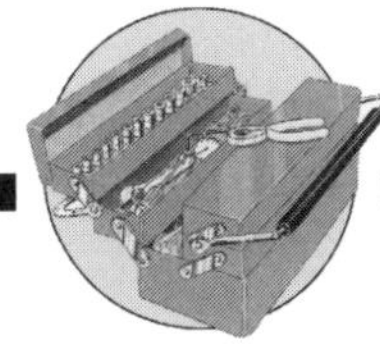

CHAPTER 2

Investing in Car-Care Tools

Every automobile owner needs some tools. There are some basic instruments that are necessary just to keep everything under the hood and in the passenger compartment tight. Others are less of a necessity but can be useful to own. This chapter helps you figure out exactly what you will need.

Checking Out Basic Tools

The amount of vibration to which a car is subjected is quite remarkable. Add in the constant pumping and spinning of the engine, the extremes in temperature, and sudden changes in road condition from smooth to washboard, and it's a wonder the car doesn't shake itself apart. It doesn't take expensive tools to keep the car "tight": hoses in place and doorknobs doing their jobs. Cheap tools will work okay, but where tools are concerned, you get what you pay for.

If you plan to do any of your own work, at a minimum, you'll want to obtain the tools listed in this section.

FACT

In the 1960s, the basic tool, apart from a wrench, a screwdriver, and a timing light, was a baseball bat. Sometimes when the battery seemed dead, you could tap on the posts and that 1965 Mustang would fire; when the alternator belt loosened, a bat wedged between the engine and alternator provided the right amount of tension to tighten the bolt.

A Set of Screwdrivers

Screwdrivers come in two types: flat head and Phillips head. The flat head has a straight blade that fits in screws that have one slit across the center of the screw head. The Phillips head screwdriver has a crossed blade that fits into a screw that has a crossed slit in the head.

Screwdrivers are essential. Many air-filter housings are held on by screws. If ever you change your own oil, it's good to check the air filter at the same time. You'll need a screwdriver to open the air filter housing. All the clamps under the hood, the clamp between the air breather and the engine, and clamps on the hoses use a flat blade fitting. Inside the car, door panels are held on with trim screws. These and some window cranks are held in place by Phillips screws. The dashboard is held in place by Phillips screws and some plastic clips.

ALERT!

Keep a set of screwdrivers that contains both flat and Phillips heads in various lengths. If the screwdriver must fit in a small space, you'll need one with a short, stubby shaft. If it must slip in a narrow space with no place for your hand, you'll need one with an extra-long shaft.

A Set of Torx Bits or Torx Head Screwdrivers

Newer cars are using a new style of opening on some screws. The opening is shaped like a fat star, called a torx head. They are designed to allow for more torque (more twist) to be applied to a screw with less likelihood of a screwdriver slipping. There may be no other place save the family car where you'll use torx bits, but if your car is new or nearly new, you may need a torx bit in the interior.

A High-Quality Adjustable Wrench

An adjustable wrench should be next on your list of acquisitions. Anywhere there is a bolt, you can apply an adjustable wrench. All right, there are some spaces where one might not fit, but it is a handy tool with many uses. If you do invest in an adjustable wrench, make sure to get a good one. An adjustable wrench has a screw-type mechanism that you work with the thumb to make it fit tight around a bolt. With cheaper ones, that tightening mechanism seems to work itself a little looser with each turn, until the wrench slips and a pair of catastrophes happen all at once: the head of the bolt gets ever-so-slightly rounded, so you won't be able to grip it with a wrench; and you'll scrape your knuckles when the wrench slips. Better adjustables hold to the adjusted position more reliably.

A Pair of Vise-Grip Pliers

It is truly a tough call to say which of these first sets of single tools is the most valuable. If you own a pair of vise-grip pliers, you already understand their value. If not, here is why you need them. Vise-grip pliers

(Vise Grip is also a name brand) grip anything in a vise-like grip. There is an adjustable screw-type element in the bottom of one piece of the handle that allows the mechanic to open or narrow the gap between the jaws so that when the jaws are locked into place, the object clamped in the vise cannot move. Vise-grips are terrific when dealing with rounded bolts.

A Set of Wrenches

There are extensive sets that contain rarely used wrenches and small sets that seek to anticipate the most common bolt size a person is apt to run into. The advantage of a set of wrenches over an adjustable wrench is that matching the proper-size wrench to the proper-size bolt results in less chance of rounding the edges of that bolt. Sometimes, though, unless you have spent a bundle on a huge set, you will find that you need the adjustable wrench.

When buying a set of wrenches for your car, be certain which type of set you need to purchase: standard or metric. Imports are easy—they always need metric wrenches—but even cars made in the United States usually require some metric wrenches. Unfortunately, practically every domestic automobile currently made requires some metric and some standard wrenches.

A Ratchet Set

Ratchet sets usually come with both standard and metric fittings. Be certain you are getting what you need. Ratchets have the advantage of allowing the mechanic to work a bolt loose or tighten a bolt in a very small space. The ratchet action allows the mechanic to use a short back and forth action of the hand to tighten or loosen a bolt. It can speed the job of tightening and loosening.

> The tools listed in this section are the bare-bones tools. Throw out the costs of the absolute cheapest and also the highest-quality varieties, and the tools described can be acquired for around $45.

Adding Battery-Care Tools

With just a bit more effort and not much more expense, you can keep your car's battery (see Chapter 6) in tiptop shape with a few tools. The lure of adding the battery to the easy tasks of keeping things tight is that you may be able to avoid being stranded because the heart of your electrical system went dead. To do the battery job thoroughly, you'll need one tool, two sprays, and a tester.

The One Battery Tool

Terminal cleaners come in a couple of different styles, depending on the design of the battery in your car. What these cleaners do is scrape away a thin layer of metal from the terminal posts and from the battery cables to ensure excellent contact between them. Don't worry about sparking. Battery terminals are soft lead, so there is no danger of sparking during the cleaning process.

As long as you do not see corrosion, there is little need to remove the battery cables from the battery and clean them. But corrosion can spring up quickly. If it does, you'll be prepared.

The Two Sprays

One of the sprays will clean corrosion from the battery cables. It is possible to scrape the corrosion from the cables, but often the corrosion gets in between the bundle of copper wires that make up the battery cable, making it difficult to clear away all corrosion. The cable cleaner spray will penetrate better, more effectively preventing corrosion's return.

The second is a spray can of corrosion prevenetive. Once the battery and cables are corrosion free, reattach the cables to the terminals and spray. This will seal out moisture and air, and help maintain the good contact with the cables a battery needs to remain healthy. For this part of the procedure, Vaseline will work, too, but it is a bit messy and will have to be reapplied from time to time, since it tends to dissipate. The spray is more convenient. It behaves almost like a paint, forming a thin, long-lasting protective shell.

A Battery Tester

The battery tester comes with a pair of cables and clamps, one cable and clamp for the positive terminal and one for the negative terminal. Once hooked to the battery, a look at the scale on the tester will indicate whether the voltage in the battery is normal or low. A tester will also have a load capability, meaning that the tester can actually put a load on the battery (i.e., make the battery work as if starting the car) to see if the battery will hold voltage.

There will be a switch on the tester for loading the battery. The load test will indicate the reserve strength of the battery. For example, if you load-test your car's battery and the voltage drops from 12 volts to 7 volts, the battery is weak. But if you load-test the battery for ten to fifteen seconds and the voltage doesn't drop below 9.5 or 10 volts, the battery is strong.

If the battery is weak, you'll be able to take it to a service station or a repair shop, or often even a parts store, and have it charged. Then if the battery won't hold good voltage after a second load test, you know the battery is weak, and you can replace it before you wind up stuck in the middle of nowhere.

FACT

Want to know how much battery tools will cost? The tool total for this section tallies a maximum of $36. Add this to the basic tools, and you'll ring up a grand total in the neighborhood of $80 or $90.

Buying Oil- and Coolant-Change Tools

Given the tools compiled in the preceding sections, you can almost do your own oil changes (see Chapter 5), and can definitely maintain or change (when necessary) your coolant (see Chapter 7). But there are a few additional tools that will make the jobs easier on some vehicles, while on other vehicles they'll be a necessity.

A Droplight and Safety Glasses

You can never have too much light under the hood. A droplight is a must if you want to be able to see everything lurking in the dark corners of your engine. You can buy either an incandescent droplight (for under $10) or a fluorescent droplight (for right around $40), but the latter is recommended, because the bulb stays cool. A fluorescent light reduces the danger of a bulb break as the result of a spray striking the glass.

Everyone is much more safety-conscious these days. Safety glasses come in a variety of styles, and reliable pairs can be purchased for just a few dollars. Some are tinted to reduce glare when used in certain environments. You only have one pair of eyes.

An Oil Filter Wrench

FIGURE 2-1: Using an oil filter wrench

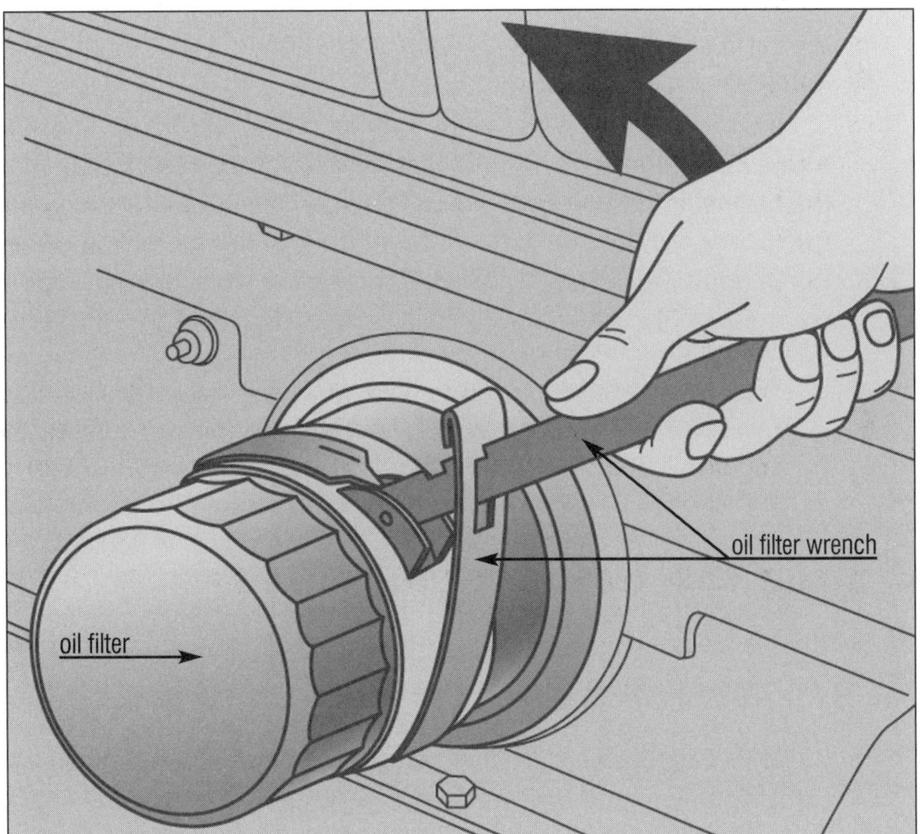

Unless you are an Olympic lifter, buy an oil filter wrench (see **FIGURE 2-1**). And be sure to purchase the correct size wrench for the filter in your car. The filter wrench provides all the leverage necessary to make changing the oil filter a breeze. Occasionally someone will say it is not necessary to change the filter every time you change oil, and if you don't have an oil filter wrench, that wrongheaded thought might prove tempting. Think of it like this: If the oil is dirty, so is the filter. Besides, filters are cheap. And so is a good oil filter wrench.

No, don't buy a cheap filter wrench. For $2 to $4 more, get a good one. You may ruin a cheap wrench in just one oil change.

A Drain Pan

It is illegal to dump motor oil, coolant, or any other automotive fluid on the ground. And it is bad for the environment, too. Many parts stores, some service stations, and some repair shops will accept the used fluids from your car.

Some drain pans come with funnels built in. Some are even designed with a wide mouth on top to catch the fluid, a screw-on lid to seal the large opening for transport, and a smaller, capped, pour-type opening for eliminating the fluid once you have taken it to the collection center.

Certainly you can save $7 or $8 and make your own. But remember, many cars hold five quarts of oil and several gallons of coolant.

E ALERT!

Don't expect that your favorite parts store or service station or even your repair shop will take your used oil or coolant without first asking. This seems to be the case in smaller communities more often than larger ones. Larger communities do have collection centers, usually plenty of them.

Oil Dry (Glorified Kitty Litter)

Spills happen. This product makes cleanup much less messy. It comes in fifty-pound bags and costs under $10. Whether the spill under the car is oil or coolant, pour out the granulated product, allowing it time to absorb the spill, and sweep it up.

In a pinch, some kitty litters will do a pretty good job, too.

Jack Stands and a Hydraulic Jack

On some vehicles, a person can wiggle up underneath the car, position the drain pan, remove the oil plug, drain the oil, even reach the oil filter without ever jacking up the front end of the car. Some other cars allow easy access to the oil filter by just leaning over the engine. The same can be true on some vehicles for draining the coolant and replacing old radiator hoses. But on many cars the clearance with the ground is so low it is nearly impossible to work from underneath.

FIGURE 2-2: Jack stands and a hydraulic jack

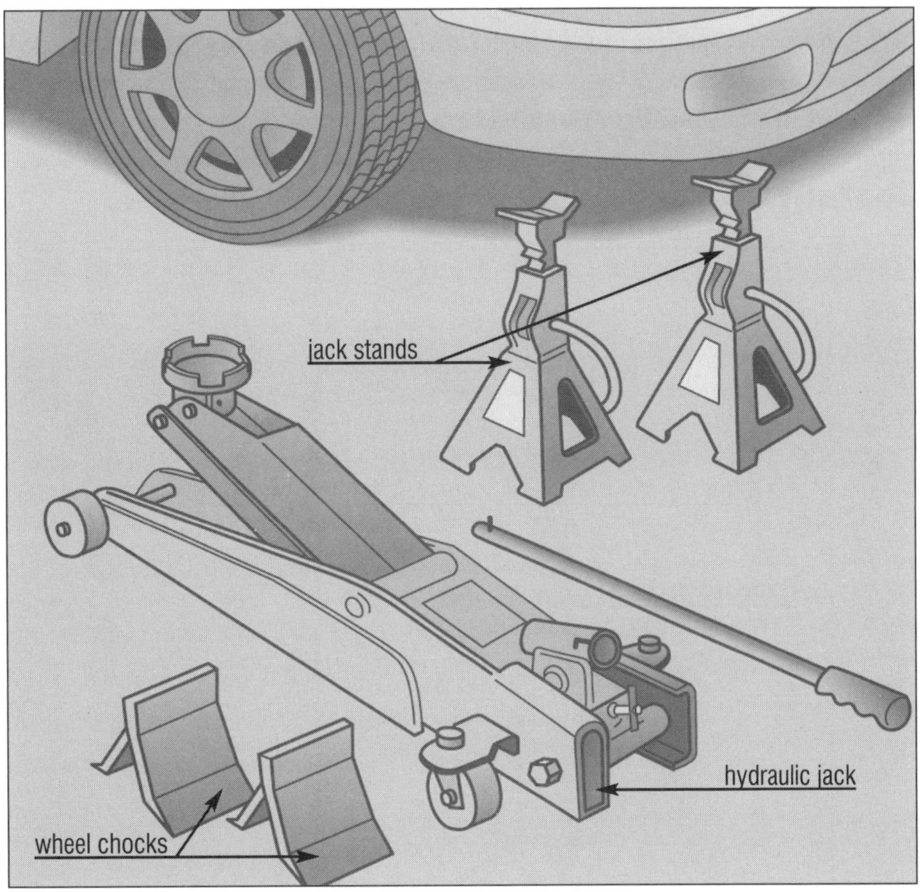

Even if you have found that with effort and shallow breathing you can stay beneath your car long enough to make it feasible to take care of your own oil changes and coolant system, you may find the time involved drops dramatically when you use jack stands.

Here's a general rule for purchasing both jack stands and hydraulic jacks (shown in **FIGURE 2-2**). Always buy a set rated to hold more weight than you'll ever put on them. For most cars a set of jack stands (that's two of them) rated at two tons is plenty. The same is true with a hydraulic jack. A jack rated at two tons could lift most cars completely off the ground. Jacks vary greatly in price, from very cheap (around $15) to expensive. Don't buy the cheapest or the most expensive kind for home use. You can find good jacks ranging from around $40 to $150. For jobs that will leave some of your car's tires on the ground, you will need wheel chocks, which are placed on either side of the tire to prevent it from rolling (also see **FIGURE 2-2**).

Coolant Tester

FIGURE 2-3: Coolant testers

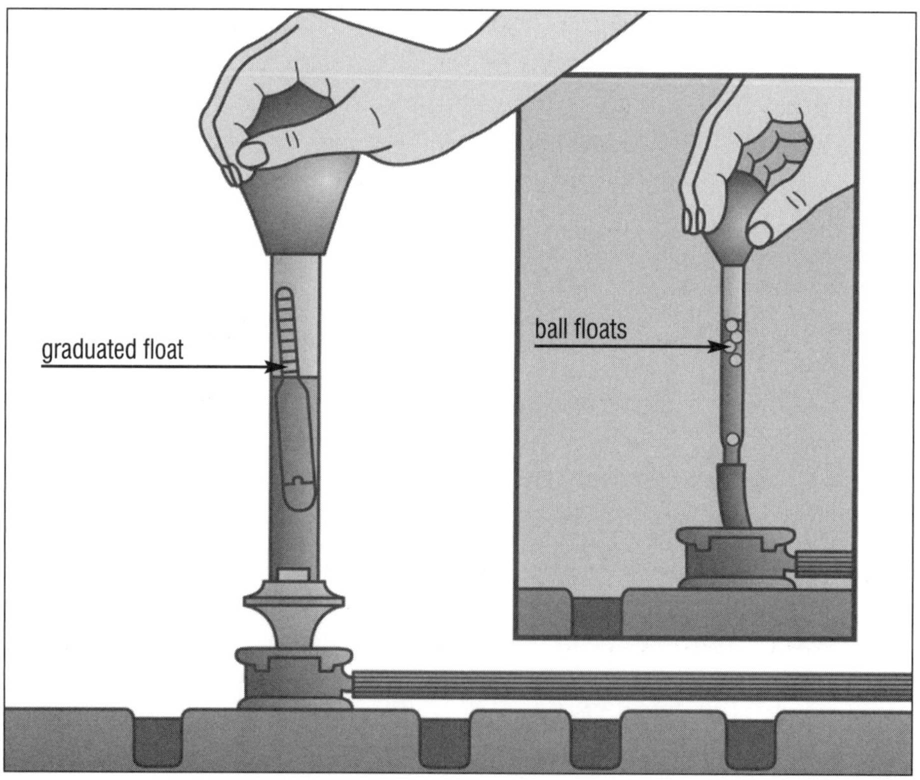

You won't need to use a coolant tester more than a couple times a year, but testers are cheap. You can buy one for $2 to $4, and it will tell you what you need to know. Most of the cheap testers use floating balls; those that have a graduated float are better (see **FIGURE 2-3**). The number of balls that are floating after the coolant has been siphoned into the tester indicates the coolant's strength: the heat within the engine that the solution in your car's radiator can withstand, and the coldest outdoor temperature to which it can be subjected without danger of freezing.

The automotive world is undergoing some shifts in coolant types. You will need to know what coolant type (not brand, type) your car uses—it'll be in the owner's manual, or the dealer or your mechanic can tell you. Testers are coolant-type specific. Be sure you have the right tester.

A Grease Gun

Maybe you need one, maybe you don't. Most late-model cars don't need to be greased anymore. The systems are sealed in most new cars. It used to be that with every oil change, the technician pumped a little grease into the grease fittings. Have a mechanic tell you about your car or pickup and point out to you the grease fittings, if there are any. If your vehicle does have them, purchase a small grease gun (under $10). Small will be perfect for someone maintaining just one car or three.

Getting Tools to Rotate Your Tires

If you plan on rotating your own tires (see Chapter 4), you'll need to lift all four wheels off the ground. Don't try to save money by dividing the weight of your car by 4 and figuring that a half-ton car (your car probably weighs less) divided by 4 equals a weight per jack stand of one-half ton. In the first place, the weight of an automobile is not evenly distributed over all four wheels. In the second place, is your life worth more than the cost of a half-ton jack stand under each wheel? Buy heavier than you need for an extra margin of safety. And always work on a hard surface: Never roll your car into the yard and place it on a jack stand in the grass.

The same is true with the hydraulic jack. Buy heavier than you need and be confident that it will always do the job.

If you are going to rotate your own tires, purchase a four-way lug wrench. The lug wrench is x-shaped, and each end of the wrench is designed for a different-sized lug, handy if you own multiple cars. Expect to pay from $5 to $7.

FACT

Ramps are designed so that a car may be driven into an elevated position up the steep incline. If you opt to use ramps instead of a hydraulic jack and jack stands, put the car in gear (manual transmission) or in park (automatic). Be certain the emergency (hand) brake is activated. And chock the wheels still on the ground to prevent the car from rolling off the ramps.

Collecting a Tool Kit for Your Car

So you've got everything you need to take good care of your car at home in the garage, but what happens if something goes wrong on the road? True, sometimes there will be absolutely nothing you can do, not even if you were surrounded by the tools that you have collected to do a good job of car care and maintenance.

But often there is something that you could do if you just had a few tools. And sometimes a little forethought can save a lot of time sitting and waiting for help to arrive.

Purchase a small toolbox and stock it with the following tools:

- **Adjustable wrench:** Not a cheap one, a good one that will fit practically every bolt.
- **Two screwdrivers:** One flat head, one Phillips.
- **A pair of vise-grip pliers:** They hold onto anything.
- **A combo set of fuses:** No matter the size of fuse that may go out, the kit will have one to replace it.
- **Electrical tape:** Use it to reinsulate an electrical wire and temporarily reduce or eliminate the leak from a radiator hose.

- **Jumper cables:** You just never know!
- **Rags:** Good for cleanup and for gripping hot hoses.
- **Waterless hand cleaner.**

You may hope to never need this kit, but won't it be nice to know it's there?

Staying Safe

All roadside emergencies don't take place on bright sunny days. Perhaps when traveling down a dark road or when stuck in a line of interstate traffic at night, you've whizzed right by someone changing a tire who doesn't notice how close they are coming to . . . denting your fender.

The following are some items to add to your car kit. Not one of them will help you do a roadside job faster, but any one of them may ensure that you are able to complete the job.

- **Flares:** They are extremely bright and signal unsuspecting drivers to slow down and watch for a dangerous situation. Never, never strike a flare if you smell a fuel leak.
- **Flashlight:** Good for seeing under the hood and for signaling to passersby.
- **Safety triangles:** Large trucks stopped on the side of the road use them. Space a couple of those reflective triangles behind your car, and the drivers in oncoming vehicles will be more alert.
- **Safety vest:** You may have seen nighttime runners light up when your headlights bounced beams off their vests. Wearing one while inches from the road just may prevent someone from hitting you, or prevent a driver from suddenly swerving into another lane and causing an accident when surprised by your proximity.
- **Flashing strobe light:** Perhaps waterproof flares are enough, but a battery-powered flashing strobe is sure to attract attention and alert unsuspecting traffic.

CHAPTER 3

Cleaning Your Car

The simplest place to start taking care of your car is to clean and maintain it. If you're just dipping your toes into the cold waters of car maintenance, start here. Not only will you feel better about taking care of your car, but you'll also get the best bang for your buck at selling time.

Giving Your Car a Good Basic Wash

Every truly clean car has it—a shine and luster that glistens in the sun. It doesn't matter whether you want to turn heads or not; an automobile dripping with color and sparkle is just plain beautiful.

Before adding that showroom shine to your car, it must be properly washed. This section gives you the lowdown.

Starting with a Cool Car

Heat is an enemy to the post-washed appearance of your car. Heat will cause the soap to dry onto the surface, leaving streaks and spots. It aids in the formation of water spots. And you will begin to work too fast as you become aware that the car is drying before you have finished washing your targeted area.

Wash indoors, if you can. If your garage isn't properly set up with the drainage to do this, plan to wash your car in the shade. Just by starting with a cool car, you're already on the way to a splendid result.

Hosing the car down first helps ensure that the car will be cool when you begin to wash. It also helps loosen dirt. After hosing the car, hose inside each of the wheel wells, and hose the tires and underneath the car, too.

Cleaning the Wheel Wells

Nearly all automatic car washes have pressurized sprays that are designed to spray around the tire areas. Some even have sprays that are angled so that as the washer machinery passes by the car, or the car rolls slowly past the various spraying attachments, soapy water is forced into the wheel well area.

If your car never leaves the highway, and never squishes through thick mud in a puddle, that may be adequate. But if you do occasionally roll through mud, or if you live where road salts are used in the winter, a complete cleaning of your wheel wells is a good idea. That can only happen when you do the job yourself or when you pay someone to hand-wash the vehicle.

FACT

If you can make it part of your wash cycle to include a preservative every time you wash, you car's appearance will stay tiptop for many years. Avoid products that aren't clear in color (they're milky), because with prolonged use, you may begin to notice a slightly white tint building up on your car's rubber and vinyl surfaces.

Thoroughly Cleaning the Entrance of the Car

Whether seeking to make a good impression at trade-in time or just wanting to clean up the car completely, don't forget to open the doors and clean the entire entrance way. Clean all the surfaces, metal and plastic, with soap and water, and once the car is dry, treat the plastic surfaces with a preservative.

Raising the Hood and Trunk and Cleaning Around the Openings

Leaving the edges beneath the hood and trunk wet and uncleaned, without at least a rubdown to wipe off surface dirt around the edges, may cause water from a washing to loosen the dirt and send it dribbling down the freshly washed car. It will add only a minute to a wash job, but it can make a lot of difference, especially on light-colored cars.

Cleaning the Pedals

Sorry, but these parts are going to show more wear eventually, no matter what you do. They can be cleaned with soapy water, and you may decide to use a stiff brush, especially if grit and small pebbles get trapped in the pedal surfaces.

Polishing the Windows

What kind of cleaning product you should use on the glass in your automobile depends on the glass in your car. If your car came equipped with factory-installed tinted glass, practically every product for glass cleaning is fine. With factory-tinted glass, the tint and the glass are one. But if you opted for tint after purchasing the car, the tint is a coating on the glass. Any product for glass cleaning that contains ammonia is bad for automobile glass that has been coated to achieve tint. Ammonia will turn coated glass purple.

Why do people use newspapers to clean car windows?
Newspaper is terrific for car windows. It really does help prevent streaking. But watch where you set down the wet newspaper, since the wet ink will come off.

Drying the Car with a Chamois

Most automated car places save you time and money by attempting to blow-dry your car when the wash is finished. Usually it takes a little more blowing in order to dry the car than the cost of the automated service allows. At a few places there are workers who do rub the car down; fewer still do the job effectively.

You can expect more from a hand wash car service. Most often, after washing the car, the car will be rubbed down with a chamois. Certainly you can cut corners at home, or you can do the job completely, but this step begins the process of preparing the surface of the car for a lustrous appearance. Consider wiping the water away with the chamois a mini–buff job.

Waxing for the Fabulous Wet Look

Washing alone doesn't complete the car-cleaning process. Washing is a great start, and waxing is the great finish. There are a variety of products on the market that will work. With experience you'll find the type of product that suits you best. Some of them are more convenient to use, and faster to apply and to buff out, liquids mostly. Some of these you simply wipe off. Others require a bit more effort. Most of these are paste waxes that contain carnauba wax.

Applying and Removing Carnauba Wax

The directions on the can of wax are always the place to start. As with most projects, people can reduce potential complications to a minimum by following directions. These points of emphasis are most likely built into the instructions of every brand containing carnauba. Keep them in mind and you will achieve long-lasting protection for your car and the fabulous wet look:

- **Start with a clean car.** Yes, wax does help clean an automobile, but for the best finish, wash first.
- **Make certain the car is cool.** A hot car will "bake" the wax, making it extremely difficult to remove.
- **Work small sections at a time.** Waxing a section of the car the size of the sections described for washing may be too large, even for some people with plenty of experience. You may discover you can work larger sections . . . great. Better to expand the section size as you go along than to apply the wax to too large a section at the start.
- **Apply the wax in a circular motion with overlapping small circles.** This helps ensure an even finish.
- **Allow the wax to haze over.** This is how the wax works. When the wax turns slightly milky in color and does not wipe off with a light swipe of the finger, the wax is ready to buff off.
- **Use a buffing cloth or a cotton T-shirt, not a terry cloth towel, and buff away the milky colored wax.** This advice comes from an experienced detailer with three decades of experience. Try a section with a towel and another section with the recommended cloth, and see if it makes a difference to your eye.

Just as with washing the car, keep the car in the shade. It will help prevent a "baking" effect. However, with waxing, if you have lost your shade, just drive the car into the garage and finish it. Or if the day is nice and you can find a lovely place where the shade will last, go park under the trees and wax away. Sure, driving a few miles or even a few dozen miles will cause the car to pick up a small amount of grime, but wax cleans, too. The drive won't make any noticeable difference in the shine or in the protection you are applying to your car's finish.

If your car has a good wax job on it, the next time you wash, as you start the final rinse, remove the nozzle and rinse with the water bubbling gently from the hose. You may find that your wax pushes the water off, leaving you much less car to dry.

Using an Old Toothbrush

You may decide that you'd prefer to wax or polish with a liquid and do the process three or four times a year, rather than use a carnauba product and wax only twice a year. With the liquids, less of the shining material will end up glaring white in the seams.

To finish the wax job, be certain you get rid of all of the hazy buildup. Take a toothbrush and rub away all the dried white wax from the seams and from the black rubber around the windows. If your car has a chrome plate proudly announcing where it was purchased or its distinguished make or model, you may find the toothbrush handy for lifting the dried wax from the loops and the spaces between the letters.

The last step in this process, of course, is to step back and admire the work you've done . . . and pray for an extended period of sunshine.

ALERT!

Beware of applying wax to a hot car or to too large a section. You may discover that you don't have the stamina to rub and rub and rub away the hardened carnauba. No, the finish isn't ruined, but it may require a power buffer.

Cleaning the Car's Carpet

There is no interior surface in an automobile that is forced to stand up to such intense and constant abuse as the carpet. People who are fussy about the carpet at home will enter and exit an automobile without a thought for what their feet are tracking in, and then grind mystery grit and goo into the car's carpet.

There are two different cleaning methods you will need to consider. Neither of which is daunting to a detailer, but the second, and most thorough, may seem downright overwhelming if you've never done it before (and you probably haven't).

> Stains from coffee, tea, chocolate milk, orange juice, and blood can all be treated in the same manner: First treat the stain with Woolite carpet cleaner. If some stain remains, treat with Spray Power, a product made by Crown. (Always follow package instructions.)

Shampooing the Car's Carpet

Yes, you can use a product designed for the household for this job. Make certain it is a heavy-duty carpet shampoo. The carpet in your car is rugged stuff. And all the grime, mud, sand, road salt, and oil, the sticky gross things that your shoes deliver straight to its surface, accumulate in the fibers and settle down to the rubber matting. That carpet is tough, but the unseemly substances your shoes have ground into it are tough to remove, so you'll need a product with cleaning chemicals as tough as the carpet is designed to withstand.

There are carpet cleaners and shampoos designed to do the job in your car. Try these products rather than ones by the same companies but designed for the home.

Follow the directions on the package. Briefly, those directions will be similar to this: Spray the carpet; let it sit, allowing the foam to soak into the fibers; then take a stiff brush (absolutely no metal bristles) and scrub the area, and blot up the cleaning residue with a cotton towel.

Going Beyond Shampoo Clean

There is an even more effective cleaning technique for automobile carpet. Take the carpet completely out of the car and clean it. No, not just the floor mats, which you should remove and clean separately whenever you shampoo the carpet. Remove the entire carpet. The job is either easier than you might think or every bit the hassle you can envision. To get the carpet out, you'll have to unbolt the seats and remove them. There are four bolts beneath each of the front seats. Yes, even power seats can be removed. Beneath each power seat you'll find a plug. Unplug it. And remove the seat belts.

Once you get the carpet out of the car, hang it over a fence, or better still, a small swing set, the kind with a frame shaped like the letter *A*. Follow the directions on the cleaning product you choose, and then take a water hose with a nozzle you can adjust to a firm spray, and hose it down. This may seem harsh or damaging, but remember, automobile carpet is tough, tough stuff. It has to be.

Hanging the carpet over an A-framed swing set helps promote drying. The carpet will dry pretty quickly; if cleaned in the morning in the garage, by late afternoon it will be dry. If you notice that the lower edges of the carpet are slow to dry, use an air hose or a blow dryer, taking care about wet floors and electrical appliances. If the weather is nice, wash the carpet outside and it will dry even faster.

FACT

Taking out the carpet can seem an imposing job, and it will be the first time, should you decide to try it. Of course, you can always leave the headaches and the hassle to a professional detailer. An experienced detailer will have the carpet out of your car in around twenty minutes.

Cleaning Your Car's Seats

Since you have to detach the seats of the car to remove the carpet, you may as well deep-clean the seats, too. The kind of cleaning you can give automobile seats once they have been removed from the car can be dramatically greater than the cleaning you can give them while they're still bolted inside the car.

Deep-Cleaning Car Seats

Just as with the carpet, most owners are far more likely to use products that will clean the surface cloth seats while they remain fixed in place inside the car rather than take the pains to remove the seats and clean them even more thoroughly.

And cleaning just the surface of cloth seats in a car will make for a better appearance than never cleaning them at all. But lest you think it overkill to remove the seats for a complete cleaning, here's what will happen when you leave the seats in place and clean just the surfaces.

E ALERT!

Treat water-based paint stains with Spray Power. Treat oil-based paint with lacquer thinner, then with Woolite carpet cleaner to help recondition cloth. For ink stains, blot right away, then apply hair spray and scrub with a stiff brush. Wash with Woolite carpet cleaner to recondition the cloth.

Seats have foam backing beneath the cloth. Over time, most of the dirt works below the cloth and into the foam. When the top of the seat is cleaned, the upholstery looks terrific. But in a short amount of time, the seats have a dirty appearance once again. This happens for two reasons. First, practically any cleaning product you choose to use on car seats will dampen the seats as part of the cleaning action. That moisture will seep beneath the cloth and into the foam, loosening dirt in the foam and causing it to work its way back into the seat cloth. Second, even after all the moisture has dried, the action of sitting and wiggling, pressing the cloth into the dirty foam beneath, will cause the deep dirt to rise to the surface of the cloth. The car seat looked clean, and the surface of the cloth definitely was clean, but if you are particular about your car's appearance, you'll be doing the surface cleaning over and over and over, because the dirt was never cleaned out to begin with.

You can clean the cloth car seats with the same cleaner you used on the carpets. Or find a milder product, if that makes you feel more comfortable. After scrubbing according to the directions on the product, hose down the seats. That's right, hose them down and let them dry.

Some seat covers can be taken off. They can be thrown into the washing machine, leaving the foam beneath the seat completely exposed for visual inspection. If the foam is dirty, clean it, too.

E ALERT!

Oh, no! You've just deep-cleaned the car seats, and then the kids let the family dog in the car. There's dog hair everywhere. And the shop vac just won't pull it out. Relax. The best tool for removing pet hair . . . a lint roller: you know, with the sticky tear-away covers.

Spot-Cleaning Car Seats

Light-colored seats present more of a problem when spot-cleaning than dark-colored seats. On light-colored material, getting it wet with cleaner will mean that when it dries, the seat will be left with a ring around the once dirty spot. If the upholstery in your car is light-colored and you need only to spot-clean a seat, it is best to clean the whole bottom of the seat (or the entire back of the seat, if that is where the spot is located). On dark-colored upholstery, you can try to spot-clean, but it is best just to take the extra couple of minutes and do the whole thing.

E FACT

When someone in your carpool spills coffee on your thoroughly cleaned seats, use a product designed for cleaning auto upholstery. Follow directions and repeat up to three times until the suds and the cloth come up clean. Once the suds stay white, the foam rubber beneath is also clean. No coffee stains will re-emerge from the bottom up next time a little moisture dampens the foam.

Discovering One Detailer's Secret for Leather Seats

Cleaning leather seats means using products designed for that purpose. Several companies make products for cleaning leather seats.

Experiment until you find the product you are most comfortable using. Always follow directions.

Leather is expensive, but it smells terrific and looks great in a car. And to keep it from cracking, keep it clean and treated with the right products. If your leather interior is extremely dirty, here's one expert's secret for doing a fabulous job.

Put a few drops of mild dishwashing liquid in a bucket of water as warm as you can stand. Take the leather cleaner, a cleaner designed for use inside a car, and apply it to the seat as indicated by the directions on the package. Dip a brush with plastic bristles in the sudsy water and gently scrub. Wipe down the seats until they are completely dry—completely dry. Use plenty of dry towels, or the leather will spot. Then wash the leather again, this time without the sudsy water and the brush, using the leather cleaner only.

Finally, condition the leather with a leather conditioner.

ALERT!

Use your own judgment about the types and styles of brushes and cleaning cloths you want to use inside a car. But there are always nooks and crannies that defy your most earnest cleaning attempts. Consider purchasing a detailer's brush. On one end is a small dusting device, at the other a natural bristle brush.

Cleaning and Treating Vinyl and Plastic

It is always easiest and safest to use products designed for the purpose intended. There are products made expressly for vinyl and plastic in cars: Spray Power is a terrific cleaner for vinyl and plastic. An excellent rule to follow whenever cleaning any part of a car is to make certain the car is cool before cleaning. A hot interior is prone to spotting, no matter the cleaning products you use.

Once cleaned, treat the vinyl and plastic parts to a spray of preservative. Preservatives do much more than improve the appearance of the plastic parts. They actually retard the effects of heat, cold, moisture, and dryness. If you keep a car a long time, you will add trade-in value by keeping all the plastic and vinyl and rubber parts vibrant and supple.

And don't forget the shifter boot, the rubber sleeve on the gearshift of a car equipped with a manual transmission. Those rubber boots wear out with use. But a regular treatment with a preservative (a tire conditioner is excellent for this job) will help the shifter boot last indefinitely. If the boot is leather, treat it properly, too.

Maintaining the Rubber Around Doors and Windows

The rubber materials that seal the weather out are the often-forgotten parts of car care. Use a tire conditioner on these parts. The spray-and-wipe types of tire conditioners, rather than the foam-and-wait types of conditioners, are best for this job. Tire conditioners do more than just make a car's tires look black. They condition the rubber, too. A tire conditioner will keep the rubber soft, prevent it from drying out, and has the added benefit of helping prevent a car door from sticking on a winter morning after a long overnight rain has frozen in falling temperatures.

> The key to preserving the life and looks of a car's interior is consistency. Most car-care products are designed to treat and preserve various materials of your car with prolonged use. This allows the preservative ingredients time to bond with the material. Using a product only once a year will not do the trick.

CHAPTER 4

Taking Care of Your Tires

Tires are the most crucial system of the automobile. That may sound far-fetched with all the wires and gizmos under the hood, but it is true. If something goes wrong with the engine while the car is in motion, it will coast to a stop. But if a tire fails on the highway, the odds are slightly less in your favor. A blowout can mean serious control problems.

Purchasing New Tires with Confidence

Before we talk tire care, let's begin with new tires. There are basically two types of tires on the market: bias tires and radial tires. Bias tires have layered cords that crisscross. Some bias tires have belts over the cords. However, most tires sold in the United States today are radials. Virtually all new cars are equipped with them.

The cords in radial tires run across the centerline of the tire at right angles. There are belts wrapped around the cords. The result is a tire with flexible sidewalls (radials tend to look underinflated) and a tire yielding superior gas mileage, longer tread life, and added traction.

Automobile tires are just like every other item available for purchase in the marketplace: The manufacturer wants you to buy its product. Tire companies work hard to make their tires sexy. Raised lettering, whitewalls, blackwalls, and low-profile designs are among the stylistic innovations used to get you to purchase tires. Brand names, too, are used to portray reliability and encourage purchase.

There is, however, a superior way to choose tires. Few people notice, but every tire is rated according to the same government standard for traction and heat resistance. And finding how a tire rates is easy. Every tire's rating is molded onto the sidewall along with the brand and fancy lettering.

Traction and Heat-Resistance Rating

Traction and heat resistance are graded by the first three letters of the alphabet. And the grades mean just what they meant in school: *A* is best. An *A* grade for traction means that the tire in question will stop faster on wet pavement than one with a lower grade. Likewise, a tire rated *A* for heat resistance runs "cooler" than one with a lower grade. A cooler running tire will wear out less quickly. Put another way, a tire that is less heat-resistant is more apt to blow out on the highway.

Treadwear Rating

The treadwear rating is a bit more complicated, but not much more. Treadwear is rated by numbers. The higher the number, the more miles you can expect to get out of the tire. A tire rated at 200 should give a driver twice the miles of a tire rated at 100. You can get a pretty good idea of the mileage you'll get from a set of tires by multiplying the treadwear rating by 200. A tire with a treadwear rating of 200, multiplied by 200, means a treadwear life of roughly 40,000 miles. Of course, if your driving habits are those of the little old lady who drives only to the grocery and to church, your mileage will be higher than the driver treating the highway as a racetrack.

ALERT!

The traction and heat-resistance ratings are vital. You can forget the treadwear rating if you want: There is no Department of Transportation standard for rating treadwear. But most tires are advertised as guaranteed for a certain number of miles by their particular manufacturer, and priced accordingly.

Load Range

There is one other rating to consider when purchasing tires, the load-range rating. Like the rest of the information, it, too, is printed on the tire. The load range tells you the number of pounds a particular tire can carry. Here's how to figure the load you expect your tires to carry. Take the weight of your automobile (found in the owner's manual) and add the weight of the passengers plus luggage, then divide by four (the number of tires). That gives you the tire load. Obviously, you do not want to exceed the maximum load-range rating. But most of us find ways to do it.

Tires sold for passenger cars are going to be fine for the way most of us use our passenger cars. But if you own a pickup or SUV, make an honest appraisal of the way you intend to use your vehicle and plan your tire purchases accordingly.

FACT

Most shops also balance the tires they've sold you. The mechanic will make certain the tire rolls evenly on the road by adding small weights to certain "light" spots on each tire. Today's standards for tires are so good that usually after the first rotation, the tires no longer have to be balanced.

Size

Now that you've learned everything about a tire, you are ready to stride up to the desk at the tire store and announce your selection, right? Not just yet. The salesperson is going to ask you what size tire you want to purchase.

FIGURE 4-1: Typical tire information

Yes, the owner's manual will tell you the size, but then, so does each sidewall of your current set of tires. Printed on each sidewall is a series of letters and numbers that indicate everything (and more) that the tire salesman will ask you. Here's a typical number: P205/70R15 89H (see **FIGURE 4-1**).

Each ingredient of information in that series is defined as follows:

P: Passenger car tire
205: Tread width in millimeters
/70: Aspect ratio, the ratio of sidewall height to tread width
R: Radial tire
15: Diameter of wheel in inches
89H: Load index and speed symbol (highest speed this tire is designed to handle)

The higher the aspect ratio number, the softer the ride. Performance tires have stiffer rides and lower aspect ratios. And in place of a speed symbol, *H*, a tire on a Viper should have a *Z*.

Valve Stems

FIGURE 4-2: Valve stem

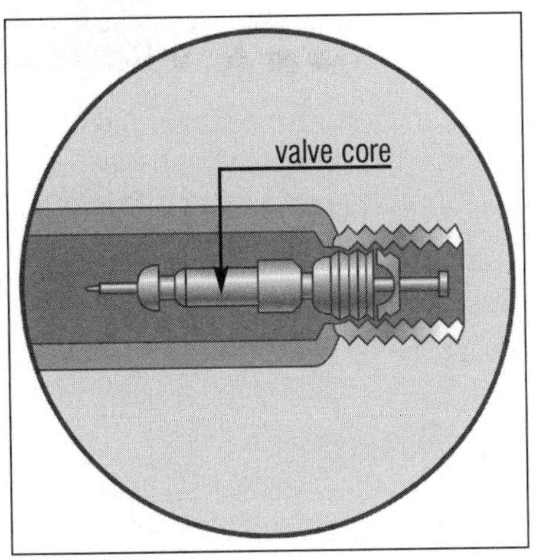

People who buy new tires frequently ignore valve stems—the little rubber protrusions with brass threads around the top that allow a tire to be inflated (see **FIGURE 4-2**). Some dealers automatically include new valve stems, while others will ask if you want new ones. Always say yes. Give new tires new valve stems. The stems are made of the same kind of rubber as a tire. And after taking the same abuse as your tires have taken for 60,000 miles, their modest replacement cost is worth it.

Most tire dealerships don't include the cost of disposing of your worn-out tire carcasses in their advertised price. Unless you know of profit to be made in mosquito breeding, pay the $1 to $2 per tire fee for the store to dispose of your old tires.

Looking at an Alternative to New Tires

Before leaving behind this section on tire purchase. . . . There is another group of tires worthy of consideration, especially if you need to keep costs down. Retreads.

Retreads are just what the name suggests. Think of it this way. The tire company installs the tread—the rubber that hits the road—last in the tire-making process. With a retread, the original treading is stripped from used, undamaged tires and replaced with new tread. Ba-da-bing: an almost new tire.

Plants that retread tires are rated on a scale of *A* to *F*. Again, the ratings are just like school grades.

With retreads, there are a couple of caveats. First, remember that the tread may be new, as good as that on a new tire, but the tire itself is older. Road salts, extremes in temperature, and general wear and tear take a toll on the whole tire, not just on the part that kisses the road. If you choose to save big bucks and purchase retreads, make a habit of inspecting the sidewalls and pay attention to the area where the retread mates with the rest of the tire.

And second, while most people who use excellent quality retreads never have any problems, those big, black, alligator-looking things frequently found sunning in the middle of the interstate? Faulty retreads.

Keeping Tires in Great Shape

Nothing is easier about auto maintenance than keeping your tires in top shape. It is so easy to do, in fact, that much tire maintenance is neglected. There are two things you can do to avoid most of the problems associated with tires: Keep tires properly inflated, and rotate.

Many gas stations have an air pump. And all good-old-fashioned service stations do. Many do-it-yourself car washes do, too. Some air pumps are free to use; the rest cost up to fifty cents. Either way, the cost is dirt cheap compared to replacing a tire worn out from improper inflation. Some of the air pumps available for the car owner's use have built-in pressure gauges, allowing you to pump and check the pressure, and some pumps don't. Go to an auto parts store and purchase a good quality pressure gauge, and keep it in the glove compartment.

FACT

For normal use, tire pressure is simple. Keep the tire inflated according to the specifications stamped on the sidewall—32 PSI means 32 pounds per square inch, and that's how the pressure gauge measures the pressure, no conversions necessary.

Inflation

Underinflated tires are arguably the most common problem on tires. Over time tires will leak a little air. When the weather turns from hot to cold, tire pressure decreases. Underinflated tires present blowout possibilities, control problems, and reduced gas mileage.

Fuel mileage drops about 1 percent for every 2 PSI (2 pounds per square inch) of underinflation. That may not sound like too much, so let's do the math.

Suppose a person drives 20,000 miles a year. This number is a bit random but is a nice round one. Besides, do you really think the manufacturers that guarantee your new car for ten years or 100,000 miles and the dealerships that want to lease you a vehicle for 15,000 miles a year are crazy? Oh, no. They know that on average you are going to drive more than that. So 10,000 to 12,000 is a little on the skimpy side. Maybe 20,000 is a smidgen high, but sooner or later you are going to drive a bunch of miles. If you maintain your car the way this book suggests, you will certainly drive into the six figures. Now back to the math: 20,000 miles . . . hmmm. The fuel it took to take your car those 20,000 miles would have carried you 200 miles farther with a mere two more pounds of air in each tire. Okay, so that doesn't seem like a terrific savings, but over the life of your automobile, say 100,000 miles, that 200 becomes 1,000 miles' worth of fuel.

> By the time a tire "looks" low on pressure, it may be only half inflated! By then, you have become the gas station's best customer and a potential hazard on the road.

Temperature and Tire Pressure

The hotter the air temperature inside the tire, the higher the tire pressure. Merely driving the car will raise the temperature and thus the tire pressure. It's always best to check tire pressure after the car has been on the road, and the tires—just like the engine—have warmed to "normal" operating temperature.

Obviously, tires warm up more in July than in January. In fact, if you only checked your tires on the first day of those two months, chances are good that you'll be letting pressure out in the summer, and adding air in January.

> If you know of a service station that offers a free tire-pressure check when you get gas there, it might be worth the few extra cents a gallon of gasoline to fill up there once in a while.

Load and Tire Pressure

Load is the other variable in tire inflation. A vehicle maximally loaded needs more tire pressure for safe handling. Why? Added weight presses down the tires, makes them bulge on the sides, causing the tires to generate more heat than normal. Those tires probably won't fail in a single overloaded trip, or even on 100 overloaded jaunts, but that extra tire strain will have an effect on the longevity of a set of tires. And the highway at seventy miles an hour is no place to learn about tire failure.

How do you know if your car is carrying more than a normal load? If your car is designed to carry four adults and has a small trunk, chances are you aren't going to put enough weight on the tires to have to do a thing. If, on the other hand, your automobile has a large trunk and you fill it with bags of mulch from the home improvement store, you've definitely exceeded the normal range.

Just because it will fit in the trunk is no measure that the load you carry isn't excessive. Forget poundage for a moment. The following will be of help:

- Normal load equals four or five adults comfortably seated in a car designed to carry four to five adults plus two to four suitcases
- Maximal load equals a normal load, plus a filled luggage rack or just one adult, plus ten or more bags of mulch in the trunk from the home improvement store; or a half-ton pickup loaded with fifty bags of mulch; or an SUV with seven adults and full luggage rack

FACT

If you are going to carry a maximal load, increase tire pressure as indicated on the tire, but don't forget to readjust the pressure when you return the vehicle to normal use. Simply put, if you have the vehicle loaded down for a camping trip, adjust PSI, and when you return from vacation, adjust it again.

Rotating Tires

Tire rotation prolongs the life of a set of tires by making them wear down evenly. It also provides an extra measure of safety by putting a mechanic's eye close to possible tire, brake, and other problems on a regular basis.

Rotating tires is a task the backyard mechanic can do at home, but why bother? Here's a list of equipment you should have in order to carry out the operation: a torque wrench, one floor jack, and four jack stands (see **FIGURE 4-3**). Never support the weight of a car on just a jack if you plan to work beneath the car. Instead, lift the car and position a jack stand beneath it.

FIGURE 4-3: Hydraulic jack and jack stands

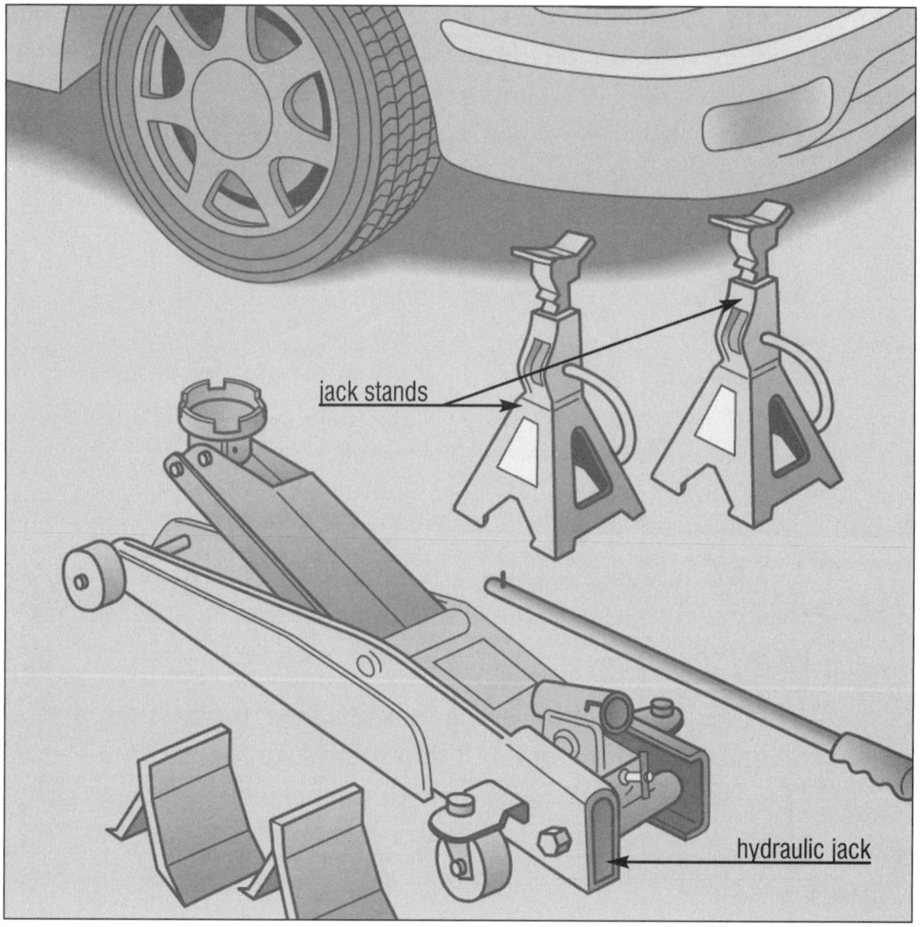

A professional mechanic will have the car up on the hydraulic lift and be halfway finished with the procedure before the home mechanic is certain the jacks and stands are properly positioned. Plus, most places that sell tires will rotate the tires they have sold for a nominal fee. Some even do it for free. An added advantage of getting tires professionally rotated is that every good mechanic will also check the brakes and C-V joint boots (rubber or plastic covers protecting the constant velocity joints from road debris and dirt).

Most new car manuals will indicate how tires for that model should be rotated. There are two basic rotational patterns: one rotating four tires, the other rotating the four plus a full-sized spare.

To see the pattern for rotating four tires, see **FIGURE 4-4**.

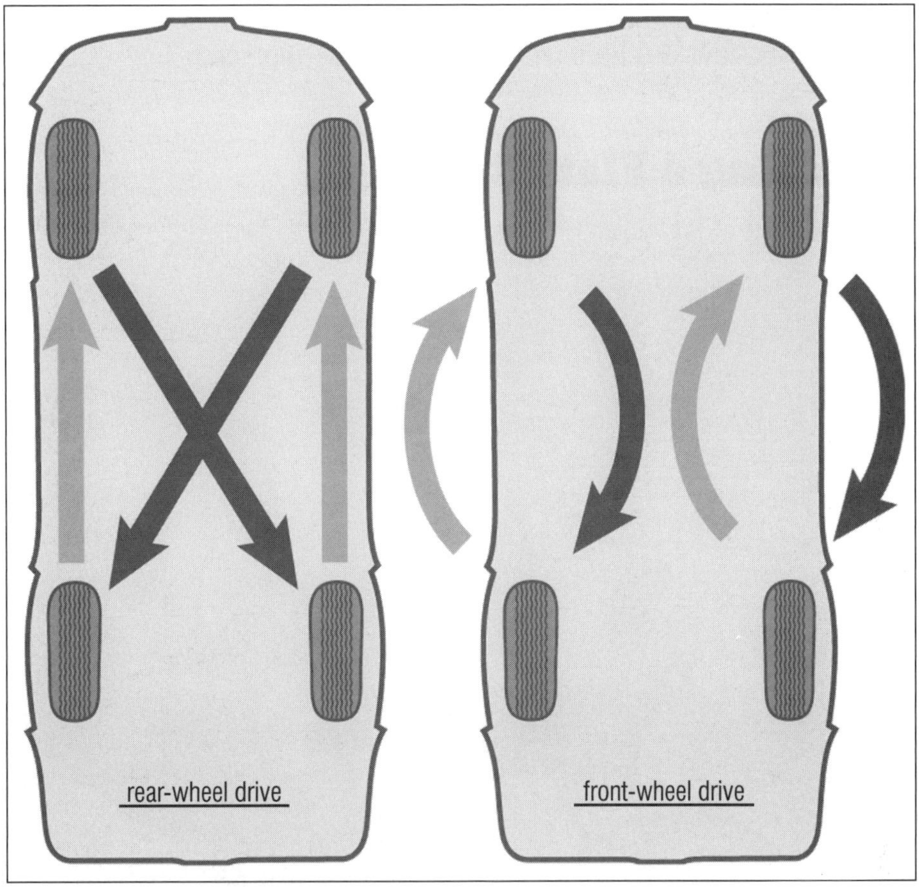

FIGURE 4-4: Four-tire rotation

The advantages of the five-tire rotation are obvious. Five tires carrying out the duties of four boosts tire life by 25 percent. It carries the added bonus of a close inspection of each tire at each rotation. All it takes is one roadside flat tire emergency with a neglected, and flat, spare tire to convince any driver of the merits of five-tire rotation.

The disadvantage of a full-sized spare tire is obvious, too. A full-sized spare is more expensive. Many new cars come with a small spare, making the five-tire rotation impractical. If the new car you are considering to purchase has a full-sized spare tire well, try negotiating for a full-sized spare or consider purchasing one.

Rotating at proper intervals makes plain the danger signs, if there are any. When tires are rotated, blemishes, bumps, cracks, and tread separation stand out. No mechanic worth his or her fee will neglect to tell you that you have a tire needing to be replaced.

Replacing a Flat Tire

FIGURE 4-5: Operating a jack

Even though many people pay a few bucks a month for the privilege of roadside assistance, sometimes the situation will dictate the best means to change the flat: How long it will take a technician to come to your location, five minutes or half an hour? How nicely are you dressed? Do you really want to get out of the car and change the tire in this downpour? But there are times that it just makes more sense to change the flat yourself than to waste time waiting. Everyone ought to know how to change a flat.

On a nice day while all four tires on your car are still in great shape, spend fifteen minutes following the instructions in your owner's manual showing you where to place your car's jack to properly effect a lift.

In a perfect world, there would only be one kind of jack, and it would fit only one way under every automobile made. Alas! Every new car brings with it the possibility of a different jack and a new manner of proper placement. If you have misplaced the owner's manual, instructions for using the jack can often be found in the spare tire well. If those directions are gone, a mechanic will probably be able to help. Or study the end of the jack, the part designed to fit against the car. That part will either be flat, or have a protrusion. If it is flat, locate a similar flat space—usually slightly indented—underneath the car. There will be four of them, one near each tire. If at the business end of the jack there is a protrusion, usually between one-half inch and three-quarters of an inch long, locate the slot into which it will be inserted. There will be four slots, one near each tire. Learn how to use the jack now, before you need it. **FIGURE 4-5** may be of help.

> When you plan to purchase a used car, have the vehicle checked out by a mechanic before you buy. Ask him to check the spare tire and the jack, making certain that both fit the car.

Before Lifting the Car with the Jack

Put the car in park and set the emergency brake. Be sure to do both. "Park" locks only the end of the car that actually drives the car. In a car with front-wheel drive, only the front tires are prevented from rolling when the car is in park. If you are lifting the front end of the car off the ground to repair the flat, the car may roll backward off the jack.

FIGURE 4-6: Lug nut tightening pattern

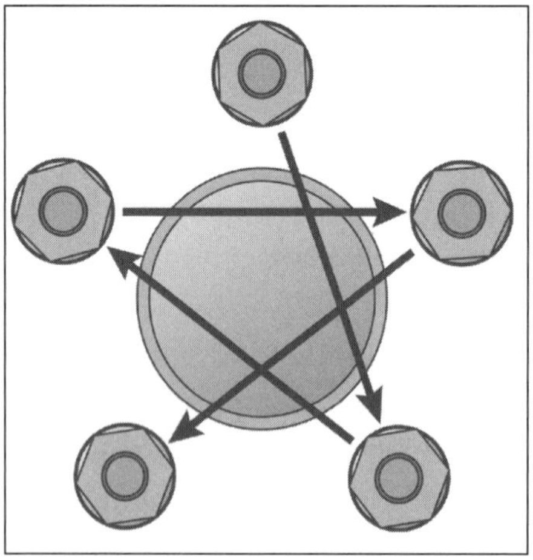

Loosen the lug nuts before you lift the car on the jack. Don't loosen the lug nuts all the way, just enough so that they will turn. Remember: righty, tighty; lefty, loosey. Put another way, clockwise tightens, counterclockwise loosens. Also, loosen them in opposing pairs (for four lug nuts) or a star pattern (for five), as shown in **FIGURE 4-6**.

There is a risk of the car falling off the jack if you wait to loosen tight lug nuts until the car is in the air. If you've had your mechanic rotating your tires regularly, the torque pressure (90–100 foot pounds for cars, 95–115 for light trucks) could make loosening the nuts difficult.

ALERT!

Begin to lift the car on the jack only after the lug nuts have lost their grip. Waiting until the tire is off the ground to attempt to loosen the nuts can create a dangerous situation. Often so much force must be applied to the lug nuts that the car can fall off the jack.

After You Lift the Car

Lift the car only enough for the tire to clear the ground. Loosen and remove the lug nuts. Set them inside the hubcap or inside the still-opened trunk, safe from accidental loss. Then remove the flat tire. Tires are heavy. You may find it easier, and safer for your back, to put a knee on the ground and work the flat off its mount slowly.

Line up the holes in the wheel of the spare with the bolts or studs extending out from the hub. Don't get confused. The hub is the round part to which the spare tire will connect. The metal part in the middle of the spare tire is called the wheel, while the metal part to which it will be attached is the wheel hub. "Studs" and "bolts" are the screw-like projections extending from the hub. Some cars use "bolts" that actually extend through the back of the hub, while most cars employ "studs" that are attached to the hub as one unit. Both do the same thing.

You may need to raise the car an inch or two at this point, since the flat will have cleared the ground more quickly than a spare filled with air. You may be able to line the tire and the wheel up so precisely that the bolts will catch in the holes and lift the tire almost perfectly into place with a couple more turns of the jack.

Tighten the lugs in a crisscross pattern. Just a smidgen more than hand-tightened. Most cars have five nuts. Assuming the five points of a star with the highest point being one and moving around the star clockwise, tighten one, then three, then five, then two, then four. On cars with four, tighten top, bottom, left, right.

This tightening procedure may seem silly, and chances are reasonable that if you were to tighten each nut in succession—that is, one, then two, then three, and so on—you would successfully complete your chore. But there is the possibility that you might tighten the wheel so that it did not rest in perfect alignment with the hub: wheel of the tire flat against the wheel hub. In that case, there eventually would be a wobble, then a bigger wobble, then the lugs would fail or fall off, then you'd be walking.

The crisscross method prevents that catastrophe.

After Lowering the Car

Once you've lowered the car from the jack, complete the tightening, again with the crisscross pattern, only now, bear down and wrench those lugs with all your might.

How tight? If you're large and very powerful, it is possible you could overtighten the lug nuts. If you weigh around 110, you could stand on the end of the lug wrench and bounce on it without overtightening.

Use your best judgment, then get the car to a shop, and before they remove your spare and return your repaired tire to its rightful place, ask about the torque pressure on the lugs you tightened. Hey! At least you'll know how close you came to perfection. Besides, the mechanic will be impressed that you know about torque pressure. And if you are in a strange town, he'll think twice before trying to pull a fast one on you, auto genius.

Checking Your Tires for Wear

We've now done almost everything to keep this most important part of the automobile reliable. Almost. But how do you know when you need new tires? That mileage guarantee you received when you purchased those tires new is partly dependent on your driving habits. Your tires may have worn quicker or slower, depending on how you drive.

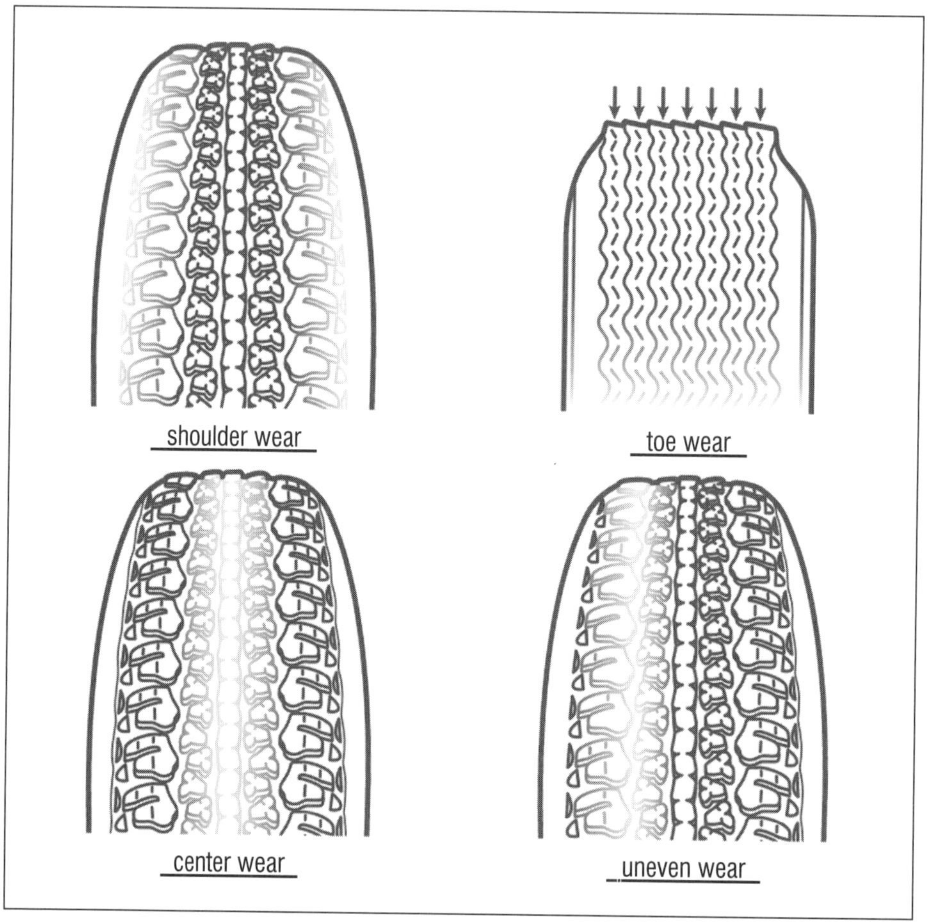

FIGURE 4-7: Tire wear

To determine if enough tread remains for driving safely, dig into your pocket and pull out a penny. Stand Abe on his head in the groove between the treads. If you can see the very top of the president's head, it is time to get new tires.

Along with Honest Abe, the other excellent and inexpensive tool for measuring tire safety is a decent pair of eyes. See **FIGURE 4-7**, but also look for the following:

- More wear in the middle of the tread than on the sides means overinflation.
- More wear on the sides of the tread means underinflation.
- Areas of wear surrounded by areas of normal tread means a tire is out of balance or the wheel rim is bent.

Obviously, a chunk out of the tread is not a good sign, either; nor are cracks in a tire's sidewalls. Both indicate that the tire should probably be replaced. Don't panic. But don't dawdle, either. Get rid of that tire.

CHAPTER 5

Finding Out Everything about Oil

Running out of fuel on the highway is an inconvenience. Running out of oil is a catastrophe. People never think about checking their oil. Many don't even know what the oil dipstick is and how to read it, and how to add fresh oil when the dipstick indicates the need. The result is reduced gas mileage, and worse, an engine that will wear out faster.

Understanding What Oil Does

Oil keeps the engine's moving parts moving. It reduces friction between the metal parts moving rapidly past each other, and it holds down the heat that friction causes. Oil picks up dirt and the small pieces of metal produced by all the movement, and deposits it in the oil filter to prevent excessive wear of the engine parts.

Can an engine run without oil? Sure. For a few minutes, maybe a little longer. But when an engine that has been starved of oil stops, it probably won't run again—ever.

> It is vital to engine health to maintain the proper level of clean oil in your car. Dirty oil makes engines work harder, reducing gas mileage and increasing exhaust emissions. Engines wear out faster if the oil is poorly maintained.

Finding the Oil Dipstick

The owner's manual should indicate where under the hood to locate the oil dipstick. Every auto manufacturer and design engineer configures an engine differently, depending upon engine size and the space available under the hood, among other considerations.

Without an owner's manual, you can still locate the dipstick, it just may take a little effort. Many of today's cars employ a plastic T-shaped handle on top of the oil dipstick, with the words "oil dipstick" printed in white letters. Other cars use a handle with a loop on top to hook a finger through and draw the dipstick out.

There are other dipsticks in the engine, too. Perhaps the simplest way not to get confused is to remember that the oil dipstick is usually the longest one. You will find two additional dipsticks, one for power steering and one for the transmission. Pull them out for comparison. The oil dipstick is usually much longer, and the fluids dripping from each will look different.

Reading the Oil Dipstick

Before pulling out the oil dipstick to determine the oil level of your car, first turn off the engine. When the engine is running, oil splashes up the dipstick, making an accurate reading impossible. Now pull out the oil dipstick. Wipe it clean with a paper towel or a clean rag and plunge it all the way back in. Now pull it out once more.

Dipsticks with Lines

Every dipstick will have a mark on it indicating the proper oil level. On the dipsticks of most American-made cars, that indicator is a line. Beneath the line is a section etched in a crisscross pattern, and below the pattern will appear the word "add." When the word "add" can be read above the oil line, the engine is one quart low. Then, and only then, should oil be added, one full quart, the standard-size container for automobile engine oil. Pretty easy, huh?

Dipsticks with Dots or Notches

Many foreign manufacturers use another set of marks on the dipstick. Some employ a pair of dots. The top dot indicates full; the bottom dot indicates "add." Other foreign manufacturers use a pair of notches on the dipstick the same way. Easy enough so far. But on many of the autos using the dots and notches, the add mark does not indicate the need to add a full quart.

So if your car indicates oil levels with dots or notches, add about half a quart, wait a bit, and check the oil level again. From then on, you'll know how much to add.

FACT

The dipstick can also indicate how clean the oil is. If it is difficult to read the oil level because the oil is transparent with a slight golden hue to it, the oil is clean and new. If the oil is dark and impossible to see through, making its level on the dipstick easy to read, the oil is dirty and needs to be replaced.

Changing Your Own Oil—Maybe

If there is only one nice thing you do for your car, change the oil regularly. Changing oil is one of the things you can do at home to save a few bucks—about half (maybe a bit more) of what it costs to take the car to the shop. Some models of automobile make servicing your oil an easy operation, while on others, the job—even for a mechanic who changes oil all day long—is a royal pain.

Here are the basics. If you can wiggle beneath your car and touch the bolt on the oil pan (the big reservoir that holds the oil), you may be able to change your own oil. And while on your back under the engine, if you can reach up and grab the oil filter with your hand—or if you can lean over your engine from the topside and grab your oil filter, you may be able to change your own oil.

If you can do both of these simple tasks easily, you can probably change your own oil in under half an hour, less time than it takes to drive to the lube joint, sit and leaf through old magazines, and drive home again.

If you can't reach the oil filter when leaning over the engine, but you know you could reach it from the bottom if only the oil pan didn't sit so close to the pavement that you can't wiggle under it, you are going to need a floor jack and a couple of jack stands to do the operation.

ALERT!

Never crawl beneath your car while it is propped up on your emergency jack—unless you want to be the top story on the local news the next morning.

Changing the oil is an easy project. To do it right you will need a wrench that fits the plug on the oil pan (see **FIGURE 5-1** for the type of plug you may expect to find on your oil filter), a container to catch the old oil, an oil filter wrench—a good one is inexpensive, a cheap one, almost worthless—and oil, of course. See Chapter 19 for more information about oil-changing tools.

Removing the Plug from the Oil Pan

With the wrench, loosen the plug on the oil pan. When you can turn it with your fingers, stop for a moment, and position the container for catching the used oil. By the way, a gallon milk jug won't work. For starters, the hole in the top is too small, and you will make a mess. And don't try to cut off the top, since many cars hold five quarts of oil.

FIGURE 5-1: Oil-pan plugs

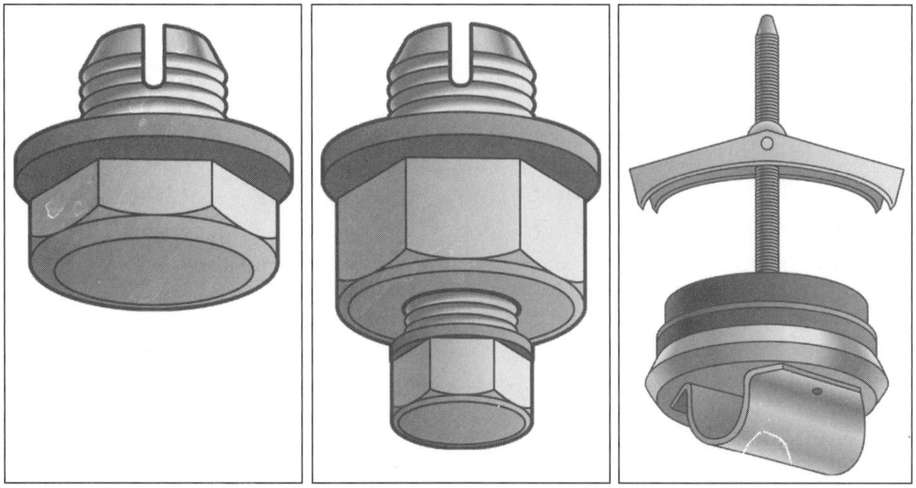

Containers to catch used oil can be purchased at most auto parts stores and large discount chains. They have a wide top with a screw-on lid, and a small opening low on the side for disposing of the oil later.

Take the plug out and be ready to make a quick adjustment with the oil container to avoid spillage.

FACT

Many auto parts stores and some service stations are equipped to receive used oil from home mechanics. Old, dirty oil is cleaned and retreated with additives. It is then resold as a deeply discounted, off-brand oil. Call around to see who will take your old oil.

Replacing the Oil Plug

This step sounds painfully obvious, but people forget to put the plug back in sometimes. Occasionally, it even happens at businesses specializing in oil changes. Or sometimes it is improperly replaced.

When the oil has drained, tighten the plug back into position in the oil pan with your fingers. Then tighten one-quarter turn with the wrench (you can use a socket wrench—see **FIGURE 5-2**). The one-quarter turn with the wrench is crucial. It ensures that the plug will remain in place and not work itself loose, and it prevents the plug from working itself so tight that removal becomes next to impossible.

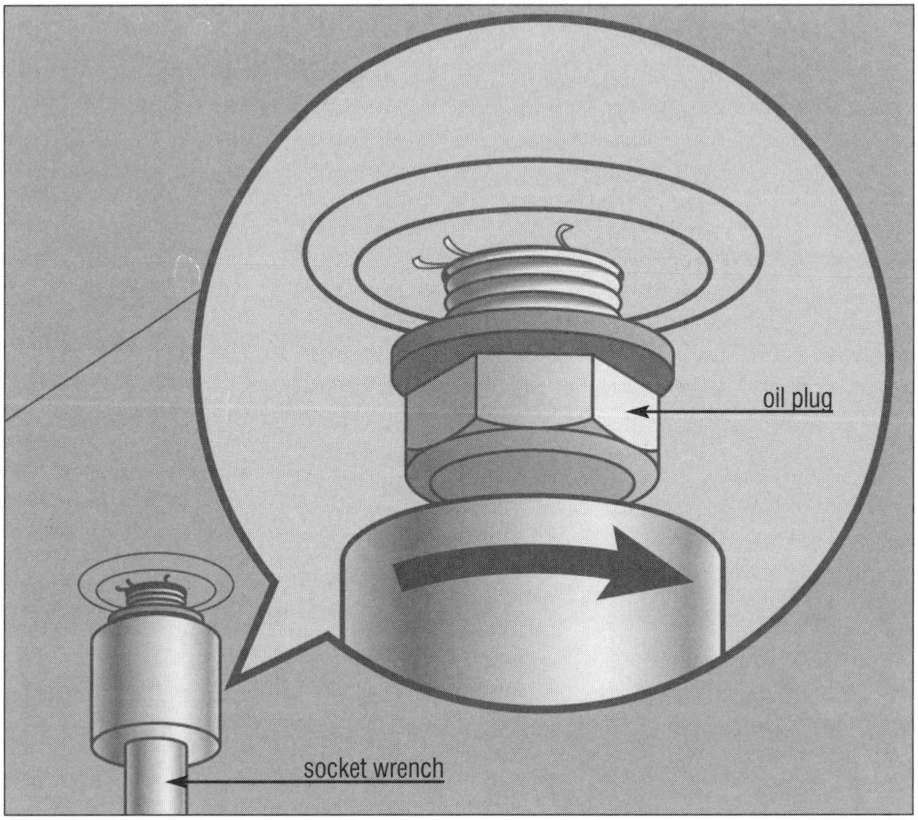

FIGURE 5-2: Replacing the oil plug

Replacing the Oil Filter

Yes, change the oil filter every time you change the oil. If the oil is dirty, so is the filter. To remove it, remember: righty tighty, lefty loosey. Use a screwdriver (see **FIGURE 5-3**), an oil filter wrench (see **FIGURE 5-4**), or—as a last resort—a chisel (see **FIGURE 5-5**), and give it a twist

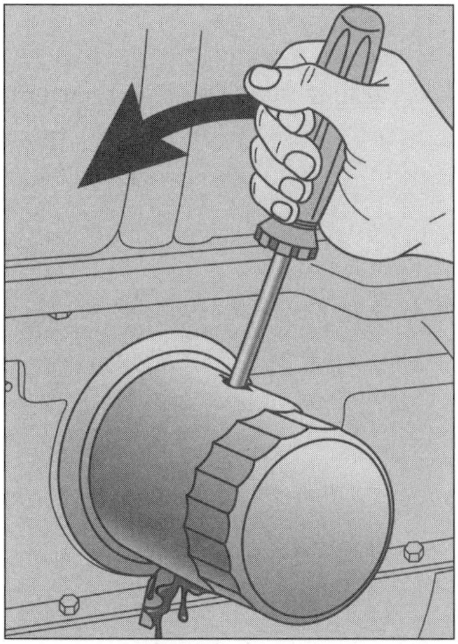

FIGURE 5-3: Replacing the oil filter with a screwdriver

to the left until it comes off (see **FIGURE 5-3**). The oil filter will be full of oil. Likely, it will spill. Be ready with a rag.

Before installing the new oil filter, clean the area where the filter will go. If this is your first oil change, relax. This is not a big deal. Just use a rag and wipe off whatever oil and grime comes up.

Dip a finger into the new oil and coat the rubber gasket (the ring) attached to the oil filter. Twist the filter into place as tightly as you can by hand. Then, with the oil filter wrench, tighten another quarter turn.

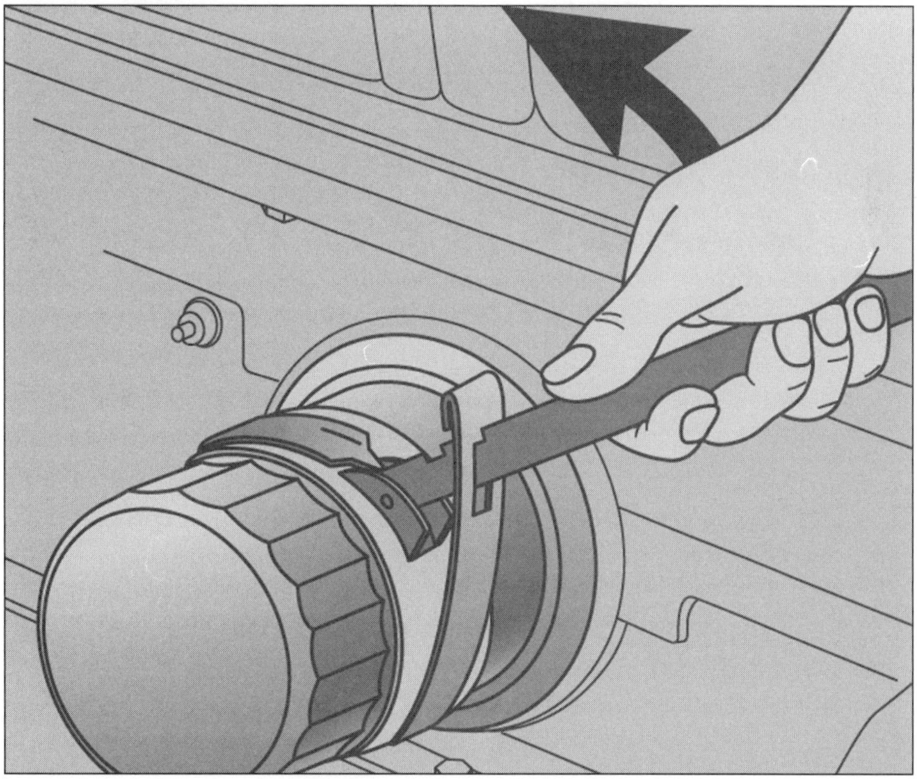

FIGURE 5-4: Replacing the oil filter with an oil filter wrench

FIGURE 5-5: Replacing the oil filter with a chisel

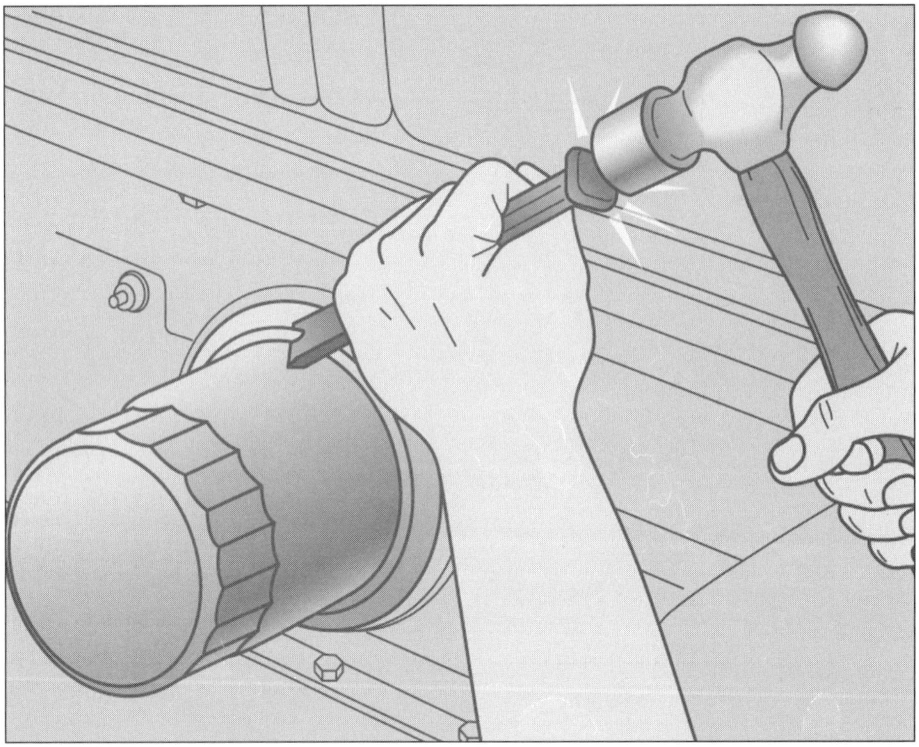

Adding the New Oil

What? Not through the dipstick opening with the quarter-inch diameter. On top of the engine, locate a metal, rubber, or plastic top that is capping a hole about the size of the opening on top of the radiator. Add the oil here. Then replug the opening, and take the old oil to your local collection location—usually a nearby garage or service station—and that's it. A half-hour well spent.

One drawback to doing your own oil up until the early '90s was that your car didn't get lubricated, or "lubed" (greased at certain joints where metal rubs against metal), unless of course you had your own grease gun. But since the early '90s, most new cars are sealed so that there are no grease fittings at all. If you're maintaining an older car, you might need to lube the car at the spots shown in **FIGURE 5-6**.

FIGURE 5-6: Car parts to lubricate

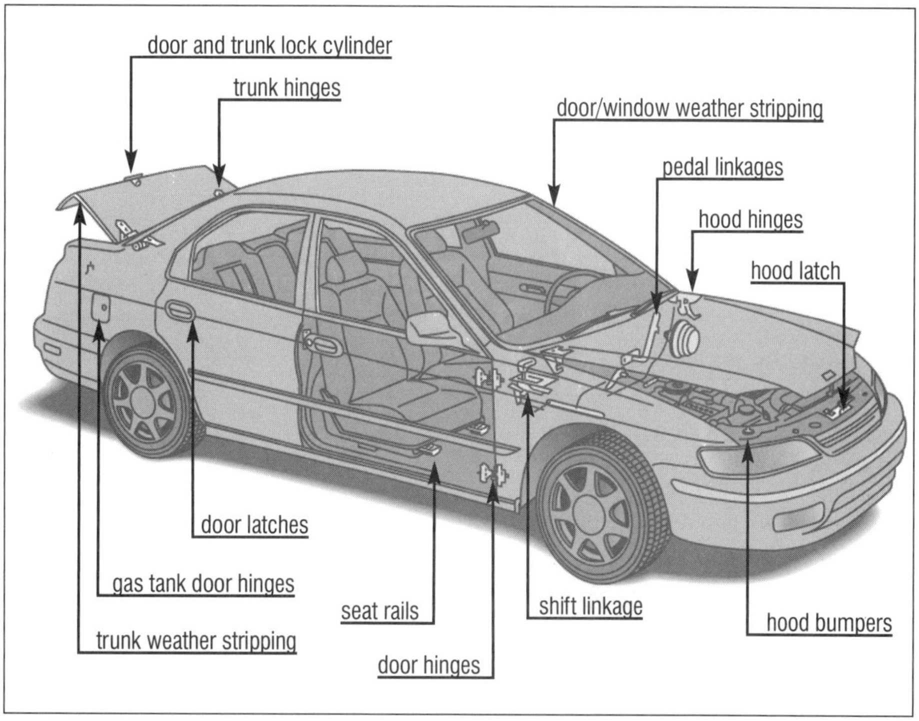

Have an oil drip after changing your oil? Assuming that there were no drips before, there are only three sources for the drip: the oil plug, the oil filter, or some spillage of oil on the engine, which might have occurred when you added the oil or when you removed the oil filter.

Figuring Out What Kind of Oil to Use

Whether you are changing your own oil or having a mechanic do it for you, a decision has to be made about the kind of oil to use. There are many fine brands, each with its own set of special additives. All top-quality oils have loyal adherents to the brand. Many mechanics will speak with conviction about the oil they prefer. But beyond brand, there are certain types of oil on the market. Knowing the difference will help you make the right decision for your car.

Checking the Owner's Manual Recommendation and API Service Categories

Your owner's manual will recommend an oil category for your car. It will show you a picture of the circle of information you are to look for when you purchase oil. At the center of the circle is the viscosity range rating, which will be explained a little later on. At the top of the circle is the oil's API (American Petroleum Institute) service category, an *S* followed by one of the first eight letters of the alphabet. At the bottom of the circle will be the words "Energy Conserving," or "Energy Conserving II." *SA* through *SG* oils are outdated. If your car is an older model and the owner's manual calls for a service rating other than *SH*, relax.

You may choose any oil that exceeds the manual recommendation. An *SH* designation will work fine as a substitute for any manual recommendation designation of *SA* through *SG*. The designation of each successive letter of the alphabet is given with new oil performance categories, where the new category is an improvement over the previous one. With each new designation there are significant improvements over the previous service classification.

The following shows the performance improvements of American Petroleum Institute service category *H* over the previous category, *G*:

- 20 percent less cam wear
- 19 percent less engine sludge
- 5 percent less engine varnish
- 21 percent improved oxidation
- 7 percent less piston varnish
- 17 percent less cam and lifter wear
- 3 percent less engine rust
- 13 percent less bearing wear
- 9 percent less piston skirt varnish

Don't worry if you don't know what these things mean—just keep in mind that they're all good!

FACT

Some motor oils have an "Energy Conserving" or "Energy Conserving II" certification. An oil certified as "Energy Conserving" yields improved gas mileage of 1.5 percent or better. An oil with the "Energy Conserving II" certification boosts mileage by at least 2.7 percent.

Deciding Between Synthetic and Regular Oil

Synthetic oil has the same molecular structure as the regular stuff. But it does not break down as quickly. In fact, it will last twice as long as regular motor oil. Sounds good so far, but the problem with synthetic oil is that it costs about twice as much. So you really won't save any money using synthetic oil. What you may save is time: If synthetic lasts twice as long, you have half as many oil changes. Right? Well, maybe.

Before switching to a synthetic oil, take a close look at the kind of miles you put on your car. If most of your mileage comes from longer distance driving (highway miles), a synthetic oil might be a good idea. If much of your mileage is stop and go, mostly short trips, it probably does not make good economic sense to use the synthetic oil.

Even though the synthetic doesn't break down as rapidly (that is, it keeps on doing the lubricating that oil is supposed to do for longer than other oils), in stop-and-go driving, a car picks up a lot of impurities, dirt, and metal particles from engine wear. In stop-and-go driving, synthetics get just as dirty. And dirty oil, no matter the type, needs to be changed.

Should you choose to use a synthetic oil in your car, in a pinch—out in the middle of nowhere, with no synthetic oil to be found—if you need to add a quart of oil, you can use standard motor oil. The molecular structure of synthetic and the real deal are the same.

Checking Out Multigrade Oil

If you're an old hand at changing your own oil, the number on an oil can may not confuse you. But if ever a mechanic or service station attendant has asked, "What grade?" and after your confused silence, the mechanic asked if you wanted 10W30 or 10W40, maybe you'd better read this section.

A car needs thinner oil in the winter and thicker oil in the summer. The number on the oil can, 10W30, for example, indicates the thinness/thickness of the oil for winter and summer driving. Here are two other words for "thinness/thickness" you may have heard, one in high school physics, the other at the garage: viscosity and weight.

10W30 means the viscosity of the oil is 10 at zero degrees Fahrenheit (*W* stands for winter), and 30 in the heat. The oil gets thicker as the engine gets hotter to better protect the moving parts. It is thinner when the engine is cold to make the car easier to start.

If you live in a colder climate, consider 5W30. If you live in the Deep South, think about 10W40. Another way to consider it: When changing oil near winter, go with a 5W, when changing oil as summer approaches consider 40 for the last number.

E ALERT!

There is a new multigrade oil being put in some new cars: 5W20. If from what you've read that sounds a bit thin, remember that auto engines and motor oils remain in a continuous cycle of innovation and improvement. Stay with the manual recommendations, and your new car warranty against engine failure is good.

Using Straight (or Single) Weight Oil

Service stations, gas stations, and auto parts places all carry single-weight oils. The one most typically seen is a 30-weight oil. Just like the 30 in 10W30, only without the ability to become thinner, to become the 10. The 30 on the can indicates the viscosity, the thinness/thickness properties, so 30-weight oil maintains a constant viscosity once the engine has warmed up. Until the engine has warmed, especially on a cold day, straight weight oil is thicker than honey. Your car's oil pump will have to work much harder and longer to distribute a cold 30-weight oil around the engine.

For most cars, most of the time, it is best not to consider a single-weight oil. But just so you'll know the full story before the neighborhood grease monkey tries to confuse and astound you: Most new cars come with 30-weight oil in them. It helps "break in" the engine.

Older readers will remember when purchasing a new car meant following a procedure in the owner's manual for "breaking in" a new car, driving a number of miles without exceeding a certain speed, then driving another number of miles without exceeding a higher speed. Now auto engines are "broken in" before the new car is delivered to the show room.

Most owner's manuals will tell you to change the oil after the first few hundred miles. Without giving you all the details, the manufacturers are telling you to drain the 30-weight (your car is "broken in" now) and treat the engine to multigrade.

Chances are good that if you were to pick up a bottle of multigrade oil off the shelf, it would be a detergent oil. As a rule, always use a detergent oil in your car. It helps keep the engine clean and reduces sludge build-up, and keeps the engine running more efficiently.

Oil Myths Your Granddad Told You

You are about to become an oil scholar, able to service your car with ease, and look at your mechanic with a confident gaze and say, "Put 10W30 in my crankcase." But there is always someone out there, usually an older family member, who will shake you to your boots with an oil myth. A story they believe in, but it just isn't true.

Myth No. 1: Overfilling the crankcase will destroy the engine.
Overfilling the crankcase (the casing that encloses the crankshaft–see Chapter 1) is not a good idea. It won't ruin the engine, but it will make

the engine work harder because the crankshaft will have to push through the oil instead of working above it. It may make the engine work at a slightly higher temperature, and overfilling the oil pan will definitely cause the car to lose gas mileage.

Myth No. 2: A car runs better one quart of oil low.

The proper level of oil helps keep the engine cool. And the proper level of oil is the full mark on the oil dipstick. Some people think that keeping the oil level one quart low helps keep an older car from burning oil, from smoking. It does, sort of. But only because running a car without the proper amount of oil keeps some oil from getting sucked past worn piston rings and burning with the fuel (see Chapter 1). The car may not smoke for a while, but the engine is wearing out a tad faster than with its proper level.

FACT

Many owner's manuals make big claims, such as changing the oil only every 7,500 miles, or even once every 10,000 miles. That is probably true for some cars with very high fuel efficiency. But dirt still gets into the oil pan. The best thing to do is make plans to change oil regularly, about every 3,000 miles.

CHAPTER 6

Taking Care of Your Electrical System

The battery is the heart and soul of your car's electrical system, which includes the ignition switch, the starter, the alternator (which generates electricity), the circuits, the fuses, and the circuit breakers. A bit of knowledge about how the system works will help you prevent quite a few headaches.

Understanding How the Car Battery Works

A battery is an electrochemical device. The key word is "electrochemical." A battery produces electrical current chemically. It does not "store" electricity. After firing up the engine, the alternator gives it a small recharge, and the battery converts the electricity it receives from the alternator into chemical energy.

Anatomy of a Car Battery

The battery has a noncorrosive plastic or rubber shell. This shell contains five noncorrosive dividers, creating six open spaces on the inside. These open spaces are each filled with a series of lead plates sandwiched close together so that a positive plate is adjacent to a negative plate: positive, negative, positive, negative.

The plates are fixed so that they do not touch. That way the fluid in the battery can flow freely between all the plates in each cell. Each cell, that combination of plates and the fluid better known as battery acid, generates 2 volts of electricity. Batteries in today's cars are 12-volt batteries. Without the battery acid, the electrolyte, a battery cannot generate electrical power.

The Electrolyte

The chemical in which the electrical energy is held is called the "electrolyte." In a car battery, the electrolyte is made of distilled water and sulfuric acid. By weight the mixture is roughly two-thirds distilled water and one-third sulfuric acid, as measured with a hydrometer. Usually when we think of liquids, we think of measuring by volume. But with a car battery, the specific gravity of the liquid is key to the balance. Water is assigned a specific gravity of 1.0. The density of all other fluids is measured relative to water. Sulfuric acid of the identical volume as water has a specific gravity of 1.835, which means it is almost twice as heavy.

Combined in the proportion required by the car battery, the specific gravity of the electrolyte is 1.270. Tuck this little number away, because it will help you to understand a battery's health. And it is a key feature used to sell you a new one: All batteries boast about cold cranking amps.

How the Lead and Acid Make Electricity

When electricity is needed from the battery, the sulfate in the electrolyte combines with the battery's lead plates and releases electrons that flow as electrical energy from the negative post to the positive post of the battery. To speak of this process chemically, the battery acid (the electrolyte) is forming lead sulfate. To say the same thing electrically, the battery is discharging.

Once the engine is running, the alternator acts as a battery recharger and passes electrical current back into the battery, reversing the chemical action. The sulfate leaves the lead plates and returns to the electrolyte, restoring the acid's specific gravity to about 1.270. If you have ever had to take your battery to the shop to have it charged, this is what the charger is also doing. And the higher the charge a battery receives, the higher the recovery of specific gravity of the battery acid. Of course, this chemical reaction does have a gradual cost. Every time the sulfates release from the lead, a small bit of residue from the plates falls to the bottom of the battery. Over time, it is this accumulation of residue that causes the battery to fail. The material builds up until it begins to touch the bottom of the plates, causing an internal short.

Battery Power and Potency

If you go to an auto parts store, two batteries of the same size can weigh noticeably different amounts. Unless there is a special sale on certain batteries, the heavier battery will cost more. Why? It has more plates. And/or it has heavier plates stacked close in each cell. That means more power, usually for many more months.

Battery power is about that simple. More plates mean more electrochemical reaction. Heavier plates mean that the cycle of sulfate clinging to lead and then releasing, clinging and releasing, can go on for longer.

Purchasing a New Battery

Your choices for new battery purchase, when that time comes, can be confusing. The place to begin is with the owner's manual. It will provide the minimum battery capacity ratings: twenty-hour rating, reserve capacity, and the one most popular in winter advertising on television, cranking performance. Keep in mind that these are minimum standards. That doesn't mean that you need to purchase a stronger, larger battery. If you purchased your car new, or if you previously purchased a battery for your car and its performance pleased you (i.e., it started when you needed it to and it lasted as long or longer than it was guaranteed to last) why spend extra money for more battery?

However, if you have moved and the climate in which you now live is colder or hotter, or if your battery underperformed—usually that means it didn't start up every time the previous winter—you should consider buying a more powerful battery.

Battery Capacity Ratings

Every battery will list its ratings right on the case. Again, you don't need to consider higher ratings unless your previous battery failed to perform as expected or you've had a change of climate. But if you want more battery, the following tells what the ratings mean:

- **Twenty-hour rating:** Determines the lighting capacity of a battery in amps. A battery rated as a 120-amp per hour battery should be able to withstand a 6-amp drain for twenty hours before dropping below 10.5 volts (120 amps divided by 20).
- **Reserve capacity rating:** The length of time that the battery will supply current to the electrical system if the alternator fails. Both of these ratings are determined at a balmy eighty degrees Fahrenheit.
- **Cranking performance:** Indicates how large a discharge a battery can generate in thirty seconds. This is usually advertised as cold cranking amps (CCA). The test is conducted at zero degrees Fahrenheit. For example, a battery rated at 750 CCA means that the driver can turn the ignition key to crank the engine, and the battery will deliver 750 amps for thirty seconds at zero degrees Fahrenheit.

The colder the temperature, the lower the specific gravity of the battery acid (electrolyte). The lower the specific gravity, the less power it can generate. Hotter temperatures increase specific gravity. That's why a car that ordinarily starts up in the morning may not start when the weather is really cold.

The Alternator and the Regulator

Once the battery has provided the electrical power to start the engine, the alternator provides all the rest of the electrical power the car requires to run its systems, including the computer, the lights, the radio, the power windows, and the power outlet once known only as the cigarette lighter. And of course, the alternator recharges the battery.

The alternator, then, is the electrical generator. Once, in fact, the alternator was known as the generator. Today it is usually called an alternator because the kind of electrical current it generates is AC, or alternating current. In an earlier era, the generator produced DC, direct current.

Why Most Modern Cars Use Alternators

Most cars today use an alternator, not a generator. Given the huge demands placed on a modern automotive electrical system, an alternator is more efficient. It is able to generate more electrical power at lower engine speeds, in stop-and-go traffic, than a generator can.

Simply put, an alternator generates electrical power by rotating magnetic fields through a conductor. This action generates voltage.

Why Alternators and Batteries Need a Voltage Regulator

Regulators, or more properly, voltage regulators, regulate the voltage generated by the alternator. An automotive electrical system typically will operate on voltages ranging from 9 volts to 18 volts. It operates optimally at around 14.5 volts. It can tolerate a bit less voltage and a bit more, but variances in voltage much above or below 14.5 will have an adverse effect on the operation of the electrical system.

The regulator works to smooth the voltage curve. When the engine spins faster, and thus turns the alternator at a faster rate, the regulator restricts the voltage. When a regulator fails, it can fail to regulate excessive voltage, or it can fail by restricting too much voltage.

FACT

A dead battery does not necessarily mean that the battery is/was bad. Have the mechanic test the voltage regulator. Too much voltage restriction will drain the battery. Too little voltage restriction will overcharge the battery. Both conditions jeopardize the longevity of the battery and also that of the alternator. Unless a battery is old, have it checked; otherwise you may just be throwing away good money.

Getting to Know the Starter System

The car's engine will start only after another motor cranks it. Do you remember old films (usually comedies) showing someone standing in front of an old automobile turning a crank to start a car? That is the same idea behind a starter motor, only it is much more efficient.

The starter motor is an electric motor that uses current from the battery. The ignition switch completes the circuit between the battery and the starter motor, causing a small gear to move outward as it spins rapidly and engage a larger gear called a ring gear. This gear, in turn, engages the flywheel and starts the engine. When the engine starts, the circuit breaks and the starter stops spinning its gear.

The rapid spinning action of the starter requires a lot of electrical energy, causing the starter to generate a lot of heat. It is never a good idea to try to start the car by turning the ignition switch and engaging the starter for more than thirty seconds at a time.

You can't start the starter with the ignition switch when a car with automatic transmission is in gear, because a switch has been used that prevents the circuit from being completed unless the car is in park. Similar switches are used on manual transmissions that are operated by the clutch pedal.

Fuses, Circuit Breakers, and Fusible Links

The electrical systems of an automobile are designed to endure extremes in temperature from well below zero to well above 200. (Today's cars operate at an engine temperature of around 250 degrees Fahrenheit.) They withstand vibrations from hours of constant use and month after month of complete neglect. Eventually the insulation from a wire will wear out, or wires will work free. And even with good wiring, there is always a chance of an overload.

Fuses, circuit breakers, and fusible links protect the electrical wiring from burning up, and from damaging other systems in the case of an overload or ground (i.e., a wire breaks free or loses insulation and touches metal). Your car may be using all three.

Fuses

Up under the dash (or sometimes in the glove compartment), your car has a fuse box. It is easily accessible, and worth getting to know. Each fuse in the box joins wires to make a circuit. A fuse consists of metal ends and a conductor strip covered by a glass tube (see **FIGURE 6-1**). You'll also find a map of the fuses—called a fuse panel—that will look something like **FIGURE 6-2**.

FIGURE 6-1: Fuses

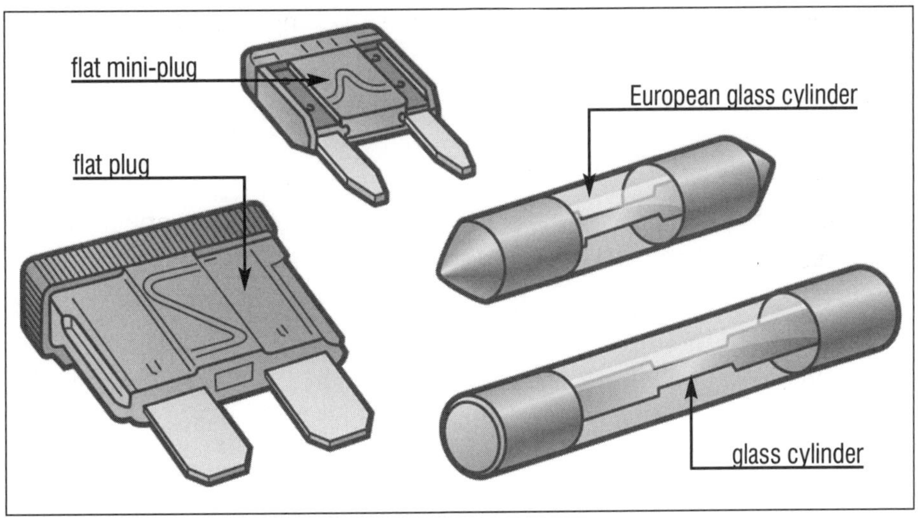

FIGURE 6-2: Typical fuse panel

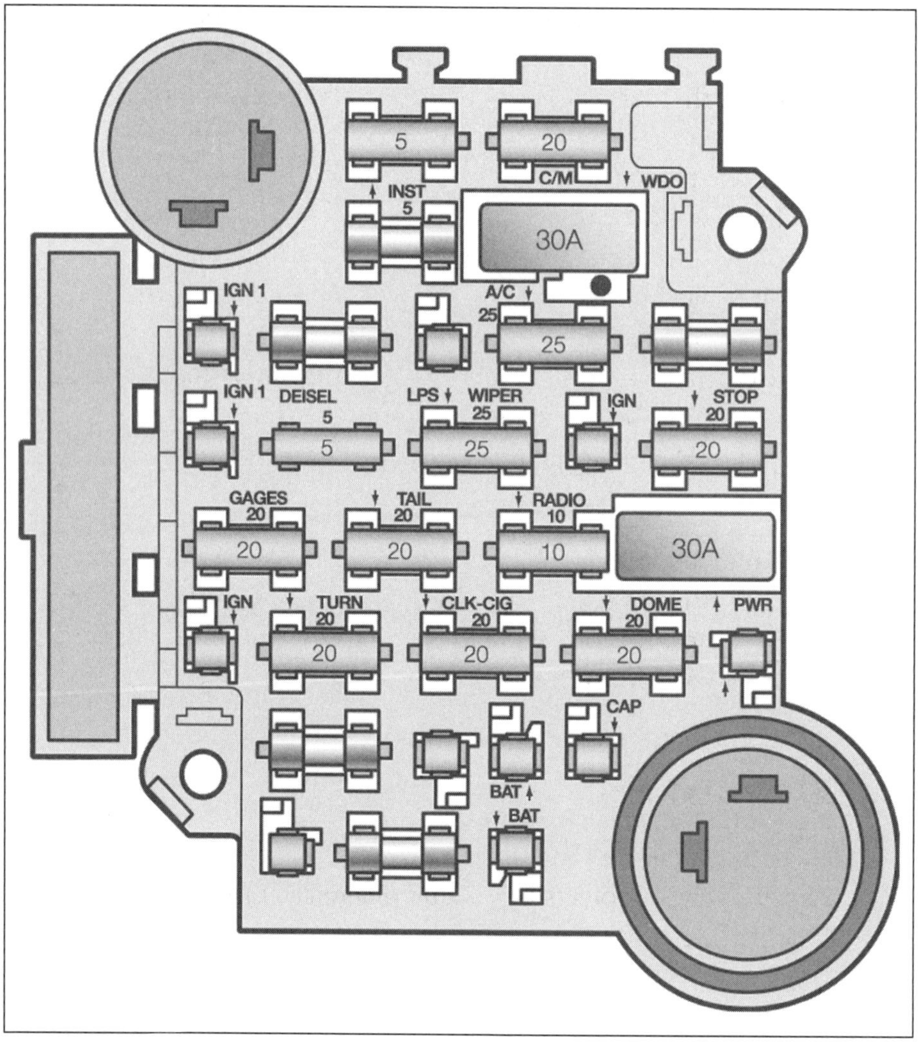

Every circuit in the car is designed to handle a certain number of amperes (amps). An amp is a unit measuring the current flow through a circuit. A fuse placed in the fuse box to protect a particular circuit is designed to handle the number of amps for which that circuit is intended. If a wire somewhere on that circuit goes to ground, the conductor strip in the fuse burns through and breaks the circuit, thereby protecting the wires, motors, and equipment in the system.

When a fuse burns through, you will notice that some electrical system on your car doesn't operate: the remote in your hand or the button in the car will not open the trunk, or the courtesy light fails, or the stereo is silent. Before spending time and money on a mechanic, check the fuse box.

Pull out the fuses one by one, then inspect and replace them. The conductor strip in a blown fuse will be separated near the middle, where the strip has burned itself in two. If you locate a blown fuse, take it down to the auto parts store, match it up, and replace it.

Sometimes a fuse clouds with age, making it impossible to determine if the fuse has blown. Replace it, just to be sure. Fuses are a wonderfully cheap fix. Most fuses can be bought for pocket change.

ALERT!

Don't try to out-think the people who designed your car. Replace a 15-amp fuse with another 15-amp fuse only! Replacing it with a 20-amp fuse may serve only to protect the fuse, not the circuit. It will not strengthen the circuit. It may lead to greater damage.

Circuit Breakers

A circuit breaker does the same job as the fuse does: It protects a circuit. Only it protects the circuit differently. Like the fuse, a circuit breaker completes the circuit, and protects the circuit from excess amperage. When such a surge in electricity occurs, the breaker overheats, and its metallic strip bends, disconnecting (opening) the circuit. When it cools, it reconnects (closes) the circuit.

This heating and cooling process can happen quite rapidly, allowing a circuit breaker to open and close the circuit over and over in quick succession. The best examples of electrical circuits that need a breaker rather than a fuse include the headlights (on some cars), power windows, and power seats. Every time these circuits are activated, they receive a jolt of electrical power greater than the circuit is designed to handle. The circuit breaker opens (breaks) the circuit, and almost instantly closes (connects) the circuit as the amps settle into the proper operating range. The rapid opening and closing of the circuit breaker averts an unnecessary circuit failure.

FACT

If the same fuse keeps blowing (and a fuse should hardly ever go bad), something is wrong elsewhere in your electrical system. Your blown fuse is telling you something. Take the car in and have the electrical system checked.

Fusible Links

A fusible link serves a purpose similar to a circuit breaker. It is placed in electrical circuits that, given the accessories for which they provide power, pull more amperes when turned on than will be needed to continue in operation. Fusible links are used by some auto makers rather than circuit breakers to control the same types of accessories: headlights, power windows, and power seats. The best description of how a fusible link operates? It is an extra-tough fuse with a conductor strip designed not to burn through on circuits that by design turn on equipment that demands an initial jolt of excessive amps.

Reviewing the Electrical System Maintenance

There are a few things you can do to reduce the chances of electrical system failure. Failure can range from a blown fuse to an engine fire. Fortunately most problems are on the bothersome end of the spectrum, not the catastrophic end. A good pair of eyes taking a long look under the hood every once in a while, some electrician's tape, liquid dish detergent, and petroleum jelly will serve as excellent and cheap tools to prevent more costly repairs.

Looking for Loose Wires and Worn Insulation

If you have a brand-new car, now is the perfect time to gaze under the hood and get a picture of how everything is supposed to look. Every wire will be secured. Some wiring will be bunched together and snugly bound by plastic tubing. Go ahead. Put a hand around some of the wiring and give it a gentle tug. The strain on the wires over the coming months and years with periods of cold followed by periods of prolonged, intensive heat and continuous engine vibration will be far more stress than you will put on the new wiring now. The wires do not flop around and their connections are tight. Where wires may eventually come in contact with the hot engine or are subject to movement and bending with the opening and closing of the hood, they are bound in an extra sheath of protective plastic.

Even if your car is no longer new, look around. If certain wires sprawl more closely in the direction of the engine than you think they ought, you are probably right. Or if there are plastic sheaths bundling wires that are cracking or are half-missing, now is the time to apply a wrapping of common electrician's tape. The following list shows where extra protection for the wiring can help:

- Hood hinges
- Door hinges
- Brake/clutch pedal
- Under the vehicle, open to the elements
- Near the serpentine belt
- Close to heat sources
- Close to sharp edges

E ALERT!

When wrapping wiring with electrician's tape, take care to overlap as you wrap. That way the tape doesn't just protect worn insulation from contact with metal, it also protects the wires from moisture.

Cleaning Away Corrosion

Most corrosive build-ups happen at the battery terminals where the cables connect to the battery posts. Corrosion adds resistance, meaning electricity is not as efficiently conducted when corrosion is present. It hampers current flow, preventing the battery from delivering the power it has converted from chemical energy, and just as importantly, it prevents the alternator from helping the battery convert enough electrical energy back into chemical energy. Corrosion will eventually eat completely through neglected wires.

Remove the battery cable from the battery post. With a plastic, stiff-bristled brush (or any brush that is not made of metal), clean away the corrosion. A mild liquid detergent can also be used.

Most home mechanics will suggest a mixture of baking soda and water to scrub away corrosion. It works. But a battery contains sulfuric acid, and baking soda is alkaline. If enough of the solution found its way into the battery, there could be an explosion.

After cleaning the battery cables, clean the terminal. Then reattach the cables to the posts, and apply a smooth coating of petroleum jelly to the posts and terminals and all exposed metal areas of the connection. There is also a convenient and inexpensive spray carried by auto parts stores that will do the same job. Both work well.

Using Jumper Cables

Sooner or later, every driver will insert the car key and turn the ignition switch, and nothing will happen. The headlights were left on, or even the map light left on overnight will drain the battery. It is for times such as these that everyone needs a set of jumper cables in the trunk. Even if you never find yourself in need of a "jump," someone in the same parking lot will.

Cheap jumper cables will work about as well as expensive ones, but the differences are worth a brief note. Cheap cables may not have the same heavy gauge wiring as more expensive cables for transferring electrical power. They tend to heat up to the point of being uncomfortable to the touch, and the rubber on their grips is not as thick. But the biggest difference is that cheaper cables are shorter. Sometimes it is impossible to move cars front to front for the procedure. Given the variety of designs under the hood, you have a 50 percent chance of the batteries being on opposite sides. Cheaper cables may not reach across two full-size cars to connect with the batteries.

To jump-start a car, do the following (see **FIGURE 6-3**):

1. Connect each end of the red cable (or the red grippers) to the positive terminal of both batteries. The positive terminal can be identified in one, two, or three ways: by a plus (+) etched into the battery post, and/or by "pos," usually printed beneath the post on the battery, and/or by the color red, usually on the cable connected to it.
2. Connect the black cable (black grippers) to the negative terminal of the good battery. The negative terminal (–) can be identified similarly to the positive cable.
3. Connect the other black cable to the engine block, or other exposed metal of the car to be started. This reduces the chance of an accidental spark.
4. Start the car and disconnect the cables in reverse order.

FIGURE 6-3: Connecting the batteries

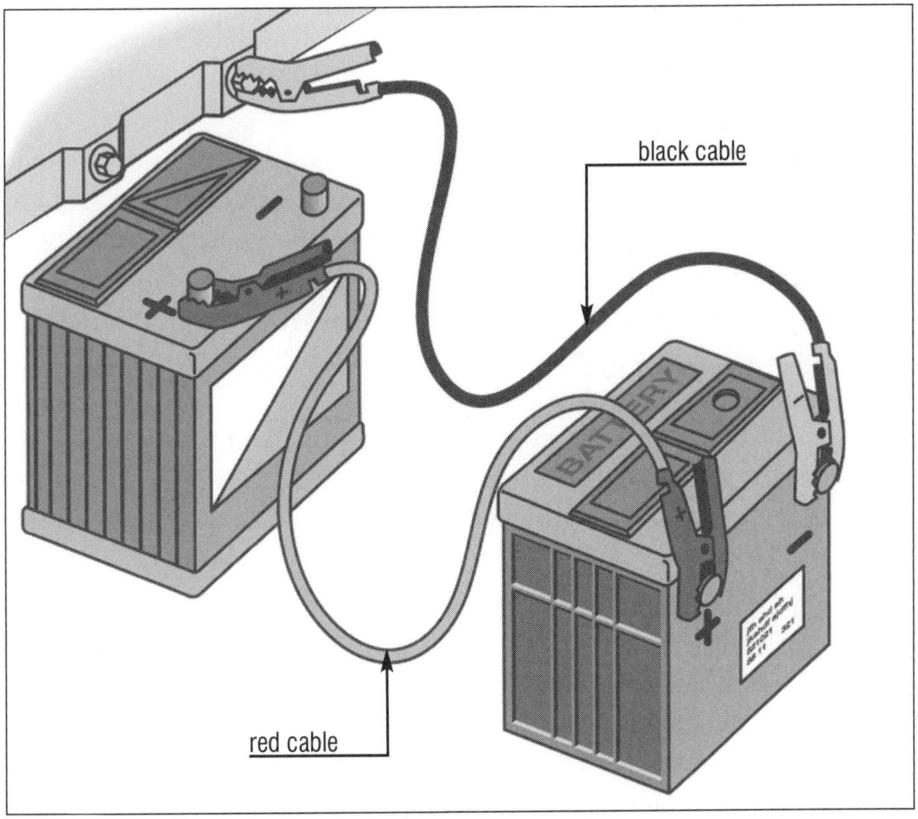

FACT

One of the by-products of the electrochemical reaction within the battery is hydrogen gas. A spark can cause a serious explosion and send sulfuric acid into your face. Should that ever happen (it is rare), baking soda will counteract the battery acid.

Reviewing the Electrical System in Thirty Seconds

The battery stores and generates electrical power. It starts the car. The alternator sustains the power the rest of the time the car is running. It used to be that one of the functions of the alternator was to recharge the battery. It still does that to a small degree, and can do it completely, but batteries do an excellent job of recharging themselves. And it's a good thing, because today's alternators are busy running the onboard computer, the mega-amp stereos, the lights, the A/C, and every imaginable item plugged into the cigarette lighter: small refrigerators, fax machines, cell phones, televisions, and fuzz busters.

Beginning in the 1990s, batteries on newer cars had to become more independent. Today's alternators do more once the car is started, and can actually overheat and wear out faster if required to recharge a nearly dead battery.

A battery can run down when it has to carry part of the load that the alternator is supposed to be carrying. The alternator can cause the battery to run down. One pitfall for the home mechanic—and a pitfall of a lazy mechanic—is to assume that a discharged battery is a failed battery. It may well be that once the car has been started, the alternator hasn't been doing its job and the battery is discharging to support one of the many systems.

A battery can run down because any number of the other systems requiring electrical current continue to run. Even when the car is off, the computer continues to draw power, and there could be a short: a wire not making a good connection, a light that is not going off when it is supposed to (the map light, the trunk light), or the cell phone kept plugged into the cigarette lighter.

Just because you get in your car one morning and it won't start, don't assume that the battery is at fault. It may be "dead" in the sense that it will not start the car, but it may just be completely drained from some other source.

In a perfect world, the battery would renew itself forever. Alas. Some of the very forces at work to make the engine go will sooner or later threaten the life of a battery. Indeed, a battery's own mechanism for sustaining itself works against it.

The battery's process of making electricity eventually works to "short-circuit" it. The battery acid reacting with the lead to produce electrical power also produces hydrogen gas. And hydrogen gas interacts with the electrical cables to produce corrosion. And corrosion short-circuits the flow of electricity through the cables, preventing the starter from getting an adequate jolt.

The battery that starts the car eventually prevents itself from doing its own job. Corrosion cakes around the battery posts and creeps beneath the protective rubber shields on the cables connecting the battery to all the rest of the electrical system, creating the possibility of an overworked alternator and an undercharging battery.

CHAPTER 7

Understanding the Cooling System

Picture the cooling system as an oval-shaped complex of hoses and metal parts with the thermostat at one end and the water pump at the other. On one long side of the oval is the radiator and the radiator fan; on the other long side of the oval is the engine. This chapter helps you see how they all work together.

The Job of the Cooling System

The cooling system's job consists of three tasks: first, it brings an engine up to efficient operating temperature; second, it maintains that temperature; and third, it removes unwanted heat. Regardless of the season of the year, the cooling system is designed to keep your car's engine operating at the same temperature, that particular engine's proper temperature for maximum efficiency.

The System's Parts for Heating and Cooling

Some mechanics may explain the cooling system differently, but none will argue what each part does. The engine generates heat, the radiator dissipates heat, and the coolant flowing between them absorbs the engine's heat and dispels it as it flows throughout the radiator.

The Coolant (Antifreeze)

A mechanic working on your car's cooling system may refer to this fluid by one of three names. The mechanic may say, "water," but he doesn't mean H_2O. Or he may refer to the liquid in the radiator as antifreeze, which is one of the two main properties of the coolant. Or the fluid may be labeled "coolant," its other main property.

The coolant is a mixture of antifreeze and distilled water mixed proportionately according to specifications found in the owner's manual. The coolant enters the engine via the water pump. It flows through passages in the engine and comes out through the opening controlled by the thermostat. It absorbs engine heat and releases it when cooled by the radiator.

It is referred to as "antifreeze" because it has properties that prevent it from freezing in severe winter weather and damaging the engine with ice. And it may also be referred to as water, because decades ago water was often used as the coolant.

There is a third property to this vital liquid that has an indirect impact on keeping the engine at the right temperature. Coolant contains additives that help prevent corrosion in the engine and in the other parts of the system through which it flows. Over time these properties are destroyed by engine heat, and coolant must be replaced. Proper care is vital in the long run, because rust in the cooling system will reduce the system's ability to do its job.

FACT

Virtually all coolant/antifreezes were at one time interchangeable. No more. There are now three types of antifreeze/coolants on the market. Consult your owner's manual for the correct type for your car. The good thing about the types of coolant is that each has its own color dye. If you need to add coolant, just use a brand of the same color.

The Engine

The engine is a system all to itself, but it plays a major function in the regulation of heat. The engine's major job for the cooling system is to generate heat, up to the point of maximum engine operating efficiency. To arrive at that temperature, the coolant locked in the engine is quickly warmed (within a few minutes) to somewhere above 200 degrees Fahrenheit. The engine has done its major job for the cooling system. Now it is up to the rest of the system to keep the coolant and the engine from getting too hot.

The Radiator

The radiator sits in front of the engine and just behind the grill. It is nothing more than aluminum tubing with fins and a coolant tank. The "fins" are those nearly knife-blade thin pieces of metal stacked side by side to direct the air to the tubing. Think of a window air-conditioning unit: The fins resemble the wafer-thin metal strips that face outdoors.

The air flowing across the tubing cools the fluid in the radiator. Air flows across the tubing as the car moves down the road. Air can also be blown across the tubing from the cooling fan, which sits between the radiator and the engine. When the cooling system is operating efficiently, the cooling fan probably will never run while the car is in motion. The fan should come on only when the engine reaches a preset (and high) temperature.

FACT

New cars run at higher temperatures than the cars of more than a decade ago—this improves fuel efficiency. They achieve that higher temperature with pressurized cooling systems. For every degree of pressure, the boiling point of the coolant is raised three degrees. A radiator designed to operate under fifteen pounds of pressure means the engine operating temperature is around 255 degrees Fahrenheit.

The Radiator Fan

Years ago when the car started, the fan began to spin. In today's cars, there is a thermostat on the radiator fan. When the engine temperature gets too hot, the fan comes on, blowing air across the radiator. In normal operation, with the car moving forward down the road, the radiator fan probably never comes on. It comes on only when the car is stuck in a traffic jam or is idling in park for a long time.

The System's Parts for Controlling the Flow

It is important to remember that this division of the cooling system into parts that heat and cool and parts that control the flow, while accurate, is a tad arbitrary. That's because each part relies on every other part for the system to function. Without these parts to control the flow of the coolant/antifreeze, the heat would continue to build past—far past!—optimal operating temperature.

The Thermostat

Once the engine heats to the proper level, it is the job of the thermostat to maintain the correct coolant temperature. The thermostat is a rounded metal plug usually located on the engine—front or top—near the radiator. It is connected to the radiator by a large hose. The thermostat prevents the flow of coolant out of the engine, until the engine temperature reaches a predetermined level.

When the right temperature is reached, a metal-encased pellet of wax in the thermostat expands and forces open a valve, sending heated coolant from the engine into the radiator on one end of the system, while at the other, coolant under pressure from the water pump floods the engine with a cooler supply. Then the thermostat closes until the coolant reaches a predetermined temperature, causing the wax to expand, opening the valve and repeating the process.

To describe the thermostat's job briefly, when the coolant is cold, the thermostat is closed; when the coolant is hot, the thermostat opens, allowing a cooler supply to circulate in the engine.

> If your cooling system is functioning well yet suddenly overheats, the thermostat may be the problem. To test the thermostat, tie it to a string and place it in boiling water. If it doesn't open, it's bad. Because each thermostat is different (and some are easy to replace while others are difficult), check your owner's manual for instructions. If you don't see instructions, ask your mechanic to replace the thermostat. It is inexpensive to replace.

The Water Pump

Okay, so it doesn't exactly pump water. In the early auto days it did. By the way, you may hear your mechanic say that the "water" is low in your radiator. He or she knows it's not water, and so do you.

The heart of the water pump is the impeller. It consists of a shaft connected to a round disk on which there are small vanes or blades. Imagine a carousel at an amusement park with the tails of the horses pointing toward the center and the horses' heads facing directly outward toward the spectators. They are facing perpendicular to the direction of travel, so that with the carousel spinning, the motion of horse and rider is sideways, catching the air broadside, not in the face. The blades of the pump are aligned just like that. A belt connected to the shaft from the outside spins the impeller, and coolant from the radiator is spun outward through an opening and sent to the engine by centrifugal force.

The Cooling System's Minor Parts

The drive belt—the hoses that connect the radiator to the water pump and the pump to the engine and the engine (via the thermostat) back to the radiator—and the heater core serve assisting roles.

The Drive Belt

You already know that once the engine starts, all kinds of gears are spinning. At the front of the engine, the crankshaft is spinning. On the front of the crankshaft is a pulley that the drive belt fits into. On many late-model cars, the engine has been ingeniously constructed so that only one belt is now needed. This belt, the drive belt, winds its way around so that it turns the air conditioner compressor, power steering, and the alternator as well as the water pump.

FIGURE 7-1: Testing the belt wear

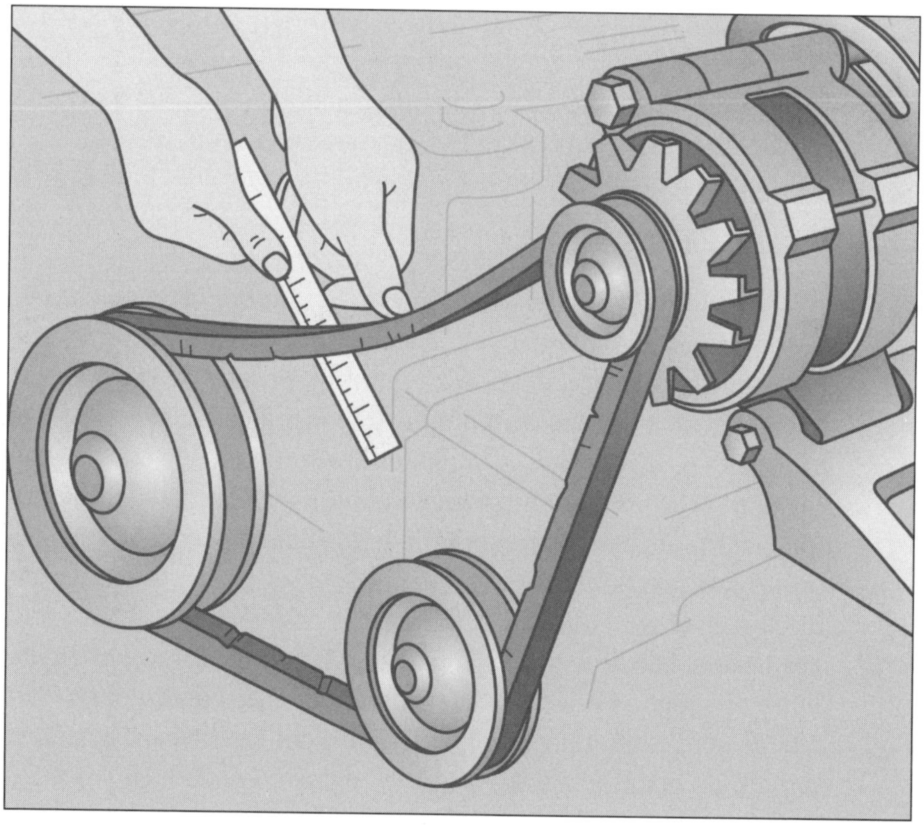

The belt itself is made of nylon cords and rubber—a long-lasting combination. If the belt breaks, the water pump will not function. And if the pump does not function, the car will overheat. No coolant will be circulated out of the radiator and back into the engine.

But this belt is one of the easiest pieces of the engine equipment to monitor to see if trouble is lurking. Bend your index finger, and fold it over tightly. The middle joint, the long flat one, is approximately one inch long. Hold that joint next to the drive belt. When you can see three cracks in the belt in one inch, change belts. (You can also use a ruler, as shown in **FIGURE 7-1**.)

Changing belts is a job you can do yourself—what you need to do is loosen the adjustment bolt (see **FIGURE 7-2**), replace the belt, and then tighten the bolt by using a wrench and a pry bar (see **FIGURE 7-3**). Under the hood of your car and in the owner's manual; there will be a diagram indicating how that belt should be looped.

FIGURE 7-2: Loosening the adjustment bolt

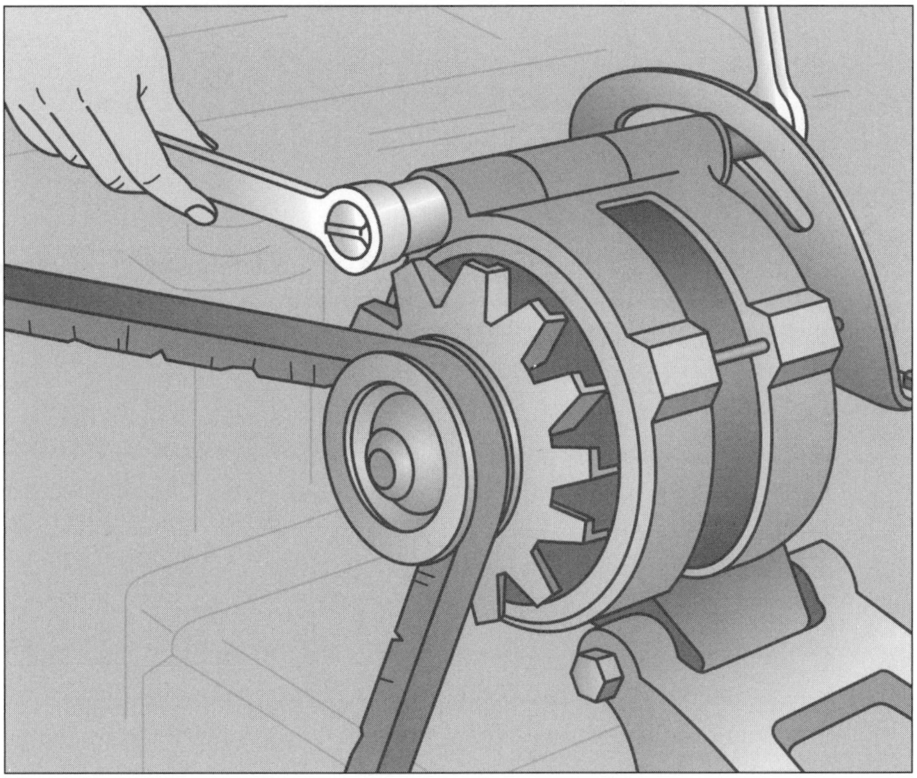

FIGURE 7-3: Readjusting tension

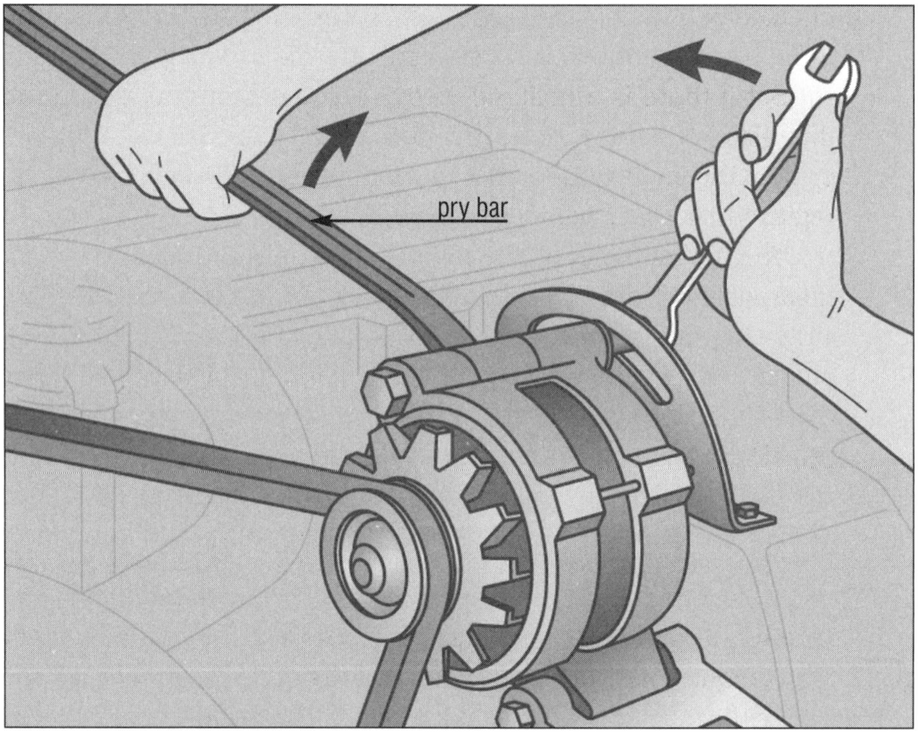

The Coolant Hoses

Given all that you now know about the cooling system itself, you can probably locate the two main coolant hoses without a diagram. Every car is different, but similar functions mean similar layouts. One hose comes directly from the engine to the radiator. The other hose goes from the radiator to the water pump. These two hoses are about as big around as an average wrist. This pair of underappreciated components of the cooling system handles liquid about twice as hot as the hot water that flows in the typical house.

Which is precisely why they, too, need occasional monitoring. Since the system is under pressure, it is possible for pinhole leaks to develop as the hoses age. You may not even notice so small a leak until your engine begins to operate at higher-than-normal temperatures, or until a hose ruptures and leaves you stranded with an engine completely devoid of coolant. To check the hoses, grab them and give them a squeeze. If the hose is flexible, with uniform suppleness, then the hose is fine.

But if there is a noticeable soft spot that seems to lack the tone of the rest of the hose, or if the hose is hard and unyielding to the grasp, or if the hose gives a bit, but feels "crunchy" when you squeeze, replace that hose.

The hoses themselves are cheap. But depending the car, replacing the hoses yourself can either be a breeze or a half-day of aggravation. Study where the hoses connect to the water pump and to the engine. Must other parts be removed to get to them, or can you see where they connect in a reasonably straight line of vision? If in doubt, take it to a pro. This is one of those jobs that won't break the bank.

ALERT!

If one radiator hose needs to be replaced, it is a good idea to replace them both. The hose coming from the engine to the radiator may carry slightly hotter coolant than the hose sending coolant back into the engine, but that coolant is still very hot. Replacing both is a cheap prevenetive measure.

The Heater Core

The heater core is the forgotten member of the cooling system. The engine of the car can operate just fine without it. But where passengers are concerned, it serves a welcome function. If it weren't for heater cores, we'd all be wearing coats in the car in the winter.

The heater core looks like a miniature radiator, and it is. It sits between the engine and the passenger compartment, under the dash. Like the radiator, it, too, draws heat from the engine. But its main purpose is to transfer that heat into the passenger compartment on demand. That is why in the winter, the car's heater doesn't immediately blow warm air onto your cold feet. The engine must heat up first.

If the heater in your car doesn't heat up as fast as it once did, a good place to begin seeking answers is with the heater core. Remember, it is part of the cooling system. Just as with other parts of the system, improperly maintained coolant can lead to deposits of rust in the heater core. And rust will diminish the core's capacity to heat your cold feet.

If the windshield fogs up when the heater or the defroster is blowing, there may be a leak in the heater core. Don't put off taking care of this problem. In some cars replacing the heater core is a snap, but for many, there's a lot of labor cost involved just getting to the part.

Maintaining the Cooling System

Most people never think about their cooling system until the engine overheats. But there are any number of reasons an engine can overheat. Most of them have to do with improper maintenance.

Replacing the Old Coolant

The most obvious threat to your automobile's ability to keep itself cool in the summer (and to keep its cooling system from freezing solid in the dead of winter—prevent one, prevent the other) is coolant that has lost its effectiveness in the radiator. Letting the volume of coolant slip too low can be bad, but a full radiator of worn-out coolant is bad, too.

Changing coolant, draining the system, and flushing and refilling it is a procedure you can do in your garage at home. Your owner's manual will probably have instructions. Unhook the two large hoses from the radiator and capture the fluid in a drain pan. Reclamp the hoses and add new coolant in the proportion to distilled water recommended by the owner's manual. This process will leave some old coolant in the engine, but if you change your own and change it at the proper intervals, the small amount of old coolant (about one-fourth of the amount) remaining should not present a problem.

To drain all the old coolant from the engine, locate the drain plug on the engine block. On some cars, it is easy to find. On others, happy hunting. If you are having the coolant drained by a professional and you insist that the block be drained, too, count on extra cost, depending on the amount of extra time required to locate and remove the plug.

If you do your own "flush and fill," there is one small extra step to the process that you absolutely must not skip.

Purging the System of Air

On many of the auto engines built since the 1990s, there are "bleed" valves, or purge valves, on the engine specifically for use when changing the coolant. Why were these valves not present on most engines built before the '90s? Because most did not need them. Sometimes it is the design of the engine—sometimes it is the angle at which the engine is mounted—but pockets of air can become trapped in most recent engines. In any vehicle in which the radiator is lower than portions of the engine, there is the potential for air to become trapped in one or more passageways of the cooling system. Air goes to the high points. The bleed valves are—as you might expect—located at those higher points.

If you don't purge the air from the system, the engine can be damaged. Trapped air—it is called an air lock—will prevent the coolant from flowing through the engine. The coolant heats and heats, and the engine "cooks."

Watching for Water-Pump Problems

Water-pump problems can come in two forms: the internal type, often undetectable because the pumps seem to keep working, and the obvious external leak. The coolant circulating through your car is a mixture that includes distilled water. Water and metal in contact eventually lead to corrosion. Of course, every coolant/antifreeze on the market touts its anticorrosive additives, and they definitely work. But just like any product subjected to cold and heat and prolonged use, over time the properties of a car's antifreeze are destroyed. Once the coolant loses its rust-prevention abilities, it assaults the metal every day as it rushes through the engine and the water pump.

It is probably more accurate to speak of the corrosion of the water pump, but if a car overheats even though the cooling system seems to be in working order, chances are the fan inside the water pump drawing the coolant through the system has "eroded" to the point of being ineffective. Take that water pump apart, and the actual pump mechanism, the blades, will have been eaten—eroded—away. As the pump slowly erodes, less and less coolant gets pumped through the engine. Finally not enough coolant flows to keep the temperature of the engine below the critical point, and it overheats.

After several years of use, the water pump may develop a leak. Even maintaining the coolant properly will not guarantee indefinite service for the water pump. Every mechanism with moving parts will one day wear out. If the water pump begins to leak, don't wait for it to fail. You know what will happen. It won't fail completely until you are somewhere help is not available. A leaking water pump is a time bomb. Replace it. Some water pumps are easy to change. Some, unfortunately, are difficult, because of the way the engineer designed everything to fit under the hood. You may have to disassemble parts of the engine to get to it.

E ALERT!

Looking to buy a used car? Remove the radiator cap and look at the coolant. Is it rusty-orange? Rub your finger on the inside surface of the radiator. Are particles of rust clinging to your finger? Is the overflow jug brown and nasty? It could be a sign of a distressed cooling system.

Monitoring the Cooling System

Every time you drive your car, you glance at the gauges on the dash. In effect you are monitoring certain systems of your car: The fuel system is the most obvious. But don't think for an instant that you are monitoring your cooling system by observing that the temperature gauge registers in the normal range. That status could change in an instant. To ensure its continued proper functioning, you will have to open the hood, or tell someone else to do it.

Keeping an Eye on the Hoses

We've already talked about the hoses, but their health is absolutely vital. You know all about the squeeze test, but watch out for the pinhole leak. If you ever hear a hiss, like a water droplet hitting a hot coal, somewhere from a radiator hose a tiny stream of coolant is spraying against the hot engine. Or you may become aware of a faint sweet odor. Same problem. Get to a service station or a shop and change both of the radiator hoses as soon as possible. The smallest leak is a signal that the hoses are at the end of their useful life.

Checking the Coolant Level and Mixture

Twice a year you should check the coolant in your car. If your car contains one of the newest coolants, orange in color, rather than an older form, which is green, all you'll need to check during the first 100,000 miles is the level of coolant. If your car uses the older, standard coolant, check the level but also check the mixture. Remember that coolant is running through your engine at a very high temperature. After a while the additives that make it effective will begin to break down.

Purchase an inexpensive coolant tester. The tester has a squeeze bulb on the end. Make sure the car is cool and open the radiator cap. Draw coolant into the tube. Count the number of balls floating; calculate according to the print on the side of the tester. That's all there is to it. Compare the result with the mixture recommended by the owner's manual. Make any adjustments you need to make.

Test your coolant on Memorial Day, to prepare for summer's heat. Test it again on Labor Day to make certain it will withstand the cold.

FACT

Modern radiators operate under pressure. The cap on your car's radiator is designed to keep the coolant at a certain number of pounds of pressure. Every pound of pressure raises the boiling point three degrees. If your car is over three years old, have the radiator cap tested every time you service any part of the cooling system.

The Fan Belt

Some cars have several belts: One to operate the alternator, another for the air conditioner, and still another for the power-steering pump. But as discussed earlier, many newer models have only one belt—a drive belt, which operates all the systems of the car that need a belt. If any one of the belts breaks, the engine's systems will fail. Every owner's manual will recommend an interval for changing the belt.

E ALERT!

If your car ever begins to overheat but the engine is still running, turning on the heat full blast will often cool the engine enough to get you safely to a mechanic. Push the heat control to its warmest setting and the fan to high.

Chapter 8

Managing the Other Fluids in Your Car

Given a car's multiple systems and the differing requirements of each, it is difficult to point to one fluid that is more vital than the others. A car needs brake fluid to make a stop, transmission fluid to convert the engine's energy into motion, and power-steering fluid to control direction.

Maintaining Your Brake Fluid

Brake fluid is the direct link between the brake pedal and the brake pads that press against the rotor (or drum) to stop the car; direct link, because the harder the pedal is pressed, the more force the brakes apply during their job. You may have heard of bleeding brake lines to remove air. Air inhibits the direct application of pressure between the foot on the pedal and brake. Or perhaps you have experienced the sudden panic of needing to stop quickly only to have the car continue to roll despite your best effort to press the pedal all the way to the floor.

Yes, the problem is often the brake pads, or shoes, or calipers. Or the problem could be the way you maintain the brake fluid. Brake fluid should be changed every two years. Nobody does that, not even the mechanics, who should know better. If you've got any curiosity at all, put down this book, go open your hood and check your brake fluid right now. Its color should be clear to light amber. Unless your car is brand-new, the odds are, your brake fluid is black. Is it still operational? It is probably performing as well as new fluid in stopping your car. Which is exactly why brake fluid is too easy to ignore.

> Adding brake fluid becomes necessary for one of two reasons: Sometimes a leak develops in a brake line. But the most common reason is that as brakes wear down, more brake fluid is required to push them into place to stop the car.

People who otherwise maintain their cars meticulously may never change their brake fluid. If you are in the habit of taking the car in to a service center for a regular oil change, the mechanic probably checks the level of the brake fluid and adds to it as necessary. But there's a good possibility that no technician has ever mentioned to you the need to change the brake fluid.

Problems Caused by Neglected Brake Fluid

Dirty brake fluid will do the job of sending the right amount of pressure from the brake pedal to the brakes for years and years. But once it is dirty, other small problems begin to develop.

Brake fluid absorbs moisture. Moisture causes corrosion. Any metal brake parts such as calipers, wheel cylinders, and master cylinders will eventually begin to rust. The small amounts of rust will cause no immediate problems, until one day a brake caliper will stick. The brake stays on after you release pressure from the brake pedal. Sometimes a mechanic will recommend replacing brake calipers when a car needs brake pads. Your mechanic is probably not ripping you off. He or she thinks there must be corrosion in the calipers. Why? Because the mechanic knows that "nobody" pays attention to brake fluid.

There is little to no difference between the moisture build-up in cars that travel only city streets or in pickup trucks that wade daily through a farm full of puddles and mud. The system is sealed. The moisture build-up has nothing to do with wheels that plow through standing water. It is the moisture within the line being pushed against the braking mechanism that does the damage. But moisture doesn't just cause corrosion of brake parts, it can also lead to a dangerous braking situation.

The moisture in the brake lines can cause the brake fluid to boil. Ever notice those signs just before a prolonged down slope on a mountain road, the sign instructing trucks to shift into a lower gear? Truckers are being instructed to use the lower (slower running) gear to reduce the need for braking and to help prevent brake fluid boiling. You, too, may have noticed the effect of overheated brake fluid. If ever you have been treating the S turns on a mountain slope as your private test track and have discovered you need to press your brakes and press them and press them until the pedal reaches the floor, that is because your fluid is boiling. Boiling reduces the brake pressure. Moisture build-up makes boiling brake fluid more likely.

Warning! If you have an antilock braking system (ABS), in addition to the possible extra increment of safety added by changing brake fluid, there is the small matter of saving some big bucks. If corrosion affects the proper function of the ABS, you may have to spend around $1,000 to replace it.

Taking Care of the Brake Fluid

On almost all non-ABS brakes, the system is gravity-fed. Above each of the four brakes is a bleeder valve. Attach one end of a section of cheap tubing to the openings at the bleeder valves and place the other end of the tubing in a container to catch the fluid. You may have to try several sizes to locate the right one, but the tubing (available at hardware stores and auto parts stores) is cheap. Open the bleeder valves and keep pouring brake fluid into the master cylinder—gravity will pull the fluid through—until the fluid bleeds out clear. (To find the location of your master cylinder, check your owner's manual.) Then you know that the brake system is flushed and filled with new fluid.

This procedure is best done as a two-person job, at least the first time. Someone to go under the car to open the bleed valves on all four wheels and someone to pour brake fluid into the master cylinder until the fluid bleeds clear at all four wheels, and until all four bleed valves are closed again.

If one person does the job alone, which is possible with experience, there is a good chance of air getting into the system (which is bad): The master cylinder may go dry while the home mechanic is scrambling beneath the wheels closing off the bleed valves. If air gets into the system, the process definitely becomes a two-person chore. If that has happened, first make certain the master cylinder is full, then open one bleeder valve. Have someone pump the brakes until the fluid begins to run out of the brake line, then close the valve. The air is out of that line. Repeat the process on all four wheels. A hassle? Sure. But it's easy.

Bleeding ABS Brakes

Don't bleed ABS brakes at home. ABS brakes need professional attention. Your mechanic will place an object on the master cylinder that forces the old fluid out. The ABS system won't allow the brake fluid to run through freely without the added pressure.

Choosing the Right Brake Fluid

There are three ratings, DOT (Department of Transportation) 3, 4, and 5. (DOT 3 and DOT 4 are alcohol-based.) DOT 3 is basic brake fluid, while DOT 4 is fluid for more extreme conditions. It contains more additives, mostly to prevent boiling, and is designed for heavier brake systems. (Braking heats up the fluid.) DOT 5 is silicon-based and used in race cars, not street cars.

ALERT!

If the owner's manual indicates that your car requires DOT 3, that is what you must put in your car. You are doing your system no favors by putting in DOT 5 (if you can even find it). Needing your brakes at seventy miles per hour is no time to realize you've made a mistake.

Caring for Your Power-Steering Fluid

Power-steering fluid is clear in color or red. Check the level of power-steering fluid by using a dipstick that is connected to the power-steering pump. Consult your owner's manual for the location of the power-steering dipstick. Most cars built in the 1990s have power-steering dipsticks clearly marked with a pair of lines. The lower one reads "Cold," and the upper one reads "Hot." The fluid level is fine if the level is even or slightly above the "Cold" line when the car is cold, or even to slightly below the "Hot" mark when the car has operated long enough to warm up.

Since a proper reading is possible whether the car is hot or cold, check it when it has been sitting awhile. No rocket science here. Given the tight spots where most engineers put the power-steering pumps, you just might get a pretty painful burn if you check it while the car is hot.

Take care not to overfill. When the fluid gets hot, it will expand. And the expanded power-steering fluid will force its way out and onto the engine. Like so many products associated with the car, power-steering fluid is petroleum-based. As such, it presents a fire hazard if it spews onto the engine. Also be careful that you don't confuse power-steering fluid with transmission fluid—both may be red.

How the Power-Steering System Works

The power-steering system is a hydraulic system. You are using the system under pressure to do work. In this case, the pressure helps turn the steering wheel. The power-steering system is basically three parts: the pump (which builds pressure and is driven off the crankshaft or the drive belt), the steering wheel, and the steering assembly, which is either a worm gearbox or a rack and pinion. The pump builds pressure. As you turn the steering wheel, the pump directs the pressure to help the wheel turn. The fluid delivers the pressure and also lubricates the system.

As with many systems that use pressure, the power-steering system builds heat. Most cars rely on the flow of air across the engine to help cool the fluid as it is working. Some cars do have a cooler for the power-steering system. Performance cars usually do; a tighter ratio of steering creates more heat.

You may have heard a whining noise when turning a steering wheel fully to the left or to the right. That whining noise is the pump trying to comply with your command and assist you in turning the wheel even farther than the steering mechanism allows. If you hear a growling noise, you'd better check the fluid level. That noise is usually air, meaning the fluid is low. And a power-steering pump low on fluid is going to burn out.

Changing Power-Steering Fluid

Over time the power-steering fluid gets contaminated and deteriorates. Power-steering fluid needs to be changed every 30,000 to 40,000 miles or every two years. But most people never change the fluid.

Changing power-steering fluid is a job some home mechanics should be confident doing, if there is easy access to the bottom of the power-steering pump. But most folk are better off letting a pro do the job. Here are the basics:

1. Take the return hose off the pump. The return hose will have a clamp on it. Not a nut, not a threaded end, but a clamp. (If you have doubts, take it to the shop.)
2. Plug up the pump so the fluid won't run out.

3. Use the return hose to dump the fluid into a drain pan.
4. Start the vehicle and pour new fluid in.
5. As you do, it pushes the old fluid out the return line.

When the fluid coming out of the hose changes from brown-black to clear (some fluid has a slight red tint to it), the system is flushed.

FACT

Cars equipped with racks or pinions present difficult power-steering problems for a home mechanic. Without know-how, there is the possibility of doing damage to the steering mechanism. Take it in and have a mechanic do the fluid change. It's about an hour's worth of a mechanic's labor, plus the cost of two quarts of fluid.

Tracking Transmission Fluid

Transmission fluid is usually red. With most cars, transmission fluid should be checked only after the car is warmed up (it should have been driven at least five miles) and with the engine running. Depending on the make and model, the fluid will be checked in one of two ways. On most cars, place the car in park with the warmed-up engine running at idle, then check the fluid level. On many Chryslers, however, the warmed engine should be placed in neutral with the emergency brake firmly deployed before reaching for the transmission dipstick. The latest model Chryslers are now checked with the car in park. Consult the owner's manual to be certain. Check your car's transmission fluid level exactly as the manual recommends, or you will get an inaccurate reading.

Some newer cars and many pickups are now operating on synthetic transmission fluid. Just like with oil, synthetics seem to maintain resistance to heat for longer. This property of synthetics should slow fluid deterioration and help lengthen the time between transmission services.

Like motor oil, you can mix synthetic transmission fluid with standard if you have to. If your car or pickup is operating with synthetic fluid and you check the level to find that your car is operating one quart low, a quart of standard transmission fluid may be added. Synthetic fluid will maintain most of its properties with up to 10 percent of its total volume derived from the standard-type transmission fluid. If the transmission holds eleven quarts, you can add a quart and still be within guidelines.

If the dipstick indicates "add" and you are in a locale somewhere in this vast country where no synthetic transmission fluid will be found for hundreds of miles, add the standard fluid. But if you are only a few miles from access to the synthetic, drive there to get it.

On the other hand, if you suspect a transmission leak—that is, you suddenly smell something you don't ordinarily smell under the hood, or you've recently noticed a puddle appearing beneath your car but haven't determined its source—add the quart. And be sure to check your transmission fluid level again soon.

As an extra fail-safe for an accurate transmission fluid reading, pull out the dipstick and read it first. Most American-made cars will indicate right on the dipstick which technique your car requires to ensure the right reading. Most imports do not provide this extra convenience.

Keeping the Fluid Level Right

Wheels may be turning in your brain right now: "If a car carries only five quarts of oil and it's okay (but not best) to drive a quart low, what difference does a quart of transmission fluid really make when the transmission holds eleven (or sometimes even more) quarts?"

Many transmissions will begin to "slip" shortly after dropping a mere quart below full. "Slipping" means that the transmission will not shift in the proper gears efficiently. If the transmission is slipping, the lower-than-normal transmission fluid level is causing excessive wear on the parts. That means that the transmission is sending more metallic fragments through its fluid, and the time before the next fluid change will have been shortened. Transmission wear means that the transmission itself will give out prematurely.

It is a good idea to keep tabs on the transmission fluid level on a regular basis. Check it once a week, and add transmission fluid through the same opening that contains the dipstick.

FACT

The two transmission hoses are attached to the same side of the radiator because the radiator contains a small coil for exclusively cooling the transmission. One hose delivers hot fluid to the coil, and the other sends cooled fluid back to the transmission. This separate system uses the air entering the grill and blowing from the fan as well as the radiator coolant to dissipate heat.

How the Transmission System Works

The transmission system, simply put, is a hydraulic pump with numerous passages that direct the fluid to clutch packs. As the fluid is routed to one clutch pack, it locks the clutch pack in place, keeping the car in a certain gear.

The heat that needs to be eliminated comes from the torque converter (see Chapter 1), the part that supplies the fluid transfer. The fluid goes directly from the torque converter to the cooler (on the radiator).

Why are there no cooling lines from a manual transmission attached to the radiator?
A manual transmission does not build the heat generated by an automatic transmission. An automatic would wear out very quickly without an efficient cooling system.

Transmission Fluid Intervals Are Determined by Vehicle Usage

Heat deteriorates transmission fluid. The way you use the car determines how rapidly the fluid will deteriorate—lose its properties of lubrication and become dirty. Transmission is about torque conversion, and torque conversion generates heat. At highway speeds, overdrive yields a 0.8 to 1 conversion, and is very easy (and cool) on the transmission. But pulling heavy loads, requiring a high torque multiple, will yield high heat, causing the transmission fluid to deteriorate much more quickly.

The more weight a vehicle is towing, the hotter the fluid gets, and the more often it needs to be changed.

Servicing the Transmission

On average, the fluid should be changed around every 30,000 miles, but that depends on usage. When the time does come to service the transmission, take care as to what service you provide for your car, whether you do it yourself or take it to the shop.

Change the filter and all the fluid, not just the three or four quarts of fluid that will drain from the transmission pan. Draining only the fluid in the transmission pan is not complete transmission service. A Ford Crown Victoria holds thirteen quarts of transmission fluid. To drain only the four quarts in the pan means 69.3 percent of the deteriorated fluid remains.

To do the job right, change all the fluid. The cost for having all of the fluid drained—flushing the system—will be approximately double the charge for just draining the pan. That may sound steep, but figure it this way: double the charge for more than twice as much brand-new transmission fluid. Besides, having to replace a transmission is much more expensive than treating the original the right way to give it a long life.

FACT

You probably don't have the machine necessary to fully flush the transmission. If you're satisfied with keeping more than two-thirds of the dirty fluid remaining, do it at home. To do the job right, take it to the shop, but be sure to request a full flush of the system.

Watching the Windshield Washer Fluid

Okay, so this isn't a vital fluid on the order of any of the others already mentioned. But it certainly is helpful. Wiper fluid is a water and alcohol mixture designed to resist freezing in the winter. It not only cleans foreign matter off the windshield, but because it freezes at a much lower temperature than water, it can be used as a deicer in the winter at start-up. There are also special additives that you can add to the fluid to help melt the windshield ice even more efficiently.

ALERT!

On bitter mornings when the washer fluid is temporarily frozen in its thin tubing, never pour warm water on your windshield to deice it. The warm water may shock the cold glass and ruin your windshield. With the wipers on, you may try pouring cold water, or just use a scraper.

The windshield washer has a pump that rests in the bottom of the washer fluid reservoir. Pressing the washer button connects the electrical circuit that starts the system. There are four reasons a washer system may fail. All of them are rare, and most of them are preventable:

- The failure of an electrical system: Check the fuse box.
- The reservoir has run dry: To prevent this, keep a large bottle or two of fluid in the garage. Whenever the hood is opened, glance at the washer fluid reservoir. If it is not full, add fluid.
- Leaks from cracks in the tubing connecting the pump to the spray nozzles: Every few years, replace the tubing.
- Debris in the system: Whenever the hood of your car is opened, make sure the cap on the plastic reservoir is sealing the opening. The fit can loosen over the years as the plastic container ages, but sometimes a top simply isn't put on properly. If there's an opening, debris from the engine will find it. If this happens, you have an expensive repair on your hands.

If you take your car in for routine maintenance, do not assume that the attendant knows what is under your hood better than you. Quick-lube places have been known to pour antifreeze in the washer tank. Numerous engine configurations make confusion possible.

Solving the Mystery of the Driveway Wet Spot

Inevitably the day will come when you will notice a puddle beneath your car. It may begin subtly as a small dot or two. Or it may appear all at once, like a seeping spreading creature in a B-horror movie, a looming threat to your personal peace.

Here's a simple solution: Buy a piece of white poster board, lay it down beneath your car overnight, trying to target the area from which the leak seems to emanate, and pull it out in the morning. If it is green, it is antifreeze. If it's orange, or a reddish color and watery, it is probably one of the newer types of antifreeze on the market. If it's black (or light-amber and slippery, and you've had the oil changed recently), it is motor oil. If it's bright red, it's transmission fluid. If it's clear and lightweight, look for power-steering leaks. And if you think it is gasoline, don't start your car!

The location of the drip can also help solve the mystery. But different engines have equipment in different spots. Still, if your car or pickup is rear-wheel drive, a transmission leak will come from beneath the middle of the car, not from beneath the front.

ALERT!

If you can tell (or show) your mechanic the color of the dripping fluid and indicate its location under your car, his job of getting to the source of the problem will be much easier.

Chapter 9

Wipers, Headlights, Fan Motors, and the Like

A car contains so many pieces of equipment for the comfort and safety of its occupants, and we take most of them for granted until something goes wrong. This chapter calls attention to a variety of those pieces of equipment that help make your car safer and more comfortable.

Windshield Wipers

Everyone knows what wipers do and how they do it. There's no need to be technical about it. Even the least mechanically gifted can keep wipers operating at their most efficient level. You can replace your own—if you choose to do so—or at least learn to distinguish which of the three parts of the wiper-blade assembly needs replacement.

Wiper rubber wears out from use, from exposure to the elements, and from lack of use. Sometimes after a prolonged drought, or if a car has been placed in storage for several months or more, the wipers will streak and skid across the windshield, no longer doing the excellent job they did the last time they were deployed several weeks ago.

Even if the rubber remains supple and the blade functions well, it is a good rule to replace wiper blades in the fall and in the spring, once every six months. Take care not to purchase more replacements than you need to.

Knowing How—and When—Wipers Are Replaced

Wipers can be replaced two ways: replacing the blade refill (the rubber squeegee itself) and replacing the blade assembly (the metal or plastic structure that comes with the refill already attached). For most of the long life of your car, you need only to replace the squeegee part, the rubber wiper blade. Over time, the blade assembly, which grips the rubber refill, can fail, but it is not a very frequent occurrence. You can tell when a blade assembly is failing, for you will notice that the wiper blade is not fully in contact with the windshield.

The wiper arm, the part of the wiper system that connects the blade assembly to the wiper motor, is a rarer replacement still. But there are times that replacement of the blade assembly won't place the blade in full contact with the windshield surface. That is when wiper arm replacement is necessary. More arms are probably replaced because the paint has worn away than because the arm itself has lost spring tension. In truth, replacing the arm rather than applying touch-up paint is probably just as cheap and much less time-consuming.

Installing a New Blade Refill

Of the three replacement pieces, the blade refill is the cheapest and probably easiest piece to install. Remove the old refill. Take care to notice how it clips into place on the wiper blade. Most refills have a pair of metal clips, one at each end of the refill. To remove the old refill, pinch the end of the clip to release its grip from the blade. Also notice that the blade assembly clasps into a groove along both sides of the refill to help hold it in place. Carefully slide the refill out of the blade assembly, and replace. Even fumbling with the clips, replacing a pair of refills shouldn't take more than a couple of minutes.

Installing a New Wiper Blade Assembly

The wiper blade assembly, that part of the wiper system that holds the refill, attaches to the arm and rivals the refill on ease of replacement. There is a bit more variation in how blade assemblies attach to wiper arms, but most replacement blades are universal, so they are constructed to adapt to the vast majority of wiper configurations. Most come with straightforward directions that indicate how to install the new blade according to the type of car to which it is being attached.

There are also blade assemblies made to fit the exact make and model of car that you drive. They may be a bit more expensive, and sometimes they are hard to find, but if you can locate them, they will be easier to install than a universal replacement.

Replacing wiper blade assemblies is rare. Only replacing refills is frequent (twice a year). If you are one of those types who squeeze every drop of value out of a car for as long as you can, in ten years, you will have replaced each pair of refills twenty times, and replaced perhaps none to three blade assemblies.

FACT

Often when it rains for several days, the auto parts store will have a run on wiper refills, and the most popular sizes will disappear fast. The next time you locate the refills that fit your car, purchase an extra set, but not more than one extra.

Headlights

Automobile headlight configurations come in two basic varieties: single lights on either side of the car and a pair of lights on each side. In the designs with a single headlight on each side, the light contains a pair of filaments aimed at differing angles. One filament is angled down toward the road surface and lights when the dimmer is engaged; the other filament aims out at the road in the distance and lights when the high beam is engaged. The headlight system utilizing two lights on each side of the car involves a similar idea, but the light with the dimmer filament remains on continuously.

Understanding the Three Types of Headlights

There are now three types of headlights available for purchase: sealed beam (incandescent) headlights, white halogen, and blue/white halogen headlights. Almost all new cars come equipped with halogen lights now. Halogens are brighter than incandescent headlights, and therefore safer. You'll simply see better with them. The new blue/white halogens, which contain xenon gas, are brighter still. If you aren't familiar with them, you will have noticed cars approaching you that use these new lights. The headlights have a bluish hue to them.

> Should a headlight ever go bad, consider replacing them all. The newer one will be considerably brighter than the other(s). Auto headlights are usually not too expensive. And an all-new set will ensure you many more years of trouble-free vision on the road at night.

Replacing Headlights

As a rule, a headlight has a very simple connection with its electrical circuit. It usually has a male connector that fits with its female counterpart. If you have a problem installing a new headlight, the problem is usually found in the manner in which the headlight mount (whether it includes a plastic cover over the headlight or not) holds the light in place. Some are just hard to figure out. (Even your mechanic may need to consult a service manual to figure some of them out. It doesn't mean that he doesn't know what he's doing. It just means there are a number of ways to do it, and some engineers have discovered the most confounding way to keep the headlight in its place.)

Once you know how to free your old headlights from their sockets, it is easy to take one down to a parts store and purchase a replacement or an upgrade. Install the new lights and replace all the mounting hardware. If you have done the job correctly, adjusting the direction of the headlight beams should not be necessary. But if you accidentally turned the wrong screws, now the fun starts.

FACT

If you have noticed that a number of people flash their brights at you at night, even though you have dimmed your headlights, your headlights are probably out of adjustment. If you have already tried the rough method just suggested, get them professionally calibrated.

The headlights must be readjusted so that the dims do not blind the oncoming driver. Most auto body shops and some mechanics have a leveling fixture, an instrument they attach to a headlight that will adjust the angle of the beams. They charge a fee to do the five-minute job that you may be willing to pay or may find unreasonable. You can do a very good approximation yourself.

There is a pair of adjusting screws on each headlight. One directs the beam side to side, the other up and down. Stand directly in front of the headlight on the driver's side of the car. Measure the height of the headlight from the ground; then measure to the same height on your leg. For an average person, that spot will be near your knee. Turn the dim lights on. Stand five feet from the headlight. Adjust the light up or down so that the dim beam is centered on that spot. Once centered, move toward the center of the car about five inches. Adjust the beam side to side until it again is centered on your knee. (The actual measurement is around four degrees off center.)

The dim light on the passenger side is slightly different. The height of the beam is identical, but this beam should remain aimed in a straight line in front of the headlight.

Taillights and Blinker Lights

If a taillight or blinker light goes out, check the fuse. (See Chapter 6 for details on how to find the fuse box.) If the fuse is good, replace the bulb. The bulb is as cheap a fix as the fuse. So cheap that if it doesn't fix the problem, bulb replacement was worth it as a troubleshooting step.

Removing the Light

Remove the taillight housing, then remove the bulb socket from the housing. The bulb will employ a short pair of metallic pegs to hold itself in place. To prevent a possible cut, place a rag over the bulb and press straight in, firmly but gently. The bulb should "give," moving in the direction of your push about a quarter of an inch. If the bulb gives, twist the bulb to the left, and release. One-eighth to one-quarter of a full turn should be enough to free the bulb. If the bulb resists and will not push back deeper into the socket, try pulling the bulb straight out from the socket, or perhaps the bulb is a twist-in type. Be certain you understand how bulbs on your make and model of car connect to their sockets. Lighting fixes are usually very easy.

Replacing the Light

Once you have freed the bulb, take it to a parts store and purchase another one. If there was no corrosion in the socket from which the bulb was removed, replace the bulb. This is usually the only repair task required. But if there is corrosion, it is best to replace the socket and stop corrosion at its source. If you are uncertain about replacing a light socket, your mechanic can do it for you quickly. And you will have saved money, having done the troubleshooting yourself.

E ALERT!

Whenever you take a minute to inspect your car, look closely at the covers over your lights. If you can see condensation on the inside of a cover, a corrosive environment exists. Remove and repair the cover seal, and check the bulb before reassembling.

The usual culprit is a seal around the light that has begun to leak. Replace the seal if possible, but since many cars today use one-piece housing assemblies, you may have to replace the whole assembly.

The Fan Motor and Vent Doors

Take good care of the fan motor that blows cool air in the summer and hot air in the winter, and keeps your windshield clear all the year through. If the fan motor fails—and oh, are they rugged!—some mechanics will refer you to another mechanic rather than work on the motor themselves. Why? Well, the motor is an inexpensive part, but getting to the motor on some vehicles is a royal pain in the toolbox. It is half a day's job to take everything out of the way just to get to the troublesome area. More work for the mechanic, more cost to you. And often they fail simply because a small object catches between the blades of the fan motor.

FACT

Do you remember what Mom always said about inserting objects in your ear? "Don't put anything in your ear smaller than your elbow." To save the life of your fan motor, don't put anything on top of your car's dash smaller than your elbow. Pencils and lollipop sticks or any small item able to slip through the defrost vent in the dash, sooner or later, will.

Small objects are even more likely to catch in the vent control doors. You may have owned or ridden in a car in which the air conditioning or heat was noticeably more forceful on one side or the other. Or on a frosty day with the defrost blasting at full tilt, have you noticed that one side clears significantly faster than the other, and when placing a hand over the air openings, have you noticed that the air blows with a lot more gusto through one side? The chances are extremely high that something has fallen through the defrost vents, or a child pushed something through the air-conditioning vents, and now a door will not operate properly.

If the situation doesn't present safety issues, you may just decide to live with it, but if the defrost vent on the driver's side is the one not operational, you'd better get it fixed. At least now you'll know how the doors directing the airflow got stuck, and how to prevent the problem in the future.

The Air-Conditioning (A/C) System

At the beginning of the air-conditioning season, the best thing you can do for your car's air-conditioning system (see **FIGURE 9-1**) and for your own comfort is to have the system serviced. Have the service technician check the temperature of the cold air that blows out of the vents, test the condenser pressure, clean the condenser, check the belt (see **FIGURE 9-2**), and clean the air-conditioner drain.

FIGURE 9-1: Air-conditioning system

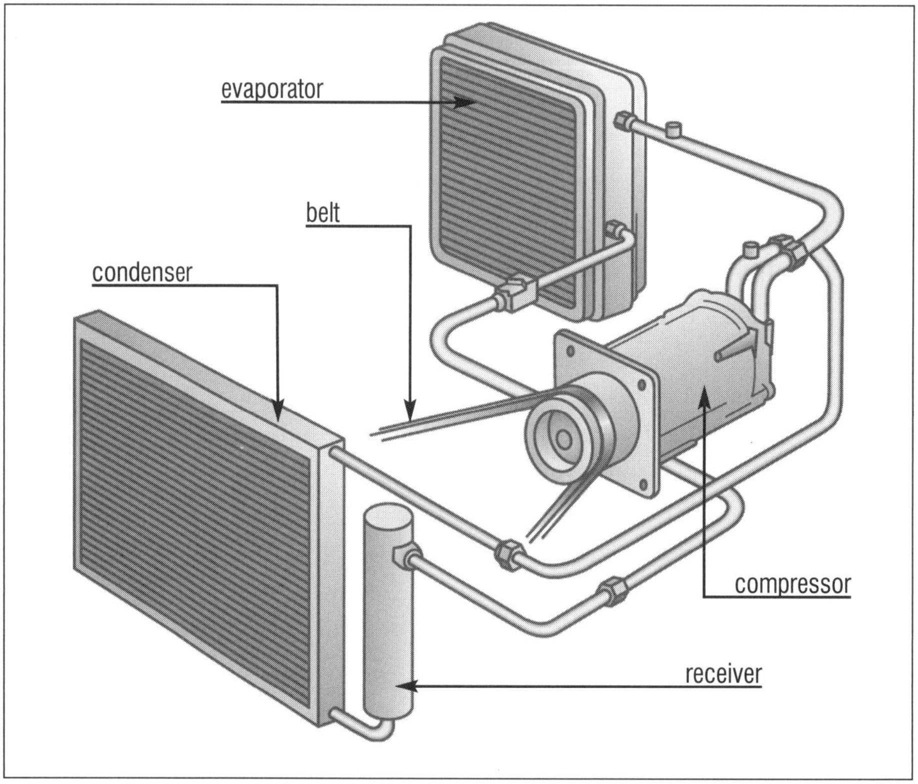

FIGURE 9-2: Worn or cracked belt

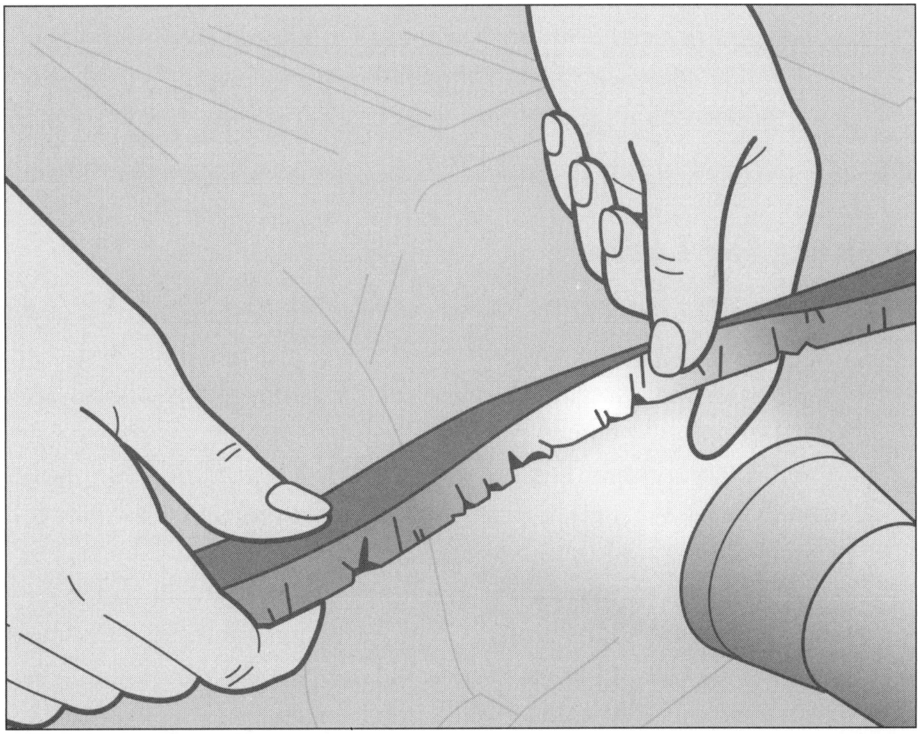

Most garages will run a special air-conditioner service each spring or summer. Yes, you could do this at home, but apart from sticking a thermometer in the vent to measure the temperature of the air coming from the A/C condenser, most home mechanics won't have the gauge for assessing condenser pressure. And cleaning the condenser is much easier with the car up on the hydraulic lift. Besides, the cost is modest, and the pro can do the job much faster.

Checking the A/C Compressor

The first thing everyone blames is the compressor. It is possible. It might have been in its death throes at the end of the previous cooling season, but as the weather began to turn, you failed to notice, or you forgot that you noticed. However, if your defroster worked well over the winter, chances are good that your compressor is fine.

ALERT!

If you noticed nothing lacking in your auto's ability to keep the windshield clear during the winter, don't give up when your mechanic says something like, "We tested the compressor, and it's fine. You'll just have to live with it."

Looking for Leaks

A good mechanic won't give up until he or she has checked the A/C system's operating pressure. This will indicate if the system has the proper gas charge. A low gas charge is the number-one reason compressors sometimes don't function as efficiently as they ought to. If the A/C compressor has lost gas, there is a leak. Check the hoses and connections attached to the compressor for areas that are oily to the touch. Such an oily spot indicates a leak.

The proper name for the electronic gizmo that will locate leaks in the A/C hoses and connections is "electronic leak detector." But most mechanics will call it a sniffer. Using the proper lingo when talking to your mechanic often gains you greater respect.

If you locate a leak in a compressor hose, replace both hoses. One leaky hose is a sure sign both hoses are weakening. A/C hoses are not inexpensive, but the cost of constantly adding refrigerant offsets the cost of the hoses.

Identifying Other Problems

If the A/C compressor is working properly, and the gas charge is correct, what then? A less-than-proficient mechanic may be stymied. The problem may be something as simple as a heat-control switch out of adjustment: that little hot/cold lever that slides along the spectrum between blue and red. Sometimes the cable to which it is attached needs some fine tuning because it is allowing heat to enter from a practically closed heat vent door (also known as a blend air door) even though the lever has been pushed to the far end of the blue.

Or if the car has front-wheel drive and you notice that each time you stop at a light the air turns warmer, the likelihood is that the cooling fan motor, which turns the fan behind the radiator, is not operating properly. This is a fine example of how interrelated the systems of a car can be. The condenser needs a positive flow of air blowing across it to operate. When the car is in motion, plenty of air is pushed through the radiator. When the car stops, the compressor relies on air circulated by the radiator fan. When the fan stops, the condenser begins to build up pressure. The compressor's high-pressure switch will cause it to shut down until the pressure decreases (when the air begins to cool the compressor again). In automobiles with front-wheel drive, that fan usually comes on with the engine warm and idling. If the fan is failing, the compressor will not yield the cool air it produces with the car in motion, and you should take it to a mechanic.

How will you know if the fan is failing, other than the loss of cool air at a traffic light? If your car is equipped with gauges, you'll notice that when stopped, your car's engine temperature will begin to rise when the fan is not working.

The Rear Defroster

Rear defrosters are a wonderful modern convenience. They are simply constructed and should provide years of maintenance-free service. But they can go bad.

If one frosty morning or one foggy night that defroster fails to do its job, check the fuses. As you know by now, anytime you have a failure of an electrical system, check fuses first (see Chapter 6). Even though you may not be able to keep straight which systems operate off of fuses, fusible links, or circuit breakers, a thirty-second study of the fuse box may provide an immediate solution, or may be the start of your troubleshooting.

However, there is a very good chance that with the rear defroster, the problem is that the grid has been broken. Look closely at those lines on the back glass. If you can see a separation in the line, there's the source of your problem.

How does a break occur? Those lines are not in the glass, they are painted on the glass. The rear defroster is a painted electrical circuit. The breaks ordinarily occur from the normal breakdown that occurs from changes in temperature and exposure to the rays of the sun.

Your local auto parts store will have a kit to repair the break in the defroster circuit. The kit will include the directions (usually instructing you to remove a short section on either side of the break), the paint, a brush, and a template to put over the area and ensure that the line you paint is Picasso perfect. When the paint dries—good as new.

If that is not the problem, you have a choice. You can pursue a fix by taking it to a mechanic, who may wind up suggesting that the deterioration of the defroster is so bad, you will need a new rear glass. At a cost of a few hundred dollars, you'll just have to decide if the defroster is a must-have, or if the people who drove cars for the first seventy years of automotive history got along fine without it.

Manual Transmission

Discussion about the manual transmission was not placed in an earlier chapter because most people don't have manual transmissions these days. They don't often fail, even if not properly serviced. But that's no license to ignore it if you have one.

Once every two years, the transmission needs to be drained and filled (see Chapter 8). Some manual transmissions use transmission fluid, others use a special synthetic, and still others use gear oil. It is vital to know what your vehicle uses. If you have no owner's manual, consult the dealer or your mechanic.

The Manual Transmission and the Clutch

Fewer people than ever even know how to drive a car with a manual transmission. Although a real sports-car nut will sneer in derision at anyone driving a performance auto containing an automatic transmission, most (not all!) manufacturers selling performance autos make them available with automatics because that's what the public wants. If you have a manual, you probably understand that engaging the clutch helps the gears mesh for a clean shift from one gear to the next. You probably also know that a clutch can burn out. If you are burning out your clutch by improper use, you will smell it. (Check out Chapter 13.)

The Manual Transmission and the Gearbox

Some people become car nuts later in life and develop the urge for a vintage sports car. It is probably a good idea to have it checked out before you write the check. Sooner or later, parts on even the best-cared-for glorious cars of the past will wear out. If you notice that when shifting gears the whole gearbox shifts to the left beneath your hand, there is probably nothing wrong with the transmission. It just has a broken transmission mount. You'll probably want a mechanic's help to repair it. It is neither too serious nor too expensive to fix. But do not write it off as a quirk of an old car. Leaving a broken transmission mount untended will strain other parts over time.

CHAPTER 10

Mastering Idiot Lights and Gauges

Idiot lights are those indicators that light up on the dash when something is wrong. Until they go on, the driver is blissfully ignorant that anything is happening to the car. Once they flash, it is often too late to do anything to prevent the very thing they are intended to warn against. Some cars have gauges instead—these gauges tend to be more useful in warning the driver about an impending problem.

Origins of the Term "Idiot Light"

While there certainly must be a definitive original meaning to the term "idiot light," a couple of meanings are used, including: "Even an idiot knows what those lights mean," and "Only an idiot relies on those lights to take care of a car."

When an idiot light flares red, the driver's eye is immediately drawn to it. It warns, it is immediate, it demands decision. Some new cars have both idiot lights and gauges (discussed in "The Value of Gauges" section, later in this chapter). For those lulled into complacency by the gauges' constant presence, or for those ill equipped to comprehend the information they provide, the lights provide a good backup. But for people who use gauges, most corrective measures will have been taken before an idiot light ever has the chance to shine.

Idiot Lights for Each Major System

All idiot lights are set up on "limit" switches. A limit switch has just two positions: on and off. The switch is off until a preset limit has been reached. When the limit is reached, the switch turns on the light.

When the engine is running, each one of these systems has a sending unit or a switch on the engine that controls the light. Said another way, the sending unit is a switch controlled by some system of the engine. The temperature light is controlled by engine temperature. The oil pressure light is controlled by oil pressure. Once the oil pressure drops, the light will come on.

The idiot light either indicates that a maximum limit has been crossed, a maximum point beyond which the manufacturer has determined it is not safe to operate the car, or the light indicates that a minimum limit has been broken, a point below which the manufacturer has determined it is not safe to operate the car. But the light is not designed to indicate both.

The Oil Pressure Light

The oil pressure switch will indicate a minimum pressure limit. The light can't tell you why engine oil pressure has dropped—neither can a gauge, for that matter—but the light signals that the oil pump can no longer pump oil. Whether your car has developed a massive oil leak, or has run low on oil, or even if your car has blown an oil galley plug, the pump no longer is squirting oil in between all those moving metallic parts. The light doesn't know the difference, but when the oil pressure drops low enough for any reason, the circuit on the oil pressure sending unit closes, and the light comes on, indicating a problem.

Engine conditions can cause the oil light to come on. When bearings begin to wear, that leaves an excessive gap between the parts, and a larger gap means oil pressure is reduced.

With some cars, the oil light will flicker when coming to a stop at a traffic light, and go off when you accelerate. This usually indicates a bearing problem. The engine can hold pressure while in motion, but not while idling. The problem hasn't gone away when the engine RPM rises, it just doesn't register as low oil pressure . . . yet.

Immediately check the oil level. The most frequent problem associated with the oil light is little or no oil in the engine.

The Temperature Light

The coolant switch indicates a maximum preset temperature. As the engine temperature reaches that predetermined level, the switch closes, and the light indicates that the engine temperature has risen above its proper operating range.

The Voltage Light

The voltage light indicates a minimum voltage limit. As the voltage drops below the right level to keep all the systems of the car operating properly, that light will come on at its preset low-end limit.

The "Check Engine" Light

This light is like big brother. Its only function is to monitor the computer, which is monitoring the car. It is not exactly an idiot light, because it doesn't tie to any system of the car. When the computer has a problem, the light comes on. "Check engine" or "service engine soon" are two common signals manufacturers use. Another one is a "power loss" light. Each of these lights means the same thing. Something is malfunctioning with the computer.

This is not one of those auto lessons Papa could hand down to Junior. Every car manufacturer places lights on the panel to help, but without reading the manual, it is easy to misinterpret the indicator. It is a common misconception that the "check engine" light indicates an oil problem or an overheating situation; in other words, that it indicates some engine situation. It doesn't.

When the "check engine" light comes on, it may only mean that the computer itself is having a problem. It will not mean an oil pressure problem or a temperature problem, although it can signify a voltage problem, since the computer needs certain voltage settings to function properly.

Some imports use a picture rather than words. A sketch of an engine will light up. This picture is still referring to an onboard computer problem, not a mechanical condition requiring service. Although on some newer cars, an ignition, a fuel injection, or an emissions problem will also light the computer light.

FACT

Sometimes the smallest goofs on the driver's part can set off the light. On new cars, if you fail to fully tighten the gas cap, the "check engine" light will come on, because fuel pressure has not climbed to the proper level.

The Engine Temperature Light

When the temperature light comes on, your car's engine is hot. The switches are set between 240 to 260 degrees, depending on the car you drive. That is on the absolute upward end of acceptability. Actually, acceptability is the wrong word. Your car's engine cannot tolerate hotter temperatures. When the temperature idiot light pops on, stop the car, or risk major to irreparable engine damage.

The problem and value of lights is one and the same: When an idiot light comes on, the car is not yet damaged, but to continue driving will cause damage.

Can an idiot light indicate that your car is running too cool for efficient operation?
Not directly. But after a certain length of time predetermined at the factory, if the computer doesn't get the proper reading on the engine temperature sensor, the "check engine" light will come on if the temperature is below normal.

The Battery Light

The battery light is a general indicator of the electrical system. A picture of a battery is often used, because most people know what the battery is. When this light comes on, it ordinarily indicates that the alternator is not putting out a charge. The problem could be the alternator itself, an electrical problem with the wiring, or a loss of power from the ignition switch circuit due to a bad connection or a broken wire.

There can be connection problems from the alternator to the battery, meaning that the alternator is not recharging the battery each time it starts the car. Sometimes the light indicates a broken belt, because a broken belt means that the alternator isn't being turned. On cars with serpentine belts, if the battery light comes on, the power steering will also fail. Usually, the battery light will come on followed immediately by harder steering. The good news is, if the battery light turns on and the steering is suddenly difficult, the troubleshooting is instantaneous: It's the serpentine belt.

Usually the light won't come on if it is just a battery problem. But it may mean that something is not right with the charging system. As long as the alternator is putting out voltage, the light will stay out. The light never means that the battery is dead; it just indicates that no voltage is being put into the battery.

A car can have a bad battery, one that has just failed after start-up, but the battery light will not light up. The battery light indicates a problem with the charging system; it really indicates nothing about the battery.

ABS and Air Bag Lights

The indicator lights for the antilock braking system (ABS) and for the air bag are not idiot lights in the purest sense. These lights are not designed to indicate a minimum or a maximum end of a range. Each time you turn the car on, the car tests to see if these systems are working. If the system is working properly, the lights go out. The lights to the ABS and air bag stay on only if there is a problem. The computer has seen a problem with that particular system that is bad enough, to the computer, at least, that it will shut the system off. If an ABS or air-bag light comes on and stays on, that system will not work. Get the system checked. Lots of new cars have traction control. This system will behave the same way. If the traction-control light on the dash stays on, the system will not work.

ALERT!

The problem can vary from minor to serious: A sensor has failed, a connection is faulty, the module is malfunctioning. If the ABS light stays on, your brakes will work, but not with the antilock feature with which they were designed.

When a Sensor Goes Bad

It is possible for a sensor to fail. A loose connection, corrosion, or a blown fuse can cause a sensor to fail. A failing idiot light may either pop on, indicating a problem when there is none, or it may not come on at all. Fortunately, it is extremely rare that a sensor light fails to come on, but it is possible to have steam rolling from beneath the hood while the idiot light maintains its ignorance.

Every time you turn the key and just before the car starts, look at the dash. All the indicator lights will light up. The onboard computer is checking every circuit of the electrical system. Every idiot light should light up. If one fails to appear, have that circuit checked.

Don't know which lights are part of your car's display panel? Check the owner's manual.

The sending units that relay info to the idiot light switches can go bad. A light can indicate a problem when one isn't there. It is always best to assume the worst; that the sensor has discovered a problem, and the light is giving an accurate warning.

The Value of Gauges

Except for vehicles used to haul or tow loads, most drivers most of the time don't need the information that gauges provide. Most trucks will have gauges. When pulling a load, the gauges will help monitor engine temperature and give the driver a "heads up" on oil pressure, lest it drop and ruin the engine. If a trailer being towed has lights, a voltage indicator gauge will alert the driver if the alternator is failing and allow the driver to react before the vehicle shuts down from a complete electrical drain.

Sports cars also use gauges. Vehicles designed to be run hard usually have gauges. Gauges allow for continuous monitoring of engine vitals. They help keep the driver from being surprised by a change in engine performance. The needles show changes in engine condition before the condition reaches a critical status.

The Problem with and Advantage of Gauges

Although you may now be scared of idiot lights, they are not without their advantages. When a light comes on, you must take immediate action. Yes, gauges alert you sooner to changes going on beneath the hood. But the gauges will do you no good unless you understand what they are telling you.

If your car is equipped with gauges, or if you've ever test-driven one that has them, the car will have been equipped with some or all of the following: a tachometer (which registers engine RPM), a temperature gauge, an oil pressure gauge, a coolant temperature gauge, a voltage gauge, and in rare cases (some trucks especially designed for towing), a transmission temperature gauge. Throw out the first and the last and you are left with the usual grouping of gauges.

Gauges are a lot like real life. There is a whole lot of ambiguity between good and bad. Look closely at a set of gauges. Notice the large space with the word "normal," or sometimes just "norm." Many people think that anytime the needle is anywhere in that wide range labeled "normal," everything is fine. (If the car is equipped only with idiot lights, there is no intermediate level of warning.) But certain variations within the so-called normal range do indicate problems, or possible problems worthy of the careful driver's attention.

The Most Important Gauges in Your Car

This section describes how the three most important gauges—oil pressure, temperature, and voltage indicator—work.

The Oil Pressure Gauge

After driving your gauge-equipped car for a few weeks, you have become acquainted with the positions at which the needles on each gauge usually stay. That nearly fixed position is the true normal position. It is giving you a "real life" reading of the pressure in the oil system.

Should the indictor needle on the oil pressure gauge shoot up, indicating extremely high oil pressure, either it's cold outside and the engine oil hasn't yet heated (the oil pump is pumping a temporarily thicker liquid), or the oil pressure sending unit (the sensor measuring oil pressure) is faulty. Only occasionally does a sending unit turn faulty, but isn't it nice to have a "heads up" about it? Why, you can drive on down to your favorite mechanic's shop at your earliest convenience and get the system checked out rather than being assaulted by that fearful red warning light on the dash, condemning your car to roadside limbo because the dreaded idiot light only just now glared.

Where the oil pressure gauge truly becomes helpful, however, is when the normally still needle begins to droop lower. If your car has some age on it, that gauge is telling you that times are a-changing, the engine is beginning to wear, and the oil can't maintain the pressure it once did because (do you remember?) the bearings are wearing and the gap between metal parts is widening.

You many have many, many miles left on your car, but the needle is telling you that you will need to keep a much closer eye on the oil level from now on. Or that you should consider rebuilding the engine, or trading cars.

Should the needle dip wildly to low and then back into norm . . . well, that will never happen to you, because you are going to keep your car well maintained. But it might happen to a friend or a careless neighbor who neglects to keep the oil level full and runs the engine even after the oil level drops dangerously low.

An oil idiot light won't come on as early as an oil pressure gauge will begin to fluctuate, indicating too little oil in the system. The gauge gives you an extra chance to prevent devastating engine damage.

FACT

All engines wear out, even with proper car maintenance. But an engine that's properly cared for in a modern car could easily last 200,000 miles. Take care of your investment (and pocket those car payments you would have been making) as the engine wears. Just plan on adding some oil between oil changes.

The Temperature Gauge

Depending on the car, you may notice very minor fluctuations in the position of the temperature needle after the car reaches its optimal operating temperature. Generally, though, it remains in a nearly still position once the car has warmed up.

Think about all the things you now know about the cooling system—about radiator pressure caps, pinhole leaks, the cooling fan, a dirty engine hampering proper cooling. Should the needle on your car's engine (or coolant) temperature gauge begin to rise, or find a new higher temperature in the "norm" range, that gauge is telling you something.

Go through a mental checklist: A pinhole leak may have been drawing off coolant in imperceptible amounts for weeks, so there is less coolant trying to do the same job as before; the cooling fan may not be coming on at a traffic stop, causing the needle to rise, then returning to its usual position once the car is at speed again; the coolant you (oops, your "friend") never changed has created corrosion in the radiator. The list can go on, but the point is, that temperature indicator is yielding valuable info you can use to keep your car from a distressing and probably damaging situation.

A needle to the lower side also yields useful info. Right off, you know that your car is not achieving the hot optimal temperature it requires for maximum efficiency. Can you guess the most likely culprit? While you search your newly developed knowledge banks, also know that anytime a gauge or idiot light gives its warning or fluctuates, it may wind up being a problem with the sensor (the sending unit) itself, but always trust your instruments first. Okay, the most likely cause of a lower-than-usual temperature reading is a faulty thermostat. Change it.

E-ALERT!

On front-wheel-drive cars, the temperature gauge may fluctuate a bit. At a stop, the temperature gauge may begin to rise, then suddenly drop. The engine fan has come on and is doing its job, but the needle movement can be unsettling if you've never noticed it before.

A coolant temperature gauge may help diagnose a cracked head or worn head gasket early enough to prevent engine damage. If driving down the road, you notice the temperature gauge jump toward hot then drop back to normal, and repeat this cycle, it may be telling you that a head is cracked or the head gasket is worn and leaking. For more on head gaskets, see Chapter 14.

The sudden jump in temperature, and the equally sudden return to normal, is a good indication that air has gotten into the system. The sudden temperature surge is caused when a pocket of super-hot steam envelops the temperature-sending unit. The temperature gauge returns to normal when coolant chases away the pocket of steam.

With an idiot light, you'd never know that it is happening.

The Voltage Indicator Gauge

A voltage indicator gauge indicates whether your car's battery is in a charge or discharge mode. There are certain things everyone does in a car that make a voltage indicator needle bounce. Raising or lowering a power window is a good example. Push the window button and watch the needle. But like the other gauges, the needle on the voltage indicator has a usual, stable position.

That stable position may change slightly but not much depending on the demand you are making on the car's electrical system. If you've got the CD pumping music, the lights on, and the heater on, and you notice that the indicator needle is indicating a higher voltage than usual, the gauge may be indicating an alternator problem; the regulator may be overcharging.

Your car is set up to run within a certain voltage range. A voltage output of 15.5 is on the highest end of normal. If your car's gauge indicates a range of 8 to 18 and the needle is near 18, the car's system is overcharging. The battery will get so hot that the acid inside will begin to boil. The computer system can be affected by an overcharging situation.

Some variables that can contribute to a higher-than-normal reading include a weak battery, which will cause the voltage indicator to register a higher reading, but never above 15.5, or a haywire voltage regulator, which can push the needle to the top end of the scale. While it will not tell you exactly what is wrong, the gauge's beauty is that it gives you the chance to check out the system before one cause or other leaves you stranded or strapped with a larger repair bill.

A lower-than-normal reading may indicate that the alternator is not charging as efficiently as it should. An easy home test for the alternator is to max out the system. Turn on the lights, turn on the blower, turn on the wipers, the radio, and punch the cigarette lighter button. If the voltage indicator needle drops below battery voltage (12 volts), then the indicator is telling you that the alternator is not charging.

If the car you drive has a separate belt for the alternator, a lower-than-normal reading could indicate a slipping or loose belt: The alternator is not turning as fast as it should; therefore, it is not charging as it should.

Most cars today use a serpentine belt, that one belt running everything. If the belt breaks, the indicator needle will drop to the bottom (to low), but that, of course, will be only one indicator of what has happened. If the belt breaks, you will have lost power steering, too. But you remembered that, didn't you?

FACT

A new battery can be so strong that it tells the alternator not to produce much voltage, which may look like an alternator problem. The needle on the gauge indicates a slight discharge, though nothing is happening. Test the system: Turn everything on, and if the indicator needle moves up a bit, the alternator is just fine.

CHAPTER 11

Wobbles, Knocks, Squeaks, and Rattles

Good maintenance makes a car last, but sometimes something goes wrong, and you hear peculiar sounds or feel your car shaking. This chapter explores the most common sounds and shakes—wobbles, knocks, squeals, and rattles—and discusses which are serious, which aren't, and how to handle all of them.

Wobbles

Wobbles—you know, when you're driving down the road and the steering wheel shakes, or you can feel part of the car shimmy—are the result of mechanical problems with tires or wheels or the driveline. There are two possible causes of a wobble: The tire is "out of round," or the wheel or something somewhere in the driveline is spinning "out of center." There is a difference between "out of round" and "out of center."

A Wobble from an Out-of-Round Tire

"Out of round" always has to do with the tire. It means that something on the outer surface of the tire is not perfectly in line with the circumference of the rest of the tire; something sticks out or indents, keeping the tire from being round.

"Out of round" tires occur when a belt inside the tire slips. This can happen with a defective new tire, or it can happen with an old tire at the end of its useful service. A lump forms on the tire, preventing it from rolling smoothly on the pavement.

Radial tires have a tendency to break belts. (Well, not much of a tendency. Most people will get the full life from their tires.) When a belt breaks, it will start raising the tread, forming a bulge on the tire that's noticeable to the eye.

> If your car is due for a tire rotation, mention the wobble to the technician. If you see a broken belt, that would explain the presence of the wobble.

A Wheel Spinning Out of Center

A wobble can be caused when the metal wheel, or rim, at the center of the tire or one of the parts of the driveline is "out of center." Out of center means that the center point around which the rest of the spinning part is supposed to rotate is not at the center of the rotation.

A bent wheel is a good example. If the wheel is bent, it means that the center of the device, that part attached to the hub, is no longer the true center. Thus when it spins, it rotates out of center. Wheels can get out of center when curbs or potholes are struck with force (called "curbing").

If the car you own has the standard steel wheels (rims), those wheels will bend in a hard collision with a curb or a deep pothole. If your car has hubcaps, your car has steel rims. If you have exchanged those wheels for something fancier, the wheels are probably aluminum. Aluminum will not bend as easily. It is harder, and also more brittle. Given a pair of identical blows against a curb, the steel wheel is more likely to bend than the aluminum wheel is to break.

FACT

It is a common misconception that an alignment problem can cause a wobble. An alignment problem will make the car pull to the left or to the right, meaning that the driver has to exert constant force in the same direction on the steering wheel to keep the car traveling in a straight line. But a wobble comes from another source.

Another Part Spinning Out of Center

Parts of the driveline can also cause wobble when spinning out of center. The driveline of the car is made of the components that transfer power to the wheels. These parts include the engine, transmission, and axle shafts.

Most of the time, if a wobble involves the driveline, it occurs in cars equipped with front-wheel drive (see **FIGURE 11-1**). It's an axle joint failure, causing the spinning shaft to run out of center. The shaft has slipped slightly to the side. Ordinarily, this will be felt as a side-to-side wobble at slower speeds and as a vibration at highway speeds, and it will not go away with a change of speeds up or down.

If a driveline wobble occurs in a car with rear-wheel drive, the wobble is most likely from a bent axle. Axles are hard to bend, except when damaged in an accident, although it is possible to "curb" a vehicle hard enough to bend an axle.

FIGURE 11-1: Car with front-wheel drive

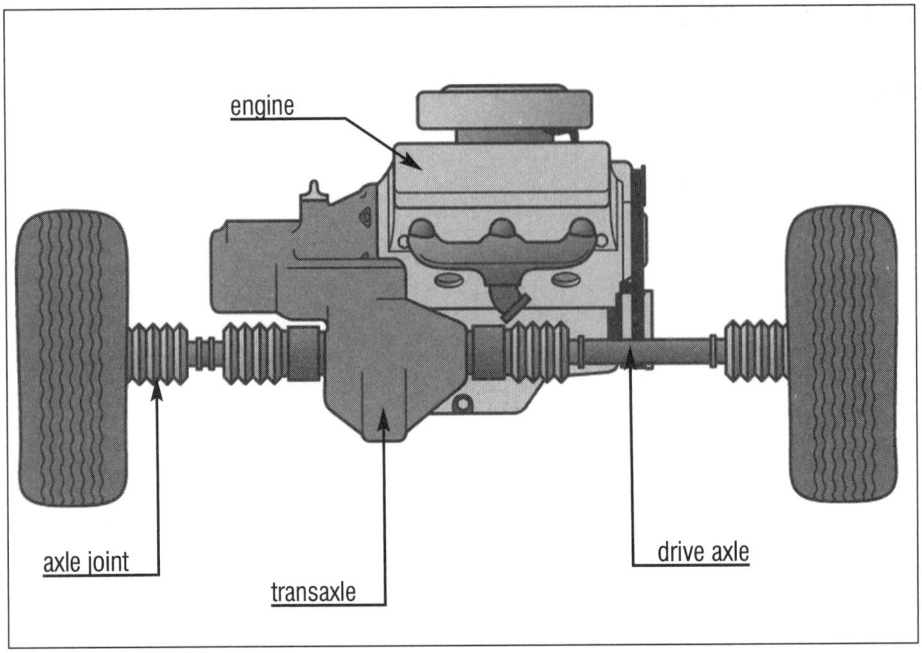

If you and your mechanic have trouble locating the wobble, try the easiest and least expensive fixes first. Have the shop spin balance the tire and wheel assembly. If the wheel is out of center, the balancing process will show it.

Whatever the cause, do not let a wobble go uncorrected for long. If left alone for many months (some drivers can get used to almost anything), the wobble may damage more parts, compounding your problems.

If your car has front-wheel drive and the wobble comes from the rear, check tires, then wheels. If the car is rear-wheel drive, do vice versa. But a front wobble in a front-wheel-drive car or a rear wobble in a rear-wheel-drive car can indicate problems with wheels, tires, or drivelines.

Drive Shaft Wobbles

FIGURE 11-2: Drive shaft on a car with rear-wheel drive

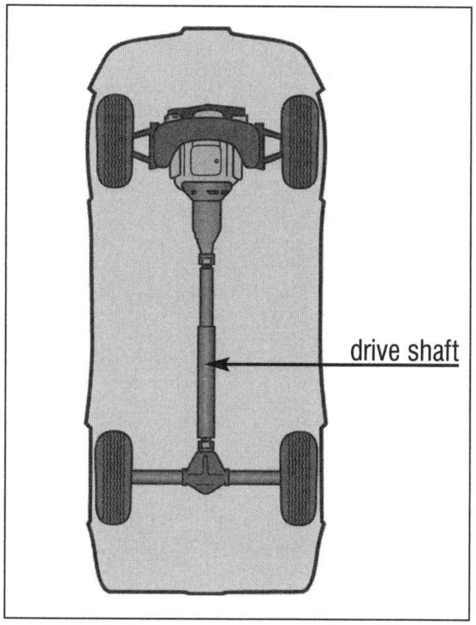

On rear-wheel-drive cars and four-wheel-drive vehicles, a wobble can develop in the drive shaft (see **FIGURE 11-2**). Drive shafts are different from the drive axles. These vibrations come from universal joint problems. As the joint wears, the shaft will run out of center. When this is the problem causing a wobble in a rear-wheel-drive car, the whole vehicle shakes. In a vehicle equipped with four-wheel drive, this same wobble problem will be felt as vibration either in the front end or under your feet.

Knocks

Knocks can come from all over the car. A knock can come from an improperly changed tire. Remember the crisscross pattern for changing a tire? Brake pads and brake calipers can knock when a warped rotor slaps them back and forth. A slight knock or pulsation can occur when a less-warped rotor vibrates against the brakes when they are applied. Knocks can come from the shocks or struts, usually when the rubber cushion (called a bushing) on either end, where the shock is connected to the car, has aged and lost its bounce or has fallen apart. But most knocks come from under the hood.

Fuel Knock

Fuel knock is the most common knock. It is caused when the fuel squirted into one or more cylinders detonates before the piston has completed its motion and fully compressed the air/fuel mixture. This early detonation is called preignition, meaning the fuel is ignited before the proper time. It ignites, in fact, before the spark plug sparks.

You will hear fuel knock when you put the car under an increased load. Pay attention now, because this distinction will help you discriminate between this knock and a knock that is much more serious.

Increasing the load on your car means that you are mashing on the gas pedal to increase acceleration, up a hill, for example. To maintain the same speed going up a hill, or to increase speed up the hill, means there is a need to use more fuel to propel the weight of the car.

If, when you increase the load on the engine, you hear a rattling or knocking noise, that noise is preignition. Preignition is caused when carbon builds up in the cylinder heads. Once the car has warmed up, the carbon that has built up gets so hot it glows red. When extra fuel is added to the cylinder, it is prone to explosion by the red-hot carbon, just a bare instant before the spark plug emits its firing spark.

In newer cars, it is quite possible to have this carbon build-up but not to hear the knocking. Why? Today's cars are so smart, a computer sensor will "hear" the knocking before you can hear it and automatically readjust the engine's timing. That is to say, the computer will readjust when the spark plug sparks. But that doesn't mean the problem is solved. It just means your engine's computer has adapted to the carbon.

Eventually you will notice that your car doesn't have the power it used to. No, it probably won't be because the engine is wearing out. It will be because that "smart" computer has continuously made timing adjustments because of the carbon build-up.

FACT

When you raise the octane of the gasoline you put in your car, you lower the explosiveness of the fuel. Lower-octane gasoline tends to explode more readily, plus the carbon that has built up in the cylinder heads gets red-hot, igniting lower-octane gasoline before the spark. Higher-octane fuel resists early explosion—that solves the knocking—and higher-octane gas has more cleaning additives, which often eliminates the carbon build-up.

If you hear engine knock "under load," or if your car has lost its power, raise the octane level of your gasoline for the next six months, then drop back to the grade of gasoline the owner's manual recommends and see if the knock is gone.

It is important not to ignore this problem, whether you hear the knocking or whether the computer has resolved it. The knocking noise is a mechanical noise. It comes from the valves being forced to move in the wrong direction at the wrong time. Eventually this valve rattling will damage the pistons. In fact, every time you hear this engine noise, you are weakening the pistons; microscopic chunks are being knocked out of them.

Now you just might be thinking, "If a higher octane will stop engine knock, why don't I just run the higher grade from the get-go?" Your car will perform better on the lower octane, if that is what it is supposed to operate on, because the computer is set to run your engine on that octane level.

ALERT!

If your car is new and rattling while using the recommended fuel octane, this is not carbon build-up. Something is not right. Take the car back to the dealership and tell them that the car is "rattling" (or knocking) under load. They'll know what to look for to correct the problem.

When Bearings Wear

This section is about bearings, not little round metallic balls, as in "ball bearings." Erase that image from your head. Bearings are hard smooth surfaces that take the wear between metallic surfaces. Or you could say, bearings "bear" the stress and the friction for the parts they are designed to protect. In essence, bearings are "throwaway" pieces protecting the surfaces of non-throwaway parts. But don't get the idea that just because they are replaceable that they are cheap to replace. They aren't. Still, it is less expensive to replace a bearing than to replace the part it protects.

FACT

If you are one of those who wants to keep a car a long time, so long that the day will come for an engine overhaul, your mechanic won't be replacing rods and crankshafts, he'll just be "remachining" them and inserting new bearings.

Bearings make noise after a certain amount of wear. When engines are new, there is a minimal amount of space between the moving parts. The space is there to allow for oil. Under pressure, the oil pushes in between parts that are separated by spaces as small as 1/2,000th of an inch. The oil holds the pieces apart.

When an automobile owner allows oil pressure to drop—not you, you are going to maintain your oil with religious fervor from now on—the oil cannot hold the hot moving parts apart, and the bearings rub together, causing wear.

Engine wear is normal over time, even with properly maintained oil. Eventually the space between the bearings widens to the point that the oil no longer completely fills the space between the parts.

The most noticeable type of bearing wear is rod-bearing wear. Once the rods begin to wear, you hear a knock when you rev up the engine, followed by a fainter knock as the RPMs come down. That's the bearings rattling in the space.

This kind of knocking noise can be distinguished from preignition knock in two ways. The first way is by sound. Preignition knocking consists of more rapid, multiple knocks in rapid succession that are higher in pitch. Bearing knocking is deeper, with a slower, more rhythmic sound. These two knocks are also distinguishable by the manner in which they occur. Preignition knocking will be heard when the car is at road speed and begins to accelerate (when extra fuel is being sent to the pistons), when load is being added to the engine. A knock from worn bearings can be heard immediately upon beginning to drive. Here's another hint: With the radio playing, you won't hear preignition knocking, but you will hear rod bearings knocking.

If you believe what you are hearing is knocking from the rod bearings, stop immediately before you inflict much greater damage to your car. If you hear it as soon as you turn on your car, shut it off and tow it to your mechanic.

How long can a car be safely driven with rod bearing damage?
If the noise is not loud and you are close to home, you may want to try. But if the noise turns loud, stop. This problem can go from bad to terrible in an instant.

Clicking Lifters

Clicking lifters have a rhythm similar to rod bearings, but the noise is lighter, less a knock, and more of a click. And the problem is somewhat less severe than rod bearings, but it is not good. It can be distinguished from preignition noise because it can be heard while the car runs in idle. Preignition noise can only be heard when you increase the load on the car, i.e, accelerate, getting the car (and not just the engine) to move faster.

A clicking lifter will have one of two causes. It may be caused by debris. Sometimes the debris frees itself and is washed into the oil filter. If you are getting a lot of lifter noise, sometimes a change of oil and a new filter will break down the debris.

A clicking lifter may also be a mechanical problem. The engine will need to be taken apart so that the lifter can be replaced. That's the bad news. The good news is, a bad lifter will not leave you stranded. That is, the car will remain drivable.

Squeaks and Squeals

Squeaks come from the rubber drive belt, which turns the alternators, power-steering pump, and water pump. When a squeak occurs, most of the time it is because the rubber belt is dry and getting hard. As the belt ages, the traction lessens, and the belt begins to slip. When the belt slips it causes a squeal.

If you hear an evenly paced "squeak . . . squeak . . . squeak" when you rev up the engine, that noise is generated each time the belt slips, usually at the same worn section of the belt.

There are also "mechanical" conditions that cause a belt to squeak. While it is possible for a belt to wear excessively fast, the chances are good that if the belt is not ready for a change, the problem is not actually the belt.

If the engine has an antifreeze leak that spurts on the belt, the antifreeze will act as a lubricant between the belt and the parts it is supposed to turn. Other leaks can have the same effect on the belt. Belt squeaks can happen when it rains and water gets on the belt. Some makes and models seem to be consistently worse than others with the water problem.

If a belt begins to squeak, check for belt wear first. If you are following this book's maintenance program, you'll be able to rule out this problem quickly. A second quick and easy troubleshooting remedy is to open the hood of the car and look up. If you see a streak across the hood, a streak directly in line with the belt, your car has a leak. Some type of liquid is spewing onto the belt, and as the belt spins, it is slinging that telltale streak across the underside of the hood. That streak will also be seen on the fender wells directly in the same line.

ALERT!

Never use belt dressing (available at all parts stores) on a serpentine belt. If a serpentine belt is slipping, belt dressing will only make it worse. It clogs the multiple grooves on the belt. Yes, it will work for about ten minutes, or maybe a whole day, but after that, the problem is back.

There is a third possible cause to squeaking belts: the belt tensioner. If your car has a lot of miles, the spring-loaded belt tensioner may have begun to wear out. This belt tensioner is the only mechanism keeping your belt tight enough to spin all the pulleys your car requires it to spin. As the tensioner weakens after tens upon tens of thousands of miles, the belt will begin to squeak. Or the belt will begin to show signs of excessive wear. If you have the gumption, you can probably tackle this job. It is usually mounted to the engine by a single bolt.

If there is still a problem with squeaks or excessive wear, let the mechanic know all the steps you have tried, and have him check the pulley alignment. Usually this is never a problem, but if your car has been in an accident, it is a possibility.

Squeaky Blower Motors

If the blower cooling and heating the passenger compartment squeaks, it usually squeaks on the low fan speeds. It can be a sign that the motor is beginning to wear, and inside the motor, metal is rubbing against metal. At slower speeds there is more contact, so the noise is louder.

Often, turning the fan to high reduces or eliminates the noise. Why? An electric motor is suspended around an electromagnet. The faster it spins, the less contact its metal parts have; it “floats” more.

If the squeaking does subside the faster you cause the blower to spin and increases when you slow the motor down, it usually means the fan motor is wearing out, although it is sometimes a hard diagnosis to make. . Once the squeaking begins, it is time to replace the fan motor. Tolerating the squeak is just a matter of personal endurance. How long can you take it? Blower motors are usually throwaway parts. Some fan motors are easy to access and replace; others are very time-consuming.

That’s the bad news, but these motors are very durable. Sometimes there is another cause to the squeak: debris–you know, the infamous lollipop stick or some other item fallen through the defrost vent. Something may be rubbing up against the fan as it turns. You may be hoping that the squeaking noise will just go away on its own. And you know what? Sometimes it does.

FACT

If a squeal or squeak emanates from a metal part, the fan motor, the water pump, or any other metal parts, the sound indicates excessive wear. The part needs to be replaced. Can you wait awhile to replace the part? How lucky do you feel?

The Groaning Water Pump

When a water pump goes bad, sometimes it groans, sometimes it chirps, sometimes it makes no noise at all. Usually (but not always) the noise is pitched lower than the noise coming from a belt: The belt sounds more like a cricket or a bird, the water pump more like a groan. If the belt is new and there are no leaks yet still there is a noise, check the water pump.

Rattling Noises

A rattling noise usually means timing system problems. Cam lobes (see Chapter 1) make certain the valves into the cylinders open and close at just the right moments—that's called timing. Your car will use one of three methods to maintain proper timing: It will use two gears and a chain (the setup looks like a bicycle chain with front and rear sprockets), or a "gear-to-gear" drive where a pair of gears mesh, or a timing belt that connects to a pair of pulleys. The belt and pulleys are notched. If you hear a rattle from under the hood, it means that your car employs one of the first two types of timing systems.

E ALERT!

To properly diagnose any engine noises, be certain you know what type of components your car has. If you don't know, and the owner's manual leaves out some of that information, even the most experienced backyard mechanic shouldn't hesitate to ask a professional for help. Cars utilize new systems so often, it is no sign of a lack of mechanical prowess if you don't know.

After many miles, the chain stretches, and it no longer fits as tightly between the gears. Now picture this: One side of the gear is pulling the chain, the other side is simply releasing it from the gear teeth. If the engine is pulling in a clockwise motion, the chain is taut on the right of the gear, but slack on the left. The slacker side now flops. The flopping causes the chain to bang against the side of the cover on the system.

The resulting noise sounds like a rock rattling in a can, a hollow, slapping noise. In gear-to-gear drive, the noise comes as the gears wear and no longer fit as tightly together as they once did.

Once the rattle starts, fix the timing system. Do not wait. If your car is equipped with the gear-to-gear system, the need to fix the timing system in a hurry is probably less essential. There are no guarantees that it will last longer than a rattling chain-drive timing system, but it could. Still, no good will come from waiting, and more harm to your car surely will. Once the chain begins to rattle, it is inclined to slip and damage the engine.

Timing belts work similarly to the chain system. And the belt is prone to stretching over time, with the pulling side taught and the opposite side slack. Once this occurs, you may detect a fluttering noise as the belt touches the cover. It is a different noise to detect because the cover is plastic, and the belt has a rubber exterior.

CHAPTER 12

Working with Whistles and Sucking Sounds

Some whistles and sucking sounds are clear warning signals that something is wrong; others are nuisances that will drive you nuts if you can't block them out. This chapter describes the ones you can ignore and those that will require your serious attention.

The Roar from Outside

Ever noticed how someone's new car always seems quieter than your older one? It's true that sometimes the reason has to do with differences in the engine or the wind-resistant shape of the newer model, but it may be nothing more than that the weather stripping around the door that seals the inside from the outside has, well, weathered.

Determining Why Weather Stripping Erodes

Hot weather followed by cold and the constant exposure to the sun eventually take their toll on an automobile, including the rubber and foam parts. The suppleness of weather stripping will change imperceptibly, but eventually it doesn't mold quite so pliably between window and doorframe, or doorframe and auto body. Outside noise leaks inside, and so does a little bit of outside moisture. The foam stays more compressed than it used to. It is no longer as elastic, and eventually it begins to crack and tear.

FACT

Keeping a car for a long time—eight, ten years, even more—makes great economic sense. But be prepared to spend money when you must to keep the car pleasant for your use. A weather stripping kit for a door is more expensive than many vital auto parts. Don't suffer with the results of your poor installation job when a pro can do it right and fast.

Fixing the Problem

There are no quick and easy fixes. You can either live with it, get a new car, or install new weather stripping. Some weather stripping designed to fit certain makes of cars may only be available from a dealer or from a body shop. Some of it is not expensive.

As easy as this job may seem in your imagination (and obviously, if you do it wrong, it won't leave you stranded in a bad part of town on a dark night), the job takes a measure of precision. All the old glue and weather stripping must be removed, and the new glue and weather stripping installed in just the proper position so that both the door and the window close effortlessly and snugly. Try it yourself if you wish, but once into this project, you may decide there are better ways to spend your money than to have someone redo your goofed-up job.

ALERT!

> Quick fixes may work, but they will not be aesthetically desirable. Some people will take the adhesive weather stripping designed for house doors and attach it to the old weather stripping of the car door. With skill, or dumb luck, it may work fine . . . for a while.

If you're keeping your car long enough for this to become a problem, you've already saved a bundle in car payments. Crack open the piggy bank and get the job done properly.

Troubleshooting Whistling and Vibrating Noises

Whistling and vibrating noises can come from a great variety of causes. Some noises your car makes you may never hear unless the car is running and you are standing beside it. Other noises can only be heard when your car is in motion. Some of those you'll hear behind the wheel with the windows up. Other noises you may not hear unless you are driving with the windows down and you catch the echo off a wall. Some noises will only be generated at fast speeds.

It is a good habit to pay attention to the noises your car makes in a variety of situations, and to vary your driving habits a bit to make certain your ears are monitoring for possible quirks in all driving circumstances. Turn off the radio occasionally and drive in silence. Roll down the windows sometimes and listen.

A Rhythmic Click at Low Speed

Driving past a wall or a large building at low speed with the window down is like seeing your reflection in the mirror. The mirror reminds you of what others see; the wall echoes what those outside your car can hear.

A rhythmic clicking sound bouncing back your way usually means something has become trapped between the treads of a tire. This usually occurs in the deeper treads of newer tires. Most of the time the click is nothing more than the nuisance noise of a stone wedged between the treads. This has probably happened to your car dozens of times that you never knew about, and the stone was eventually thrown free. But do check out the noise when you hear it. Examine your tires. Roll the car back a little at a time to inspect the tread on all four tires. It is just as possible to trap a nail, a screw, or some other hard object with puncturing potential. You just might save yourself a tire repair, or a flat tire, if the sliver of metal has already worked its sharper end into the tire.

> If your car has hubcaps, sometimes a loose hubcap will rattle or click as the tire turns. These aren't big deals, but the act of noticing noise may help prevent a real problem.

Vibration Noises and Whistles

The faster the car travels, the more air speed can play tricks. Everyone has heard the wind whistle and moan through the trees. At fifty-five to seventy-five miles per hour, there is quite a wind whisking all around your car.

Most car manufacturers are no longer using chrome trim, partly because of weight—lighter cars are more fuel efficient—and partly because it is "out of style," and certainly other reasons exist. But a piece of chrome partly detached from the body of the car with air whipping by at seventy miles an hour could provide a variety of haunting tones.

For the same reasons, but to a lesser degree, plastic and rubber trim will yield tuneful troubles when loose.

If you are maintaining your car well, don't overlook the rubber trim around windows, or the trim pieces accenting doors. A loose piece is the likely or potential culprit for noise.

Some cars are designed with extremely thin radio antennas. Have you ever watched one vibrate at highway speed? Some will produce a buzzing sound. Some will begin to whistle in the wind. People whose ears are sensitive to high-pitched noises will easily notice the sound and may take the car back to the dealer complaining.

Yet it is quite possible that no one in the dealership's shop can hear the noise. Some designers have included a plastic sheath on the thin antennas to reduce wind noise. If you have recently purchased a late-model used car and notice the whistling or buzzing, buy a plastic sheath for the antenna. There is a good chance the car originally came with one that cracked or simply was removed by the previous owner.

Interior Whistles

After a car has some miles and a few years, you may begin to notice a whistling noise when you turn on the blower—heat or air conditioning, it won't matter. The whistling or sometimes dull roaring effect may evolve so gradually that you don't notice it until someone else points it out to you. Or the noise may occur suddenly.

For most air-related noises, it probably helps to think of the brass and woodwind instruments in an orchestra. Noises erupt from air being channeled a certain way, or from air causing an object to vibrate rapidly.

Over several years, the ductwork directing air to the windshield and through the vents on the dash and down at your feet may begin to separate, creating an open space. Air that once rushed through the ducts to the destination you selected now rushes through and around the ducts, creating a breathy sound (some call it a roar) when the fan is turned on high.

Not only can you usually hear the problem, often you can feel the problem. The air now exits one or more sets of openings disproportionately. The heat, for example, may blow more vigorously on the passenger's feet than on the driver's, or more air may blow when the defrost setting is chosen than when heat is selected. You may even hear the breathy roar more on one of those settings than the other, usually on the setting that prohibits most the selected flow of air. Sometimes the same problem will create a whistle instead. The position of the opening, its size, and how the air blows across (or through) it makes the difference.

Either way, pieces of the sealing material, tape or foam, eventually make their way through a heating duct and onto the floor of the passenger compartment. Sometimes a piece may be blown through the air-conditioning vent. The gravity of the problem is mostly determined by your level of tolerance.

Or a whistling blower can be caused by an obstruction, something that has fallen through the defrost vent, maybe pushed through another opening by a child.

Whistles from the Squirrel Cage Fan

Usually the whistling noise is created as just described, and that is the most likely cause, but it is also possible that a broken fan blade in the squirrel cage fan that delivers the air creates a blower whistle. Since the fan is now off balance with a broken blade, this whistle is usually accompanied by a vibration.

The most damage that you will do leaving this problem untended is eventual destruction of the fan itself. Tolerate the noise and pay for a new fan later, or opt for quiet and pay for a replacement now.

Transmission Pump Whistles

If you've ever stood where you could hear a car coming from a long way away and could hear the car going for a long time after it has passed by, you might have heard a whistle; a whistle that preceded any motor noise generated by the automobile and lingered after the motor sounds subsided. That kind of whistle comes from the transmission. Anyone inside the car will be completely oblivious to it, unless the car's windows are down.

As the transmission wears, fluid pressure will begin to bypass some of the seals, and air may get in the system. A faulty filter in the transmission pan or a filter with a crack in the filter housing will allow air into the system and a whistle to escape.

As the transmission ages, it may develop a whine/whistle noise. If ever in doubt about the health of the car's transmission, take it to a transmission shop and have the transmission tested. The shop will road-test the car and check system pressure, shift points, and all the basics.

A Sucking Sound from the Heater Control Unit

The heater control unit, the device that controls the flow of air out of the heater, the vent, or out of the defrost, is often a vacuum-controlled unit. The sucking or hissing noise emanates from a pair of half disks that rotate against each other, sealing and unsealing, directing the flow of air.

As the disks age from use, a small gap forms. Since these disks no longer are sealed continuously, a sucking noise is created every time you change the selector, as those half disks reseal. Yes, the system is wearing, but as long as the selector keeps shifting the flow of air at your command, you have nothing to worry about.

How Vacuum Leaks Can Affect Performance

All of today's cars use a computer to control the air/fuel ratio that gets into the engine. A vacuum leak anywhere in the engine allows for extra air in the engine. The computer is being forced to make adjustments. If the leak is large enough, it will affect the way the engine runs. You may not notice it on the highway, but when idling, the engine will run rough.

It is possible that a vacuum leak is bad enough that the computer summons more fuel to compensate. Black smoke indicates that too much fuel was entering the cylinders (see Chapter 14). A vacuum leak can create this situation, too. The leak is confusing the computer; more air in the system to the computer means more fuel is needed.

FACT

Here's a quick sign of a vacuum leak. The heater control box won't send air through any exit points, but the defrost vents and the car runs rough. When vacuum is lost, the system automatically blows through the defroster (it's a safety feature designed to help keep the windshield clear). Coupled with rough idling, a vacuum leak is a sure thing.

Locating a Vacuum Leak

First, let it be said that with some cars even the vacuum hoses themselves are hard to find. If that is the case with your car, the best you can do is identify the symptoms and relay that information to your mechanic. But on some cars vacuum hoses are easy to find, and with a service manual–if you want to go that far–you can find them on every car.

To locate a vacuum leak, the engine must be running, with the hood and your ears open. When the engine is operating, it is creating vacuum. You are listening for a sucking sound; to some ears it may sound like a hiss. An enormous amount of air is being drawn into a very small area. You should be able to hear it.

Exploring Methods for Finding the Leak

One way to find the leak is to look around and move your ear around the engine, moving the vacuum tubing gently. If you hear differences in engine noise when you move a certain tube, you know that you have located the tube with the leak.

> If you have a car that is more than four years old and you are getting valve rattle, keep in mind that one possible cause is a vacuum leak to the EGR valve.

Some cars have a plastic covering that sits on top of the intake of the engine. It will have to be removed first (just a screw or two) before you will be able to hear a leak in a vacuum hose or manipulate a hose.

The other way is to take a nonflammable brake cleaner, available at parts stores, and spray the vacuum hoses one at a time, and slowly. Listen for the engine to stumble.

What you are doing is spraying a fume into the engine that is sent to the cylinders and burned. When you hit the spot with the leak, you will notice a definite drop in RPM, because the brake-cleaning fluid will shoot directly to the cylinders through the vacuum leak.

Once you hit the spot, don't keep spraying. Now search the area where you sprayed and locate the leaky hose. This is one of those jobs you can easily attempt in your garage. With a little luck and half an hour to kill, you may locate the leak. Buy some cheap new vacuum tubing and the problem is solved.

The Vacuum Needed for Fuel-Injection Systems

Most fuel-injection systems use a fuel pressure regulator; a spring-loaded device preset to open at a certain pressure according to manufacturer guidelines. The pressure regulator uses engine vacuum to vary pressure as the car accelerates. In acceleration, a car needs more fuel. The regulator increases fuel pressure when you push down on the gas pedal. Pressing the gas pedal causes the vacuum to drop in the engine. As it does, the fuel pressure regulator bumps up the fuel pressure because it is losing its vacuum source. Adding more pressure increases the fuel input to the cylinders. As the car attains the desired speed, the regulator starts drawing vacuum and the fuel pressure is reduced.

ALERT!

If troubleshooting leads you to a vacuum leak, replace all the vacuum hoses. The additional time spent, and money for that matter, is nominal. Also, in a pinch, some electrician's tape will seal a vacuum leak temporarily. But engine heat will cause the problem to return shortly. Replace the vacuum hoses.

Getting a Handle on Vacuum and the EGR Valve

EGR stands for exhaust gas recirculation. All it means is that when the EGR valve is open, a little bit of the exhaust is being returned to the engine intake. It is an emissions device designed to help the engine achieve better combustion and help stop valve rattle. It directs exhaust to be reburned and helps cool the cylinders. The system only works when the car is up to speed. On some cars this system is electrical, but roughly 90 percent of the cars on the road use vacuum to make the system work. As the car moves, the computer will open the valve up, and exhaust gases are returned to the intake.

How the Vacuum Line Goes to the Brake Booster

The vacuum line to the brake booster is the largest vacuum line in diameter on the car: A lot more vacuum is required to pull the brake booster and make braking easy.

The brake booster is the large doughnut-shaped object behind the brake master cylinder that contains a rubber diaphragm. When you press the brake pedal, a valve opens, allowing vacuum to pull on the diaphragm toward the front of the car. The brake booster is helping the driver push the brake piston in the master cylinder.

In reality, all the driver is doing when pushing the brake pedal is directing a valve to open. The more you push, the more it opens, and the harder the diaphragm pushes on the brake piston.

E FACT

The brake booster is the reason a power-brake system is so smooth and easy. You are controlling a valve, and the vacuum pressure is doing all the work for you. If you've ever used manual brakes, you know what a great invention power brakes are.

If you have a hard brake pedal—a pedal so hard to push that you must grip the steering wheel with both hands and press down on the brake with all your might—and the engine is idling extremely fast; or if the hard brake pedal is coupled with an engine that dies at a stop, both are good indications that the vacuum hose to the brake booster is off.

The key is the hard pedal. Either of the other two symptoms may exist. If the computer can cope with all the extra air (by putting enough extra fuel into the cylinders), the engine races. If the computer can't cope with all the air (can't inject enough extra fuel), the engine dies. But the hard brake pedal coupled with either symptom is a good clue that the vacuum line to the brake booster is leaking or has even been pulled off.

When replacing major parts, make sure the parts were produced by your car's manufacturer. This probably means you'll have to have your vehicle serviced at a dealer instead of an independent service station, but as a result, you'll be using parts that are made to fit the exact specifications of your vehicle.

CHAPTER 13

What's That Smell?

Ever been in a line of traffic stopped dead on the interstate? Drivers stop their cars, but don't turn off their engines, and some even get out of their cars and start making friends. Then suddenly a smell pours through your car's vents. "Is that my car?" We've all felt the fear. When it comes to cars, apart from the "new car" fragrance, all the other smells may be cause for concern.

The Moldy Smell of Summer

Okay, so maybe this first smell doesn't bode ill for your car's well-being, but it could be a problem for some folks' health. And despite all the advances in the world of cars over the last hundred years, this one stinky problem is a definite setback for automotive technology: mold in the air-conditioning system.

If you've conquered all your allergies in the house, pet hair, dust mites, you name it, but since your last car purchase you've noticed that you've begun having some trouble again, consider mold breeding and growing in an ideal climate inside your car. The problem is more pervasive than ever.

The short and most poetic answer is that we have done it to ourselves. The government we elect makes restrictive demands on the auto manufacturer, and we make selective demands on the same manufacturer to put into autos all the goodies that we desire, more power, better gas mileage, longer lasting tune-ups, heavy-duty electrical systems for televisions and video games, more leg room in the interior. The humble engineer is left to do it all with the same limited space under the hood: The air-conditioning system is confined to a much smaller space than in the past. Air flowing across the engine can't hit all the parts and systems and dry out the excess moisture that an air-conditioning system produces. Your car is a breeding ground for mold spores.

Understanding How and Where the Mold Grows

The moisture sits in the evaporator core. The evaporator core is the unit in the air-conditioning system used to transform refrigerant from a liquid to a gas. It is at this point that cooling takes place. It is also at this point that condensation occurs and water droplets can pool. Most of the moisture drains down and out onto the road, but in newer cars some of it lingers.

The mold grows in the evaporator core. Air conditioners in newer cars are designed as units—a very good idea. It saves space. If you are constantly on the go, you may never have a problem because enough air is rushing through the engine daily to control (probably not eliminate, but control) the growth of mold. But let the car sit for a couple of days and your evaporator core/breeder farm will get busy.

Start up the car, turn on the air, and the mold your car has been nurturing blows directly into your face. When the problem is bad, the moldy smell is as obvious as used sweat socks forgotten in the bottom of the hamper for too long.

The smell goes away with the air conditioner fan running on high and the car moving swiftly down the road. But think of all those mold spores that have been blowing at you. And they'll be back the next time the car sits for a day or so.

Eliminating the Mold—and the Smell

There are kits available at parts stores. The kit consists of a spray in a can and a very long tube to be attached to the business end of the can. The directions will instruct you to snake the tube down a vent from inside the passenger compartment, right into the evaporator, and spray it. End of problem.

That Sweet Smell of Heat

One chilly morning as your car blows hot air across your feet, you become aware of a sweet smell wafting through the car. Some people shut off their heaters immediately, fearful of a major problem, worried more about doing damage than about staying warm. Others keep blowing the heater, praying that the sweet smell lacks the noxious punch to overpower them. But since you are reading this book, you recognize the sweet smell of coolant, and you know it won't kill you. But you also know that it means your car has a problem: It's a leak in the heater core.

Getting a Quick Refresher about the Heater Core

The heater core is part of the cooling system (see Chapter 7). It sits beneath the dash, between the passenger compartment and the engine. Heat cannot blow across your toes until the engine has heated sufficiently to warm all the coolant in the system. Once the coolant is up to temperature, air directed across the heater core enters the passenger compartment as hot air.

FACT

Ever wondered how hot the air is that your heater delivers? Think about it. If an engine operates at nearly 250 degrees Fahrenheit, then the air coming to you must be very warm. It is. The air blowing across your feet enters the compartment at around 186 degrees.

Recognizing the Smell of Antifreeze

When the heater is blowing and the air it blows has a slightly sweet smell to it, the heater core has an antifreeze leak. The leak may be very tiny, a pinhole leak. Probably the cooling system is leaking only under pressure, as the system rises to operating temperature.

Sure, it's possible to go the entire winter with the system operating this way, keeping a close eye on the amount of coolant in the system. But a dangerous driving condition could arise. The leaking coolant could fog the windshield. And if the leak is bad enough, it could keep the windshield foggy.

The heater core itself is not very expensive. For most vehicles, the cost of the replacement part is $30 to $50. But since most of them are not easy to reach, the labor to replace the part may take the better part of a day.

Flush the cooling system when you should (see Chapter 7), and maintain the right mixture in between flushes. Help prevent corrosion and the ensuing costly repairs before they happen. If the heater core has rusted to make a leak, there will be rust in the rest of the system, too.

The Foul Smell of Heat

Any fluid in the car can and will leak through a weak or worn part. Motor oil is no exception. Oil can find its way to the surface of the engine block in a number of ways. First, let's talk about the smell.

Smells can be difficult to describe. The odor of oil burning smells metallic and hot and thick. Usually you won't just get a little whiff of it. The stench will be strong and obvious. Still, with oil burning on the engine surface, it is easier to describe when you will smell it than to describe the odor itself.

Usually, if oil is burning, you will smell it when the car is stopped at a traffic light. Sometimes you may pull to a stop behind another car, and in seconds you smell the oil. It could be coming from your own engine, or the smell could be coming out of the tailpipe of the car in front of you. Oil can be burned leaking on the engine, or oil can be burned leaking into the engine. You may need to wait until you have stopped at another traffic light at the head of the line or behind a different car just to be certain the oil smell belonged to that other vehicle and not yours.

Oil Burning on the Surface of the Engine

The valve cover gasket, intake gasket, oil pan, and the rear main seal (the seal at the back of the crankshaft) make up a likely list of oil leak locations. As bearings wear and seals and gaskets dry out, oil will leak, dripping between the engine and the transmission. Most of the time smoke burning on the engine will come from a valve cover on the top of the engine. Oil burning externally probably won't break down the car, but the problem will not go away. Gaskets and seals should be replaced.

Oil Burning on the Inside of the Engine

Oil can also leak inside the engine. When piston rings and valve stems wear, oil will seep into the cylinders and will eventually foul the plugs, keeping the plugs from sparking and burning the gasoline.

Locating the Leak

Whatever the source of the leak, it must be found. You can do some simple troubleshooting to help determine the urgency of the problem.

If your engine has too much grime to be able to determine the leak's source, degreasing the engine is a good start. Purchase a can of engine degreaser and follow the directions on the can. A big leak will show itself quickly on a clean engine.

If the leak is very small, you can also purchase oil dye at the parts store. This dye is a fluorescent chemical that you place in the crankcase, the same way you would add oil. Run the engine; then take a black light—like those ones out of the '60s, but made more rugged for this diagnostic test—and shine it around the engine. Look for a glowing. If you find the glow, you find the leak.

The Sweet Smell of Leaking Antifreeze

Often, you can use the location of the sweet smell to find the leak. If you smell it inside the car every time you blow the heater and the smell goes away after turning the heater off, the leak is in the heater core. Because you can't check out the heater core without taking it out of the car, you may as well replace it, if it must be checked.

If you smell coolant when you walk around to the front of the vehicle, the coolant leak is from the radiator, or from one of the two main coolant hoses. If you don't get a good whiff until you open the hood, the leak is probably smaller, probably a pinhole leak in a hose or a leak in the intake gasket.

Let your nose lead you. Smell is usually the first sign that you've got a problem. Often you will smell a leak before a loss of fluid or oil can even be noticed.

Brake Smells

Hot brakes will emit smells. A hot brake is a burning brake. A burning brake has an acidic smell: very strong and distinctive, a rubbery, pungent smell. (If you have a standard transmission, you can get the same smell if you overuse the clutch.)

Brake material is designed to work within a high temperature range, around 900 to 1,200 degrees in short bursts. But a brake that is sticking will overheat and can actually catch fire.

There are a variety of qualities to brake pads. Better brake pads withstand heat better. If you like driving fast and stopping quickly, a better brake pad will pay off.

If after a drive you think you smell a brake, walk around the four wheels and sniff. If you think you have located an overheated brake, put your hand on that wheel—not the tire, the center. Compare the heat you find on that suspect wheel with the heat of the others. If it is hotter than the other three, your nose and your hand have located a problem that you can point out to your mechanic.

FACT

Smell works well for clutch problems, too. If you smell a brake smell but can't pinpoint by smell any of the four wheels, if the touch test fails to turn up a hot brake, and if you have a car with a manual transmission, you've probably discovered a clutch problem.

The Rotten Egg Smell

A catalytic converter is an air-cleaning device that helps the car reburn excess fuel. One of the by-products of burning fuel is sulfur. Eventually the catalytic converter loses its effectiveness and is able to burn up less and less excess fuel. The less fuel the catalytic converter can burn, the greater the leftover sulfur being emitted from the exhaust. Sulfur smells like rotten eggs, or at least that is how most people with converter problems describe their dilemma.

You can buy additives that promise to clean a catalytic converter. Try it. But more than likely, you will wind up replacing the old converter.

Catalytic converters should last a very long time. But if your car has only 50,000 miles (or less) and your nose is complaining, the automobile has a problem elsewhere that has caused the catalytic converter to wear out much too fast.

ALERT!

Smelling rotten eggs may mean your car has a fuel-system problem. Usually the problem is an "overfuel" condition, meaning too much fuel is entering the system for too long.

When you first start your car in the morning, the computer senses that the car is cold and sends more fuel to be burned. (Prior to the mid-'80s, that was the work of the throttle and the carburetor.) The extra fuel helps the car warm up quicker, and it helps it run smoothly while it warms up.

Once the car achieves its optimal operating temperature, the computer reduces fuel to the engine, giving it just enough to keep it running smoothly with decent power. But the system isn't working properly if excess fuel continues to be delivered. The prolonged supply of excess fuel will significantly shorten the life of the catalytic converter.

Smelling rotten eggs at 100,000 miles should be considered normal. Replace the converter. But smell the same smell at 50,000, and . . . yes, you still need to replace it (your car probably won't pass its next emissions test unless you do), but have your fuel system checked out, too. You're wasting fuel.

It is possible to tolerate the offensive odor, and many people do. But eventually that converter will become so clogged with fuel by-product that it will have the same effect as a prankster stuffing a banana up the tailpipe. The fume build-up will smother your engine and make it shut down.

Even if no "check engine" light comes on, and the computer is accepting the overfuel condition, there is something wrong. The smell is the telltale sign.

Even on cars with a three-year or 36,000-mile warranty, many states require coverage on emissions parts for five years or 50,000 miles. Meaning: Even if your car is technically out of warranty, your emissions parts (catalytic converter included) may still be covered.

The Smell of Raw Fuel

The smell of gasoline can come from several sources. If the smell is the fragrance of fuel right out of the pump, it means that there is a leak somewhere between the fuel tank and the engine, a leak letting raw unburned fuel into the atmosphere. Usually it will mean corrosion in the fuel line. In the not-too-distant past, fuel lines were often made of rubber. Most of those have been replaced with steel fuel lines. They do last longer, much longer. But after many years it is possible for a line to corrode and leak.

However, these days with long-lasting steel fuel lines, there is a more likely way for gasoline fumes to reach your nostrils.

Recognizing Fumes from the Charcoal Canister

Right next to your fuel tank is a charcoal canister. It is a kind of filter designed to siphon off the fumes of raw fuel emitted from the gasoline tank, store those fumes, and slowly send them on their way to the engine to be burned. A charcoal canister is just another clever way auto engineers have come up with to reduce toxic emissions.

A charcoal canister should last forever. But many will not. Next time you are at the self-serve pump and people are busy filling up all around, watch what happens at the end of the fill-up. The fuel is pumping. The driver is either busy checking routine maintenance, just like you are doing, checking the oil and eyeballing other items under the hood, or standing by the pump waiting for it to stop pumping. Suddenly, there's the click and the pump shuts itself off. Now, then, what do you and every other driver around you do? Think. No, hardly anyone ever pulls the nozzle right from the tank and hangs it up. Try again. Yes. You, and all the rest of the people filling up, squeeze the trigger on the nozzle again until the click shuts it off, and again . . . and maybe a third time, "topping off" the tank.

Sometimes fuel spills out and splatters on the ground. Sometimes it comes right to the top where it sloshes just a bit at the lip of the fill spout.

Right there at the top is a small hole. You've probably noticed it before. A tube connected to that hole is designed to carry fumes rising from the tank to the charcoal canister. But by topping off the gas tank at fill-up, gasoline, not gasoline fumes, gets drawn into the canister, ruining its ability to function as designed. There is no immediate danger of explosion, but don't overfill. Overfilling won't ruin gas mileage, either. It just means that more fumes are escaping into the environment. When the pump shuts off the first time, stop filling. Besides, topping off the tank won't add more than half a gallon of gas.

Finding a Pinhole in the Gas Tank

Before mass panic begins, it is important to say that gasoline tanks are rugged. They are designed that way. No manufacturer wants tanks that rupture easily, even when a car is in an accident. However, most modern tanks are made of plastic. It is just possible to have an accident—be struck by another car, or run into a deep ditch—and put a tiny hole in the tank.

This is not necessarily a likely occurrence, but it does happen. Should you have had an accident, and though you're able to drive the car away, you smell gasoline fumes, have the tank checked for a rupture. The leak may be so small that the fumes sting your nose but dribble imperceptibly to the ground. Trust your nose.

Getting Gasoline Odor from the Exhaust

When a car floods, the smell of gasoline can fill the passenger compartment from the exhaust system. Even late-model cars flood. When the temperature gets down to zero, and the engine barely turns over (you know, that *nyuh, nyuh, nyuh* noise you hear just before *vwoom*), the computer won't start the car until the engine is spinning at a certain number of RPM (revolutions per minute). The computer will let the engine continue to crank, pumping fuel until the RPM rises to a certain level or until the car floods—too much, way, way too much fuel in the cylinders. So, what do if you live in the frozen north? An engine heater perhaps, or keep the car sheltered.

E ALERT!

If too much fuel continues to flow through the engine, there will be a strong, pungent smell, and the fumes may sting your eyes. (There will also be black smoke.) This, too, is a flooding condition. Too much fuel is being squirted into the cylinders, and though fuel is burning, it is not burning completely or efficiently.

Back when cars had carburetors, even older-style fuel injectors, this was less of a worry. But on newer cars with port-type or sequential fuel-injection systems, the car will not catch until the engine turns a specific number of RPMs. No doubt, solutions are on the way and may already be here for some models, but as of this writing, cold-winter starts remain quirky business for the current computer/fuel-injector duo.

A Burning Rubber Smell

Sure, if you "pop a wheelie," "get it," "peel a wheel," or accelerate too fast from a dead stop, you'll get that burning rubber smell. Or if you slam on the brakes on a car not equipped with ABS, a skid will cause that smell. But nearly the same smell can occur when the belt (or one of the belts) on the engine is slipping.

Usually you'll hear a squealing noise even before the smell smacks your nostrils. It is the sound and smell of the belt spinning faster than the part it is designed to turn is rotating. Usually it happens because the belt is aging and getting hard. It has lost moisture and now has less "grip."

The Strong Smell of Burning Wires

If you have ever conducted a home improvement project that involved your home's wiring and have done something wrong that caused a wire to burn for an instant before the circuit broke, you may have smelled the odor of high heat burning the insulation of a wire. The same thing can happen in your car.

Usually this will not happen on one of the electrical systems with fuses, but rather on one of the systems that use a fusible link or a circuit breaker. It is possible to overheat the wire without tripping the safety switch. Most of these types of problems involve battery circuits such as cigarette lighters, power windows, power locks, or headlights.

The most likely occurrence comes from use of the cigarette lighter for purposes other than for which it was designed: plugging in spotlights, fans, mini-heaters, refrigerators, cell phones, radar detectors. Just because you can plug a gadget in doesn't mean that you should.

However, many newer cars are now set up with power outlets. If in lieu of a lighter that outlet has a plug denoting voltage rating, your car is set up with heavier wiring in that circuit, wiring designed for a prolonged use of electrical power. These outlets have been re-engineered.

Shorts, and thus the burning smell, can come from wiring problems other than from circuit overload. In the most vulnerable places in a car, wires are usually covered with extra layers of insulation. Sometimes a plastic sheath will cover a group of wires all along the vulnerable space, usually where the wires bend and come in close proximity with the engine.

Eventually, the insulation may wear through. If and when that happens, a bare wire touching a metal surface will short out the circuit, producing the simultaneous foul rubber-burning smell.

Even on a circuit with a fuse, it is possible for a short to occur between the fuse box and the battery, creating the burning wire.

FACT

If your car is equipped with one or more power outlets, and these outlets will be denoted as such, don't confuse them with cigarette lighters. These outlets are heavy duty, designed for prolonged power usage. Don't plug in a cigarette lighter to one. To do so may increase the risk of fire.

The first system to check when your nose detects the smell of burning oil is the oil system. But transmission fluid is also a petroleum-based fluid. When transmission fluid squirts across a hot engine, the odor is indistinguishable from burning oil to most noses, in the same way a pair of colas are difficult to distinguish unless compared sip to sip.

But a transmission leak (and its similar smell) can be distinguished from an oil leak. When a transmission leak causes that burning oil smell, there will be a puddle on the driveway. A leaky transmission is far enough away from the engine that any dripping it does will fall beneath the center of the car rather than directly under the engine.

CHAPTER 14

Clearing the Smoke

Every driver has a pretty good idea about what normal exhaust emissions look like. If you live in a state that requires an annual exhaust emissions test, you know for certain whether your car's emissions are indeed normal (acceptable) at least once a year. This chapter gives you the lowdown on smoky emissions that aren't normal.

Tailpipe Whiffs and Plumes

It makes good sense to begin at the back of the car, because that is the first place anyone ever notices smoke. The car is designed to expel exhaust from the tailpipe. The engine fires, fuel injectors spew a mist of fuel into every cylinder, the spark plugs fire, and the fuel explodes, pushing the piston away. When the piston makes the return trip up the cylinder, it pushes out the exhaust gas, sending it through the exhaust system and out of the tailpipe.

But what comes out of the tailpipe varies with the warmth of the engine and the condition of the engine or one or more of its systems or parts.

A Billowing Plume of White Steam

On a winter morning, have you ever noticed a cloud of white smoke pouring from the back of your car or belching from every car preparing to leave for the office or wherever people need to go? It seems to billow from tailpipes, almost obscuring the back of the car. Then, if there is no wind, it rises and disappears just above the trunk with only tiny whiffs surviving to climb a few more inches.

Instinctively, you have always known that this smoke has something to do with the car not yet being warm. Because within a few minutes the white smoke is gone, and you no longer notice those puffy white clouds hovering by the trunk.

Your instincts are absolutely correct. This benign "smoke" has everything to do with that first start on a cold morning. Or any start after the engine has cooled completely during winter months. And the smoke is not smoke at all, at least not the vast majority of what you see. Mostly, it is water vapor. Your car is making a cloud by releasing hot water vapor into chilly air.

The colder the engine, the greater the amount of fuel being fed into the system to get it started, keep it running, and raise its temperature to optimal operating temperature. One of the main by-products of the process of converting gasoline into energy is water vapor. As the temperature of the air drops, the greater the visual impact of the water-vapor cloud is. And as air temperature drops, the colder the engine, so more fuel is being pumped into the system, increasing the amount of steam escaping from the tailpipe.

On a cold morning in commuter traffic, you can tell which cars have just entered the fray, and which have been traveling longest. The cars with warmer engines aren't making white water-vapor clouds.

In terms of your car's engine, the more efficient it is, the greater the amount of water vapor relative to other emissions. Water vapor generally signals that all is well with your engine. But all may not be well with your exhaust system. If you find that your muffler needs to be replaced while your neighbor, who has an identical car, has never needed to replace any part of his exhaust system, can you guess what is different?

Chances are excellent that the difference lies in the miles that you drive. If you drive short hops, never allowing your car to warm up completely, and your neighbor drives somewhat longer distances, allowing his car to warm to optimal operating temperature, the heat of your neighbor's engine and the heat of that engine's exhaust system is evaporating the water, while your cooler engine is allowing water to sit in the exhaust pipe or in the muffler. And where there is water, there is corrosion. Rust.

FACT

When you see a dribble coming from the tailpipe, that dribble is not gasoline finding its way unexploded through the system. It is water. Once a car warms to its best operating temperature, most of the water evaporates before it reaches the end of the tailpipe.

The Bluish White Puff at Start-Up

Once a car begins to wear a bit, and even with magnificent maintenance habits, engines do wear. At start-up your engine is prone to emit a puff of blue-white smoke. It may appear as nothing more than a single puff. Or for several seconds after the engine fires, the tailpipe may yield white smoke with a blue hue before the smoke quits.

Your car is telling you that while the car sat overnight, a minuscule bit of oil ran down into one (or more) of the cylinders. Usually the oil leaks in past the valve stem seals, and once the engine burns it away—really it takes just a few seconds at the car's first start-up of the day—it won't be seen the rest of the day.

Is it a problem? No, not a major problem. It is not a sign that the engine is losing oil, and not a sign of excessive wear of the pistons. It will not affect the way your car runs. Analogies between the automobile and the human body don't work very well, but this analogy is close enough. The bluish white puff at start-up is no different than getting out of bed in the morning a little stiff with age. In a few seconds everything is operating just as it ought.

The Thick White Cloud after Warm-Up

The first two "smokes" were at warm-up and were insignificant. But this thick white cloud after warm-up indicates a problem. This white cloud can become so thick that if you're standing behind the car, you may not be able to see the car through the smoke. The word "smoke" remains a misnomer. This problem, too, has a closer connection to water vapor than to smoke.

You're becoming a car whiz, so now think diagnostically for a moment. White smoke—water vapor, really—came from the tailpipe at start-up. What could thicker white smoke mean now? And why only after the car has warmed to operating temperature?

If you guessed something about more water, you are almost right. If you guessed within the ballpark of what is explained in the following text, you really are becoming a car whiz.

Coolant is being burned in the engine. And a high percentage of the coolant mixture in your radiator is water, hence the white cloud. But this much thicker white cloud is forming only after the car has warmed up. Something else is going on. Coolant is entering the parts of the engine that burn fuel.

When the engine heats, the engine metal expands. The parts between different pieces of metal that keep fluids separate and in their rightful places are called gaskets. Some gaskets are rubber and some are hardly more than glorified cardboard, but all gaskets serve as seals. On top of each cylinder is a head and a head gasket. The head serves two purposes. It holds in the explosion of fuel, forcing the piston to retreat in the opposite direction, and it holds out coolant that flows across the top of each head to cool the engine.

You probably know where this is going. When a head gasket wears out, no longer expanding and contracting to fill the very tiny space between metal engine parts, coolant seeps in. The cylinders are trying to burn a mixture of fuel, air, and coolant. Not good.

If you have been keeping a check on your cooling system (see Chapter 7) and have noticed a sudden drastic drop in the coolant level in the reservoir and have begun to notice the thick white smoke, you have coolant leaking into the engine.

Do not wait for your engine to begin to run roughly, and eventually it will. Take the car in and have the head gaskets replaced before the car begins to operate poorly. Once coolant begins to leak into the cylinders, there is a chance that it will leak into the crankcase, mixing with the oil and destroying the oil's ability to lubricate the engine.

> A "cracked" head will produce the same result as a leaky head gasket. Neither you nor your mechanic may be certain which it is until repair work has begun. A "cracked" head is just that. The metal head of the cylinder has fractured and will need to be replaced.

White Smoke That Lingers

If your car is newer than the mid-'90s, you can probably skip this section. Up through that time several cars from at least two different manufacturers used a modulator valve—a valve hooked to a vacuum line on the engine to sense load.

Using this valve, it was possible for transmission fluid to be sucked into the engine. The resulting smoke resembled the thick water vapor from antifreeze in the engine, only unlike water vapor, transmission fluid—a petroleum product—lingers in the air, a true smoke.

This problem is not so critical as the cylinder head problems described earlier. It is not good, but the potential for catastrophic engine damage is not likely. What will happen is that transmission fluid leaking into the cylinders will eventually foul the spark plugs: The plugs won't fire every time, meaning a cylinder will "miss."

ALERT!

> You may not notice the coolant vapor through your rearview mirror, but you will notice this transmission leak as you look behind. The smoke can become quite thick. It doesn't dissipate; it lingers.

Compounding Problems by Ignoring White Smoke

This situation with coolant leaking into the cylinders can grow worse very quickly. If your car has not begun to run rough (i.e., the engine shakes the car and struggles to accelerate), it will begin to run poorly soon. Enough coolant leaking into one cylinder will prevent that cylinder from firing. In a four-cylinder engine, that means 25 percent of your engine's power is suddenly gone.

With coolant leaking, there is the eventual threat that the engine may overheat. The oil, which may protect the engine from severe damage if the coolant were to leak to the outside of the automobile, will fail, and your car's engine may be destroyed if the engine overheats and the coolant has been diluting the oil in the crankcase.

It is always a temptation to put off costly repairs. But break open the piggy bank and get the job done. Putting off repair of a head gasket or a cracked head can be even more devastating.

FACT

> When coolant enters the crankcase, the action of the moving parts in the crankcase "whips" the coolant into the oil, filling it full of air. It is similar to the action of an egg beater making meringue. This lighter, airy oil is worthless to your car.

White Smoke, Not Water Vapor

With most car problems, there are several clues that lead to the proper diagnosis. With white vapors, beyond what you can see, there is also what you can smell. Water vapor smells like water, like steam. You can't successfully identify many problems simply by looking. White smoke from the tailpipe, a smoke that looks a lot like the coolant problem, can also come from a transmission leak into the engine.

Black Smoke from the Exhaust System

The color of smoke your car emits may not always indicate the severity of the problem facing your automobile's health, but color helps indicate the problem's cause. Black or charcoal-colored smoke indicates that raw, unburned fuel is getting through the system.

You may have noticed black smoke belch from a flooded automobile. "Flooded" means that too much fuel has entered into the cylinders. When a car is flooded, you can smell the gasoline fumes. When the car eventually does start, it is often accompanied by a burst of black smoke out of the exhaust pipe.

The smoke itself will smell similar to gasoline, but since it came through the cylinders and the engine attempted to burn it, the smell is somewhat different. Many people who work on cars find that this smoke will make their eyes sting.

This flooding condition in today's fuel-injected cars comes from one of two places: from the fuel-injection system or from the fuel pressure. The computer on your car's engine will try to fix the problem. It will work to reduce the amount of fuel being injected into the engine. Eventually, though, the "check engine" light will come on. That's the computer telling you that it has done all that it can to reduce fuel flow, and the engine needs more help than the computer can give.

It is possible that you haven't noticed the black smoke coming from your car, but there are some other symptoms that will signal you to look closer. The car will have a loss of power and poor fuel economy. Eventually the spark plugs will foul from so much contamination that they will no longer produce a spark.

Most newer cars require lots of technical equipment to correct this problem: equipment you won't have in your personal garage.

Continuous Bluish White Smoke

What causes bluish white smoke? Oil. Only there is a second oil smoke. The other one goes away after the car starts. This one continues. Bluish white smoke that continues from the tailpipe means that oil is finding a way into the cylinders continuously.

The oil has found an opening into the cylinder. Usually this opening is around the outer edge of one or more pistons, the area known as a piston ring, the area designed to keep a tight seal between the piston and the cylinder for maximal explosion, with no oil seepage.

In this condition, careful car maintenance will call your attention to the problem. You will notice that the car is using oil. And if not already doing so, the car will begin to foul its spark plugs, and the engine will begin to run rough.

ALERT!

This is not a puzzle to solve at home. A good shop will have the necessary equipment to test each cylinder and locate the one causing the problem.

Smoke in the Passenger Compartment

Chances are good that you have seen one of the two types of "smoke" you might see entering the passenger compartment of your car. Chances are even better that one type of "smoke" you have not and may never see. The first type is condensation from the air conditioner; the second type is smoke from an electrical short.

Air-Conditioner Condensation

During the height of the cooling season, you may have noticed "smoke" blowing into the car through an air-conditioning vent. For some people, it can be alarming—Am I breathing deadly fumes? Carbon monoxide? Is my car on fire?

This grayish fume is nothing more than water vapor. On a really hot day, when humid air outside is drawn across the evaporator—the part of the cooling system that transforms the refrigerant from liquid to gas, and is where cooling takes place—most of that hot air gives up its water in the form of droplets that fall to the ground. But some of the humid air becomes water vapor that blows through the vent. The more moisture in the air, the greater the possibility of getting vapor through the vent. As soon as the vapor travels a few inches, it disappears. Once the interior of the car has cooled, you're less likely to see the vapor.

Some people who see this happen think that it is their refrigerant leaking from the system and into the car. Nope. You couldn't see the refrigerant if it were to leak, nor would you smell it.

FACT

When a car has a refrigerant leak, the gas usually leaks directly to the ground and not into the car. The refrigerant used is heavier than the surrounding air. It will seek the lowest point, and won't climb through a vent.

Steam from the Heater Core

A leak in the heater core, which you will smell as a sweet fragrance, sometimes blows through your defroster as steam. And actually, it is steam. The interior of the car can't begin to heat until the engine has raised the temperature of the coolant. Since some modern engines operate at temperatures in the neighborhood of 250 degrees, a leak in the heater core can easily present itself as steam rising when the defrost vent is open.

You may know that when the defroster is in operation, it uses the air-conditioning system to blow-dry air onto the inside of the windshield. But if the day is cool, and comfort dictates that you apply the heat, too, then you are directing air from across the heater core up through the defrost vent. A leak in the heater core can blow as steam.

You can also get steam blowing from the heating vents on the floor. Some people see this "smoke" and immediately think there is a life-threatening problem, but if the smoke smells sweet, it's a coolant leak.

Wiring Problems

Despite the sophistication of auto electrical systems and the safeguards fuses provide, it is possible to get an electrical fire. A bad smell of charred plastic accompanies any smoke from an electrical fire. It is the smell of wires burning through their insulation and shorting themselves out.

Smoke under the Hood

Smoke from under the hood is the stuff of fear. Funny thing, though. Most smoke from under the hood is not much different from the other smokes and vapors already discussed: a fluid leaking on a hot surface, an oil gasket leaking onto the exhaust manifold—the hottest part of the engine.

Steam from a Coolant Leak

After driving the car long enough to get the engine up to operating temperature, a leak from the radiator or from a radiator hose will show as steam. Usually the steam won't show itself until the car is stopped. Then the "smoke" will appear as a small puff, or as a constant rising stream; or, if a hose has just ruptured, the vapors may billow out from under the hood, looking ominous and threatening.

If you are the curious type, take care opening the hood. Keep your face back and as protected as possible. If the steam is gushing from a large opening in the radiator or a hose under pressure, that hot liquid, hotter than water boiling, can be dangerous.

Often there is no problem locating the leak. You can usually trace the steam directly to its source with your eyes. But sometimes the leak location is relatively small, larger than pinhole size, but not exactly a complete rupture of a hose. In some cases the location of the leak or the direction at which the coolant sprays out shoots the hot stream into the cooling fan. In that case, locating the leak may not be easy.

If you can drive the car home, you can let it cool and dry off. Then start the car and allow the engine to reach operating temperature while it idles. Studying the hoses and the radiator as pressure slowly builds, you should be able to find the leak before the spray soaks the engine again.

An Electrical Fire

If the smoke coming from under the hood smells like something burning, not like oil, nor like coolant steam, it will likely be an electrical fire. Smelling oil or coolant steam will happen to practically everyone. An electrical fire is not likely to happen to anyone. But it does happen. If you live in a metro area that broadcasts traffic reports each morning and afternoon, chances are that in the course of a year, you'll hear at least one traffic report announcing an engine fire that most likely started as an electrical fire.

If the smoke under the hood billows up progressively worse, this is going to be an engine fire. If you have a fire extinguisher, carefully open the hood and try to smother the flames. If you don't carry an extinguisher, leave the hood down (it may smother the flames) and get away from the car. The damage will probably be total, and the possibility of explosion high.

Chapter 15

Worse Yet, Nothing at All

Have you ever gotten into your car, turned the key, and nothing happened? If you haven't, you are either a sure bet to win the lottery or haven't been driving very long. Sooner or later, every driver inserts the key, gives it a twist, and is greeted with a most unwelcome silence. Sometimes there's a click. And sometimes the car won't even whimper.

When There's No Noise at All

Cars can refuse to start for a number of reasons. What you check, and the ultimate solution, depends on what happens when you turn the key. Maybe it's the battery. It often is, but it can be some other problem altogether.

If there are no noises at all—no clicking noises, no lights in the dash when the ignition switch is given its first twist—the first thing to check is the battery; it might be dead.

A dead battery can occur for one of two reasons: The battery has gone bad and needs to be replaced, or the battery is drained. A drained battery is very likely still a good battery, but the map light wasn't turned off at the end of a trip, or the connection for the light in the trunk or under the hood has worked loose so that the light has stayed on since you last shut that trunk or hood. Even tiny lights like these will completely drain a battery overnight.

Checking for a Dead Battery

If another car is available, the best first step is to attempt to jump-start the car. Follow the procedure described in Chapter 6: Attach the hot (red) cable to the positive terminal of the good battery, the other to the positive terminal of the bad battery; attach the black (negative) cable to the negative post of the good battery, and the other black cable to a metal surface of the engine in the dead car. Try to start it. If the car starts, the battery has either been drained (a light that didn't go off) or the battery is truly dead. Don't think that just because the car started that the battery will recharge. It might; then again it might not. The battery needs to be tested.

The best way to check the battery is to take it out of the car and take it to a shop. Many parts stores will also be glad to test a battery for you. But if you want to try an intermediate step, try this with an assistant. Have your assistant hold apart the pair of jaws at one end of a set of jumper cables, not allowing them to touch. Attach the other end to the questionable battery. Then with the jumper cables stretched as far from the open engine hood as possible, brush the set of unattached jaws together. Do not hold them together. Pass them by each other and allow them to strike in the passing. If there is a spark, the battery is not dead. Keep the pair of jaws apart and have your assistant detach the jaws from the battery. Once the car starts, take the battery to a service center and have it tested.

If the Car Refuses to Be Jump-Started

Check the battery cable connections. If you have been eyeballing your battery with every fill-up, you no doubt will have detected corrosion building up by now. Still, if your car can't be jumped, this is the logical first step, so look again. You may have missed the corrosion with a quick glance.

If there is corrosion, enough can actually break the connection to the battery. Clean the cable ends, reconnect them to the battery, and try to jump-start the car again.

If after cleaning the cables you still get nothing, take the battery out and have it checked. The problem is that on some cars these days, that is extremely difficult to do. On many cars, you can't even see the battery. It has been installed beneath the jug of windshield washer fluid. Remote terminals have been placed on those batteries to make a jump-start possible when it becomes necessary. (But that remote terminal becomes just another area to watch for corrosion.)

> A bad cell in a car battery means that the battery, designed to deliver 12 volts to an electrical system designed for 12 volts, is capable of delivering a maximum of only 10 volts (2 volts per cell). It cannot be fixed. It can only be replaced.

The Battery's Good, but Still No Start

Suppose the battery is good, everything checks out, but still there is no power into the car. The next thing to check for is a blown fusible link or blown maxifuse. Maxifuses and fusible links are the last line of defense between the battery and the rest of the car. If there is a short, these items are designed to burn out first, protecting the onboard computer and other electronic instrumentation. When a fusible link or a maxifuse burns out, the whole system shuts down.

Checking Fusible Links

In most cars these are under the hood. Where you see a number of wires bundled together, chances are, those are the fusible links. The bundling makes tracking down a burnout, if and when it happens, much easier.

A fusible link is the one place in the electrical wiring of a circuit where the wire is thinnest and weakest. This is where the circuit will fail if a fuse or maxifuse doesn't burn through when it is supposed to. It is an extra safety measure. If a fusible link has burned out (i.e., has done its job), you can often tell, because it will be burned in two. Sometimes, however, only the wire inside the insulation has burned through, leaving the insulation intact. How can you tell if such a fusible link is burned? Pull on it. If it stretches easily, the wire is burned through, and only the rubbery insulation is intact.

How does a fusible link get its name?
A fusible link behaves just like a fuse. It is the weakest section of wiring along an electrical circuit, a thin section of wire ready to burn through to save the circuit.

Checking Maxifuses

Many new cars have switched from fusible links to maxifuses. This is good news for people who would like to do as much of their own troubleshooting as possible. Under the hood, locate a square (or rectangular) box near one of the fender wells. Usually the box will say "Distribution" or "Electrical." Take the cover off and you'll find all of the maxifuses.

Each maxifuse has a clear window. You can pull it out and look through it to see if the connection is broken. If a maxifuse is blown, replacing it may get your car started. Replace it and see what happens. Maybe it was time to head to the great junkyard in the sky. If the car starts up, all may be well and probably is, but don't drop your vigilance just yet. Just as with smaller fuses, if the same maxifuse blows again in a short length of time—a day, a week, a month, a year even—it means there is a short elsewhere in the electrical guts of the car. Get it checked out pronto.

A Clicking Noise Without a Start-Up

Most people who have had their driver's license long enough to have them renewed have probably experienced a car not starting. If not a completely silent response, then this: A twist of the ignition switch evokes a clicking noise. Yes, it is an unmistakable "clicking." If you've never experienced it, relax, one day you will. And when you do, you will know it when you hear it.

More than likely this no-start problem is a problem with the starter motor itself. When the system is working properly, the driver turns the ignition switch and makes the connection between the battery and the starter solenoid. The starter solenoid, in turn, makes electrical contact with the starter motor, and the starter motor responds by turning the engine. The starter solenoid always makes a "clicking" noise when it is doing its job, but you won't hear the noise when the system is working properly, because engine noises are louder. But when the starter motor fails, you'll hear the solenoid's "click."

FACT

If you're stranded and get the clicking noise, try this; but use extreme caution. Put the car in park, and have someone take a hard object (baseball bat or tire tool) and crawl under the car, tapping continuously on the starter as you turn the key. This tapping often unsticks the starter. The starter isn't fixed, but the remedy might save you a long walk.

If your battery is good, this step should seem appropriate. But you know the old expression, "any port in a storm." It won't hurt to try to jump the engine. Sometimes it works. That extra jolt of power from an additional battery will sometimes coax the starter into doing its job.

Even so, the starter isn't fixed. Consider yourself warned, and consider getting the starter to function a lucky break. Yes, it may work for years to come or not work on the next start-up. As soon as possible, take the starter out yourself or drive the car to the shop and have it tested. There is a remote possibility that the only problem is an electrical connection problem, but not usually. Usually the starter has gone bad.

The Car Cranks but Won't Start

This problem is just another quandary shared with the whole world of drivers. You turn the key, the engine cranks, you know, spins *nyuh, nyuh, nyuh* . . ., but it will not start.

Checking the Fuses First

Since almost every vehicle on the road today has a fuel-injection system, open the fuse box (see Chapter 6). If there is a fuse blown, it could be a fuel pump fuse or even a computer fuse. Either of those will prevent the car from starting. The engine will spin, but it will not catch.

Checking the Spark Plug Wires

Alas, this is no longer the simple task it was even five or six years ago. Many cars today no longer have spark plug wires. But some do. And if your car was made prior to the mid-'90s, this is a task you can definitely try. Pull a plug wire off a spark plug. Any spark plug wire will do. Grab a screwdriver with a head small enough to probe down into the spark plug wire opening. Put the screwdriver up against a metal part of the engine and have someone turn the engine over a couple of times. What you are doing is looking for a spark.

ALERT!

> If you have a spark, the fuel is getting ignited, and the ignition system is not the problem. If there is no spark, there is possibly a problem with the ignition system. Check fuses first. If the fuses are intact, you're better off taking the car in to a pro.

Checking Your Fuel System

Be sure the car key is in the off position. Take the cap off the fuel fill tank. Put your ear next to the opening. (This process varies slightly according to the acuity of your hearing and the noise your car's fuel pump makes.) With your ear close to the tank, have someone turn the key on. You should hear a humming noise. The noise usually lasts two or three seconds. The humming you should hear is the sound of the fuel pump priming. It means that the fuel pump is working and that your car has fuel pressure.

If the fuel pump is working, check to see if your car has fuel. A good mechanic will keep your secret, but you'd be surprised how often someone has a car towed in because it won't start, and it won't start because the fuel tank was empty.

FACT

> Just because you "know" that once the needle indicates empty, or the idiot light comes on signaling low fuel, that you have fifty more miles of driving in the tank, don't argue with your mechanic when he suggests that just maybe you have run out of gasoline.

If there is even the remotest possibility that the tank is dry, put three or four gallons in it and try to start the car before calling for advice or a tow truck. Yes, a gallon will probably work, but a gallon will barely wet the bottom of the tank. That may not be quite enough fuel volume for the fuel pump to pick up enough gasoline. This is especially true if you have parked on a hill. One gallon may not be enough to wet the pump sitting in the bottom of the tank. If you can just as easily get three gallons, get three.

If you've put in a few gallons and you can hear the pump hum for a few seconds when the key is turned from off to on, but the car still won't start, check the fuel filter next.

Before fuel injectors, most fuel filters could be checked for a clog by removing them and blowing through one end. If your breath met a great deal of resistance, then you knew that you had a fuel filter problem. That doesn't work with fuel-injector filters. If your car's fuel filter is easy to get to, go ahead and take it off and get a new one. Most of them are cheap, and when did a new filter ever hurt a car?

If you want to do this procedure yourself, first pull the fuel pump fuse. Locate your owner's manual and look for a diagram that shows you the location of the fuse box and which fuses are which. Then just open the fuse box and pull out the fuel pump fuse. Then crank the engine over a time or two. Doing so helps bleed the pressure off. But be careful. Sometimes it doesn't remove all the pressure. If the pressure wasn't relieved, fuel will spray when you disconnect the fuel line from the filter.

Maybe you aren't that well acquainted with the guts of an engine. You know you have fuel, and so far you've checked for sparks and you've heard the pump hum, telling you it is on the job. But you don't know where to locate the fuel filter, and you aren't even certain you want to know. Then it's time to have the car towed.

But take heart. Every troubleshooting step you are able to take on your own earns some respect down at the local garage.

E ALERT!

Anytime you deal with fuel, especially detaching a fuel line such as disconnecting an old fuel filter, safety is the primary concern. Fuel injectors operate under pressure. Fuel can spray out, pooling on the garage floor, or it may spray all over you. Keep all flames or potential sparks away, and prevent turning this simple procedure into a nightmare.

Don't Keep Crankin' and Crankin'

This advice is especially pertinent for fuel-injector systems. Every time the engine rotates one complete cycle, it has injected fuel into each of the cylinders. Try to start the car two or three times, then do all your troubleshooting. If you just keep on keeping on, you may end up with a crankcase (where oil and only oil is supposed to be) full of raw fuel. The gasoline will run right past the pistons and into the crankcase, thinning the oil into uselessness.

A person may try to start the engine and try over and over to start the engine. Eventually, after figuring out what the problem is, the engine starts. The gratified owner never thinks about the unfortunate change in oil condition, and the car endures hundreds or thousands of bearing-wearing miles because of fuel mixed with the oil.

An Exceedingly Cold Day Can Be the Problem

If your car is unprotected from the most brutal winter weather, and the cold has turned the oil into pudding (not a technical term, but a descriptive one), the car will crank extremely slowly. Keeping the ignition key turned to the starting position for fifteen seconds with extremely slow engine RPM may flood the engine. There may be absolutely nothing else wrong with your car other than a bitter cold temperature yielding slow turnover and a now flooded engine.

Before troubleshooting all the other possible problems on an extremely cold day, assume first that you have a flooded engine. If you have attempted to start a car with fuel injection (yours probably has it) three times for fifteen to twenty seconds each attempt, stop. Press the gas pedal and hold it to the floor, and crank the car. This cleans the engine out if it is flooded. Now take your foot off of the accelerator and try again. But if this doesn't work, don't keep trying.

Roll-Starting a Vehicle

In a standard (manual) transmission, if the starter will not work and the battery is drained, you can turn the ignition key to the on position, place the car in second or third gear in a three-speed, third or fourth gear in a four-speed. Keeping the clutch pedal mashed to the floor, roll the vehicle down a slight hill, or have some friends push the car. Once the car reaches a speed of just a few miles per hour (let's say, five), the driver releases the clutch and the car will start. You have used the transmission to turn the engine over.

With the key on, the instant you release the clutch, the injectors will pulse fuel, and the plugs will spark just as if the starter had been doing its job. The reason for using a higher gear is that there is less resistance on the engine. But if the battery is completely dead, even this won't work.

FACT

Don't let an old-timer tell you that a roll-start is possible with an automatic transmission. It was possible with cars in the '50s and '60s that had a fluid-coupling converter that would turn the engine. Not anymore. One of the most terrifying experiences one of us ever had was making that futile, idiotic, and reckless attempt to start an automatic transmission pickup truck being towed on a six-foot chain at seventy-five miles an hour; but he lived, so he can tell you—don't!

When It's Time to Give Up

If you've done everything discussed in the preceding sections and the car still won't start, tow it in. You've done everything you can do. It is time for diagnostic equipment you won't be buying for home use. Your mechanic will now start checking injector pulse and pulse width, and scanning the computer, checking for coolant temperature operation and throttle position settings, technical stuff hardly possible outside a professional garage these days.

A Pair of Special Case Start-up Problems

Those problems listed in the preceding section are the typical causes of an engine that won't start. There are a couple more problems to talk about, but these are special case problems. They aren't the normal problems, but they do occur. If you suspect one of the following, don't troubleshoot. Get the car to the shop.

A Timing Belt Break

Timing belts keep the crankshaft and camshaft turning in the same relation. When a timing belt breaks, slips, or its teeth strip off, preventing it from gripping the timing gear, only the crankshaft is spinning, moving the pistons up and down in the cylinders. The starter is spinning the crankshaft, but the camshaft is not turning. And the camshaft works the valves up and down. So if the camshaft isn't turning, the valves aren't moving.

Some engines are designed so that the valves and pistons occupy the same space but not at the same time. If the timing belt breaks on a car so designed, a piston in at least one of the cylinders is going to slam into a valve, bending it.

In some cars, the spark plugs will still spark if the timing belt breaks. But fuel is not being squirted in, nor is exhaust escaping, because the valves aren't opening and closing. The car won't start, or if it does it will only run for an instant.

If the timing belt breaks, the car won't continue to run. When you turn the key to the start position, you'll hear fuel pump noise, but your car won't have spark. The clearest sign of a timing belt problem is that the engine will crank exceptionally fast and free, and the pitch of the noise is higher.

The instant you try to start your car and hear the rapid spinning of the engine, stop, or risk possible valve damage. Have the car towed in. Unfortunately, once you hear the rapid spinning of the engine, valve damage may already have been done.

The Ignition Switch

If it ever happens that you insert the key into the ignition, and you turn the key and nothing happens, go though all the procedures suggested in the preceding section. The battery may be dead or drained. But if everything checks out, yet there is still absolutely no noise, the ignition switch is not connecting the battery with the engine.

The problem with the ignition switch is that it controls more than just turning the engine on. The ignition switch is the control center of the electrical system. All electrical circuits except for direct battery-feed circuits such as the headlights and horn—anything that comes on when the ignition switch is in the on position or in the accessory position—are controlled by that switch.

Troubleshooting ignition switch problems involves use of a test light. A test light is a very simple device for testing circuits. It's almost foolproof—almost. One of the systems tied in to the ignition switch is the passive restraint system, better known as the air bag. Touch the wrong wires with the test light and . . . *poof!* Faster than an air bag inflates you've gone from paying someone $150 to install a new ignition switch to paying somebody $800 or more to reinstall an air bag.

The Starter Fluid in the Can

Sometimes when the engine will crank but won't start up, it is because not enough fuel is getting into the cylinders. This can happen if you've run completely out of gas and have continued to try to start the car, or if you've let the car sit for several weeks or longer. There are cans of starter liquid available, and they do work, but use them carefully. These cans contain an extremely volatile gas. That's why it works. Follow the directions on the can. Usually you'll take the air duct off the breather assembly, and put the can into the ductwork, spraying into the air intake.

With the engine cranking, with spark there will be ignition. The vapor is drawn into the engine and a spark will create a terrific explosion that usually results in getting the engine going.

But take care concerning the location of your face at the time you spray and someone is trying to start the engine. This vapor is extremely volatile. We don't know of anyone killed using this product, but it can create a backfire. We do know of someone whose eyebrows and beard were burned off in the instantaneous boom.

The best, safest way to use the spray is to spray through the air cleaner assembly. Don't take the top of the cleaner off. Consider this advice backfire insurance.

This procedure is easiest with older cars equipped with carburetors or throttle-body injectors. But if this procedure doesn't start any gasoline-powered car, either the plugs are fouled or there is a problem with the ignition itself.

Chapter 16

Surviving Scratches, Dings, and Dents

You love your car. You take care of it as if it were your child. Then one day you walk out of the grocery store only to watch in horror as a runaway grocery cart races like a guided missile, gaining speed as it bears down on the best maintained car in the lot–yours. This chapter will help you recover from such a traumatic experience, as well as some others.

What Happens to the Value of Your Car

People who properly maintain their cars come from two camps: those who truly love their cars like members of their family, maybe better; and those who treat their cars well because they want to get years of excellent service from them. Those in the second group take a vicious grocery cart assault much better than those in the first camp.

So your car has a scratch, or something worse. Before deciding how much to spend, or even how much effort to put into repairing the problem, it's time to take an honest assessment of the car's value.

The Personal Value of Your Car

One measure of value is the car's value to you. Is this a car that was handed down from a family member? You got Granddad's car in the will, a car you remember as a small child, a car Granny still wants a spin in every time she visits. Or perhaps the car is a classic, a collector's car, the kind of vehicle to be maintained in pristine condition forever. Or perhaps your car is subject to some other measure of value, like your lost youth. The market value may or may not be so great, but other measures of value make the car priceless.

The Market Value of Your Car

The other measure is the car's market value—what the car is worth if you were to sell it. If you've taken excellent care of the vehicle, it will be worth more than a comparable car that has received less care. Use this car as a trade-in, and a dealer will assess the market value. Dealers can tell the kind of maintenance a car has received. A car in excellent condition will always be worth more, unless it has extremely high mileage (as a well-maintained vehicle might), in which case there will be fewer potential buyers.

> Given these two versions of value, assume that a scratch on this vehicle is worthy of repair. But do keep in mind that in certain cases, the hassle and/or the cost of repairing a scratch may not be worth it.

Surviving a Scratch

The first thing to do is to determine if the insult to your car's shiny exterior is actually a scratch. Then decide on the proper course of treatment.

Deciding Whether It's a Scratch or a Scuff

Place your fingernail on the surface of the car. Don't bear down, but slide the fingernail perpendicularly across the presumed scratch. If your fingernail doesn't catch, it isn't a scratch, it is a scuff—whatever collided with your car didn't penetrate the clear coat all the way to the car's painted surface. You should be able to buff out the scuff with a lamb's wool buffing pad designed to fit on the end of an electric buffer. With care and patience, a buffing pad on the business end of an electric drill will work, too, but you'll have to be more careful.

If the abrasion is a smudge and you choose to buff it out, be certain not to press down hard on the spinning lamb's wool pad while holding it in one place, or you may burn the car's finish.

If your fingernail catches when you run it across the blemish, it's a scratch. If it is just a scuff, you'll feel a roughness, but you will not feel an exact line.

FACT

There are three ways to repair a scratch. This is where an accurate assessment of a car's value by one or both standards becomes important. There is the expensive way to repair the scratch, the less expensive way, and the cheap way. All three ways work, but the results will be different.

Touching Up the Scratch Yourself

The least expensive way is to do the job yourself. This does not necessarily mean that the job will be done poorly, but there is an art to scratch repair. If you grew up painting intricate models, or if you simply have the knack, your efforts may yield a fine result.

Go to a parts store or a dealership for your make and model of car. At both places you should find a rack containing the amazing variety of paint colors used on today's vehicles. Select your car's paint color. The paint comes in a tube and contains a small brush. The size of the touch-up kit is about twice as large as a tube of mascara.

The next step is to wash the area of the car that was damaged. Take a small amount of car wash and water, apply with a rag, and dry. This will eradicate all the oils, road grime, or waxes that had been on the car. Do not use a harsh cleanser to clean the area of the scratch. A harsh cleanser may affect the clear-coat finish on your car.

For steadiness, brace your hand containing the brush on the car. Then with one constant motion, apply a light coat of the paint along the full length of the scratch. Using a thin coat of paint is best. A heavy coat of paint will cake up and be as noticeable as the scratch itself, so use the least amount of paint you can. This paint dries very fast—hence the reason for attempting to cover the scratch in a single stroke. If you lift the brush and place it back on the car's surface, overlapping the last swipe, you'll leave a brush stroke.

It may be impossible to cover the whole scratch in one stroke, but cover absolutely as much of the scratch as you can with the single stroke. When the paint dries in a few minutes, try another light stroke.

E ALERT!

Despite applying the paint with a skill that would make da Vinci jealous, the paint you applied will appear a shade darker than the rest of the car. Your car has probably faded in the sunlight.

Going to a Detailer

If you are reluctant to try this job yourself, you can take the car to a detailer. A detailer will use much the same technique that you did. The principal difference is that the detailer's is technique and yours is practice. A detailer will be more skilled with the brushstroke, applying less paint, and will be able to cover the scratch thoroughly with little or no caked-up paint. But the chances are very good that a detailer using the same paint as you would use will wind up with a color that is slightly darker than the rest of the car, too.

Automotive paints have changed over the past twenty years. Before then, nearly every car made used a paint with a lacquer finish. The gloss came with the paint itself. The spray contained the color and the shine.

Now cars are painted in a two-step process. (Yes, every manufacturer touting what makes their particular brand superior will speak of the paint process differently, and there probably are some differences, but all use similar techniques.) The two-step process involves the application of a base coat and the color coat, and the application of a clear coat, the coat that gives the car its shine and helps protect the color. What you are buying in a touch-up paint is the base color.

> Always cover scratches. If something has scraped off the clear coat and has cut into the paint, there will be surface rust forming on the car soon. To keep a protective shield over the exposed metal of the car, put on a blanket of paint.

Taking the Car to a Body Shop

The most expensive way to take care of a scratch is to take the car to a body shop. There they will sand out the scratch and redo the paint job in a fashion very similar to that done at the factory. The end result being that the paint matches perfectly and the scratch is absolutely gone.

Remember, let the value of the car determine the method of dealing with the scratch.

An Even Cheaper Way to Deal with a Scratch

If your car is older and has no great value but lots of scratches that you'd like to make less noticeable, go to your local hardware store and get a can of spray paint. A can of spray paint that is as close to the vehicle's color as you can find. Shake the can, and spray the paint into the plastic cap of the can. Then, using a cotton swab or a tiny artist's brush, wet it with the paint and apply it to the scratches.

Touching Up a Bad Paint Job

When you've finished repairing a scratch and come to the conclusion your work looks more like a scar than a repair, you still have other options. You can repaint. But first, purchase a small can of acetone. Acetone is a paint remover, much like the product used to remove fingernail polish. Use it with care, since it will take paint off.

Here's how you repaint a scratch: Fill a bucket with soapy water, and have a rag on standby. Pour the acetone on another rag, and gently wipe the touch-up paint out of the recently repaired scratch. Immediately use the rag in the soapy water and wipe off the spot where the acetone was just used. This will stop the ultra-deep cleaning of the acetone.

After repainting, you will need to wax or polish the area, because acetone will have cleaned everything—that means everything—off.

If you take your goofed-up scratch repair into a detailer and ask them to undo your poor job, this is what they are going to do. With a deft touch, they may add a few extra layers of paint after the first has dried. Then they'll take a buffer and work to smooth the surface.

Using Miracle Scratch Removers

You've seen the miracle scratch removers advertised on television. Wipe it on; wipe it off. *Poof!* The scratch has disappeared. Similar products are also available most places car-care products are sold.

FACT

Be sure you pick up the right "miracle" product for your car. These products are sold according to particular ranges of color. There is a product for all shades of gray to black, for example. The products aren't perfect, but they are handy and useful.

Don't expect a miracle, but these products do work to a degree. And they are absolutely better than doing nothing. They will mask the scratch and protect the car's surface from rust formation.

Dealing with Dings

A ding is a small indentation in the smooth metal of the car and is very nearly round in shape. Hail can cause dings in a car. So can falling walnuts, and errant golf balls and baseballs. Fixing a ding can sometimes be expensive. Unless money is no object, you will probably want to assess the ding to determine how noticeable it is. If you are the only one who will ever notice it, do you really want to mess with it? Yes? Well, then, read on.

A Home Remedy That Works . . . Sometimes

So you were out practicing your chip shots and accidentally misfired. Your car took a golf ball hit broadside. You've examined the damage. You can run your hand across it and feel it. No one else may ever notice it, and it shouldn't matter, but it does matter to you.

If you are going to get the thing fixed anyway, you may as well try the one completely free way first.

Place the car in the sun to heat up the ding. Summer is the best time to try this, as hotter is better. Allow plenty of time for the heat to warm the metal. Once the exterior of the car is hot, take an ice cube and hold it on the ding. Sometimes that sudden contrast between the hot and the cold will lift the ding right out.

Ding Slayers

If the ice cube trick doesn't work, or if you are not satisfied with the work you've done, there is another way to get them out. In metro areas, there are some entrepreneurial companies that seem to chase hailstorms. A hailstorm hits, and the company hangs out its shingle and takes out dings caused by hail.

The process is not something you want to try at home. Basically they gain access to the back side of the ding and massage it out, leaving the paint without a crack. The cost is not prohibitive.

Sometimes a ding may have cracked the paint, or what looks at first like a nice rounded ding is really a gouge caused by a rock bouncing off the interstate concrete and colliding with your car. In a case such as this, you may want to take the car into a body shop.

Any project pertaining to the restoration of paint or auto shape can be done by a body shop. Their techniques are usually different from what has been described. They'll sand down the damaged part, fill an indention with body putty, reshape the part, and paint it. It will then be good as new.

Moving from Ding to Dent

Determining the difference between a ding and a dent can be a judgment call. If the damage is not perfectly round, or if the concave area is more than an inch or so in diameter, it is best to consider the damage a dent.

If such a determination is not important to you, if for every blemish you race to the body shop, none of this discussion matters. But dings and scratches are certainly worth your best attempts before shelling out bigger bucks to a detailer or to the body shop.

Bumping out Bumper Bumps

Many of today's bumpers are rubber. They, too, can pick up abrasions as scratches and small indentations that to your mind mean the bumper is doing its job. Or for you it may be yet another mar in the car's surface in desperate need of attention.

A rubber putty is available at body shops for repairing bumpers. A body shop will treat a bumper in a similar fashion as a dent in a fender.

FACT

A lot of car dealers do their own repairs, coloring their scratches and scrapes to avoid sending a car to the body shop, because of the perceived value of the car. The greater the market value of the car, the more expense a dealership will incur having the car repaired.

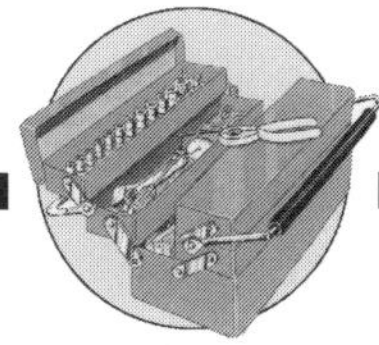

CHAPTER 17

Avoiding Amateur Mishaps

Mistakes happen. If a surgeon can accidentally sew up a surgical sponge inside a patient, a professional mechanic can goof too, and so can you. Consider your mistakes tuition payments in the college of car care. Some likely goofs can be undone—the rest, after reading about them, you might be able to avoid.

Staying Away from Brake Mistakes

Of all the systems on your car, a mistake maintaining, replacing, or repairing parts of the braking system is number one on the "to avoid" list. If you work on an engine and fail, the car won't go. But if you work on your brakes and they fail, the car won't stop. Zipping around a curve too fast and suddenly needing the brakes is no time to discover your brake job didn't take.

Adding the Wrong Fluid to the Master Cylinder

Just because the brake system is a hydraulic system doesn't mean that just any hydraulic fluid will work. In fact, most brake systems do not use hydraulic fluid at all. Hydraulic fluid is a petroleum-based fluid of a type most often used in the power-steering system. Brake fluid is alcohol-based. Big difference. When the rubber parts of the brake system come in contact with petroleum, they swell and deteriorate.

The mistake happens one of two ways. The home mechanic keeps fluids that are used in various systems of the car on a garage shelf. By mistake, a bottle of power-steering fluid is opened and poured into the master cylinder, and the home mechanic recognizes the mistake quickly. Or knowing that the brake system is hydraulic, the car owner's brain, operating on just one cylinder, makes a connection: Hydraulic brake system . . . hydraulic fluid. The deed is done, and the home mechanic is none the wiser.

Both types of problems show up in the repair shop. Usually the first type of problem is less damaging. Yes, both car owners poured the same wrong stuff into the brake systems, so what makes the first goof less damaging and more fixable? Time.

Within three days, the driver will notice that the brake pedal must be pushed farther toward the floorboard in order to slow and stop the car. And it will push too easily, perhaps feeling mushy. Upon acceleration after a stop, a brake might stick on one of the wheels, making it feel as if the car doesn't want to begin rolling as soon as it ought. These symptoms indicate system damage. Once pedal pressure has been lost or the brakes are grabbing when they should be releasing, the likely remedy will be a major brake system overhaul: Everything in the brake system that is made of rubber, including the master cylinder, calipers, wheel cylinders, and hoses, must be replaced. Brake system overhauls are expensive. All of this deterioration can take place in three days or less.

On the other hand, if this is a problem you notice in an hour or so (we hope less time than that) after pouring the contents of the wrong can into the brake system—if you haven't driven the car, haven't used the brake system—you probably will be able to take the master cylinder off and drain it, and bleed the system. With luck, that will be all there is to the lesson. However, if after draining and bleeding the system you still have a loss of brake-pedal pressure—that is, you push the brake pedal and it continues moving under your foot to the floor—the master cylinder must be replaced.

Backward Brake Pads

Some brake pads look like one solid piece of material with no front or back. Usually, it's easier to tell the front (the part that will squeeze against the rotor) from the back (the backing plate, the area affixed to the brake caliper) on better brake pads. The backing plate is larger in area than the front. This is true for most domestics. But it isn't always so with imports.

Many imports use a brake caliper into which the brake pad slides. This type of caliper calls for a brake pad that is uniform in size from front to back. On many Japanese-made cars, it is easy to mistake the front of the brake pad for the back. Often the entire pad is painted black, compounding the problem.

Even if you don't know the difference, there's a way to make sure you are installing the pad correctly. Take a key or a screwdriver and scratch one side of the brake pad. If you can see metal, that side goes against the caliper piston. If the material flakes off and looks fibrous, it's the brake pad material, the part that will press against the rotor to stop the car.

FACT

If you install a brake pad backward, you'll know it from the first application of the brakes. When you apply the brakes, the backward one(s) will growl and/or grind. And the car either won't stop as fast, or the metal of the brake backing will grab the metal rotor and lock up. But the noise will be immediate.

Putting Calipers on Upside Down

For all domestic cars, a mechanic takes the calipers off to get the brake pads out. On the front brakes usually there are two bolts that attach the caliper to the steering knuckle. The caliper can be turned upside down and remounted, and the brakes will work if there is no air in the line. And that is the problem. There will be air. Which means that the brake (usually that set of brakes—the front brakes or the rear brakes) will have little stopping power. And the pedal will press almost all the way to the floor.

If you have just done your own brake job and this is the immediate result, check the position of the brake calipers.

The problem with mounting the caliper upside down has to do with the location of the bleed screw, that part of the caliper directly connected to the brake line. If the bleed screw is positioned low when the caliper is mounted, the caliper is upside-down. A person doing a brake job at home may turn the bleed screw to make sure all the air is out of the line, get brake fluid flowing out immediately, and declare the brake line air-free.

But air rises and fluid sinks. The bleed screw must be at the top of the brake caliper to properly bleed the brake lines of air.

When considering a purchase of a used car from a private individual, check out the system if the brakes barely work. Sometimes a home mechanic sells a car when he thinks he's made a big goof. If the brake pads are new, look at the position of the bleed screw.

Patching a Brake Line

Don't. If you've begun to feel a surge of mechanical prowess and you are considering a repair to a leaking brake line, sit down and let the feeling pass.

There are a couple of different reasons a brake line may begin to leak. The first is age. If you have opted to do what practically everyone does with brake system maintenance, keep good pads in the brakes and just make certain the master cylinder stays at the full level, eventually that steel brake line will rust. Moisture building up in the system will one day take its toll. Rust will weaken the whole line, and the weakest spot will break first.

Assume, for a moment, that a repair of a rust-induced leak is feasible, and there are lots of products in a parts store that may make you think you can mix certain components together to smother a small hole and make that area harder and more durable than it ever was before.

What happens the next time you apply the brakes? The pressure building up in the brake line will seek a new weakest link, and later, if not sooner, a new leak forms. The patch of a rusted line will not work and is not safe.

There is another way to get a hole in a steel brake line: road debris flying up beneath the car on the highway. If you are in the habit of keeping a car just a few years, this is the most likely means of developing a brake line leak. The number-one rule for patching a good, strong, rust-free brake line: Don't. Any damage to a brake line requires replacement of the brake line. There simply is no way to make a good repair.

In a panic stop—that is, when you have to slam on the brakes—the pressure in that brake line can reach beyond 1,000 pounds per square inch. Do you want to entrust your car, your insurance, your health, and your life to a patch holding back that sort of pressure? If the patch fails, the car has no brakes. Replace the line. At $30 to $50, it's cheap insurance.

FACT

Draining the brake fluid when it turns black will help prevent rust in the brake lines and brake calipers. It will also prevent boiling brakes and loss of braking pressure that can happen when descending a high range of mountains where braking is frequent and sometimes hard.

Sidestepping Flubs with the Fuel System

Everyone makes mistakes. Diesel fuel in the gasoline tank and gasoline in a diesel system are out-and-out blunders that occasionally occur. Some mistakes are calculated, like putting the wrong octane fuel in the tank. And then there's patching up a leak in the gas tank.

Diesel in the Gas Tank

During the brief period when diesel cars were seen as the answer to spiraling gasoline prices, diesel in the gas tank was more likely to occur than it is today. Many self-serve gas stations placed diesel pumps right next to the pumps containing gasoline. A driver pulling in and seeking the cheapest price could insert the diesel nozzle in his gasoline-powered car and begin pumping before realizing the mistake.

It is much harder to do that these days. Diesel fuel pumps are usually separate from gasoline pumps, and the nozzles are distinctive.

Actual damage to a gasoline engine from diesel fuel is minimal, but the car won't run. Okay, it might run if the mixture in the tank heavily favors the gasoline. And if it does run, it will smoke like an old locomotive. The best remedy is to drain the fuel tank immediately. Mechanically drain it with a pump, or remove the tank and pour out the fuel. Yes, it is possible to try to drive through the problem. And you may be able to do so. But most likely, the spark plugs will be fouled and need changing.

ALERT!

If on occasion you loan your car to a friend or neighbor, make sure there is no confusion about the type of car being loaned. Make it clear that your car takes diesel fuel, lest a gesture of thanks, such as filling the tank, turns into a big boo-boo.

Gasoline in the Diesel Tank

If diesel in a gasoline engine is a mere nuisance, gasoline in a diesel engine is a problem. Gasoline is a highly volatile fuel, requiring no pressure to ignite. A diesel system is set up to generate pressure in order to allow the diesel to burn efficiently. The detonation of gasoline in a diesel engine will be enormous. Gasoline will be exploding before the diesel pistons have closed far enough for proper detonation.

The engine will hammer and knock as the pistons and gasoline battle over their shared confined space. If the tank has twenty gallons of diesel and one gallon of gasoline, more noise will be generated than harm done—maybe. But any higher percentage of gasoline than that, and the diesel owner is better off getting the tank drained immediately, to reduce the extent of engine damage.

Using a Higher-Than-Prescribed Octane Gasoline

Maybe where you live there is a day of the week or a random day of the month when certain gas stations will run specials on their highest-octane fuel. You know, "ten cents off per gallon." Maybe you are one of those who scramble to the pump, thinking that you are treating your car to something special, filet mignon instead of the usual soy burger.

If you remember a discussion in Chapter 11 about older cars, you will recall that a higher-octane gasoline used in the vehicle for a period of up to six months will help eliminate carbon build-up, preignition, and engine knock. The higher the octane, the less volatile the fuel. It is not as prone to preignite as a lower-octane fuel; therefore, valve rattle from early detonation is reduced, if not eliminated. And higher-octane fuels have more additives that help eliminate the carbon build-up.

Most people think that running a higher-octane fuel gives the car more power. Wrong. If the system is working correctly, higher-octane fuel will have the opposite effect: Power will decrease and gas mileage will diminish. You may even notice the black smoke from the tailpipe that signals raw fuel passing through the system unburned.

All you are doing is wasting your money. Doubly. There is the added expense of the fuel, and the reduced power and mileage it yields. But it will not hurt the car.

> Think of higher octane to treat carbon build-up and valve rattling as medicine to treat an illness. Follow the prescribed course, in this case, six months; then stop taking the medicine.

Using an Octane That's Too Low

Many high-performance engines require a higher-octane fuel, including turbo-charged engines and super charged engines. The owner's manual will tell you if your car requires the higher-octane fuel.

It is tempting to go for cheaper gas. If the first time you use it you don't notice any problems, it is easy to opt for the more volatile, less-additive-laden, cheaper fuel.

By putting in an octane that your car is not intended to use, you are making the onboard computer make adjustments to the system it wasn't designed to make. To prevent the predetonation of the cheaper fuel, the onboard computer will change the timing of the engine. In the long run your engine will perform at a poorer level than it was designed to run, and it will have less power and poorer mileage, just like the car using an octane that is too high.

Patching the Gas Tank

Another short answer: Don't. That certainly is the correct answer for all cars made with plastic gas tanks later than the mid-'90s.

But if you are hanging on to an older car with a metal tank, a classic, or just one that you have maintained from the mid-'90s or earlier that continues to perform well, patch kits are available.

Whether you patch an older-style metal tank depends on why it needs to be patched. Eventually all metal tanks will rust out. Condensation collects on the underside of a tank, slowly weakening the metal after many years. If the old tank is beginning to rust, you'd be better off getting a new tank. The patch will hold, but more leaks are soon to happen. If, on the other hand, that metal tank is in good shape, use a patch kit.

On today's plastic tanks, never attempt to patch a leak. Replace the tank instead. In fact, words printed on the tank will indicate that the tank cannot be repaired. A plastic tank flexes, making permanent adhesion impossible.

Installing the Wrong Battery

A good deal on a battery is great if the battery is the right size for your car. And you know enough now to realize that size means something more than the outer shell of the battery; it means power, cold cranking amps, reserve power.

The simplest approach to making certain your car gets the right new battery is to check the old battery. If the battery has always supplied all the power your car has needed to run the power windows, power seats, and every other system requiring a battery's sudden jolt, replace the worn-out one with one of the same rating.

FACT

A cheap, underpowered battery in a car loaded with electrical equipment won't last. If your car has power everything, virtually every time you start it, the systems of the car will drain the battery. A battery in constant need of recharging won't last long.

Facing Con-Fuse-Ion

Modern cars have lots of fuses. Every system on the car will have a fuse of one form or another to protect it: maxifuses, minifuses, and fusible links. Only maxifuses and minifuses are a concern here. Just as you may be tempted to outthink design engineers about fuel octane, you may be tempted to outwit the design engineers about these safety features built into your electrical systems. There is nothing you can do about fusible links, so we can ignore them.

But with fuses, the temptation exists to think that bigger is better. Here is a typical scenario. A fuse blows. You spend a buck and buy another one. It blows. Then your brain begins to overheat: "This fifteen-amp circuit keeps frying. I know! I'll insert a twenty-amp fuse instead."

A fuse is a safety for the maximum amount of power a circuit is designed to handle. Installing a larger fuse in any circuit will jeopardize other circuits of the electrical system. Sometimes a fuse wears out and blows. No other reason is necessary. But if a fuse blows again, and blows quickly, the system needs to be checked, not overridden by a larger fuse.

An override with a larger fuse will not protect that circuit. It just puts more electrical circuits and systems in harm's way.

ALERT!

> Don't bypass a fuse, either. That's worse than an oversized fuse. But here's ingenuity: Someone (nameless, to protect the lunacy of the deed-doer) wrapped a blown fuse in a metallic chewing gum wrapper, creating one all-powerful magical circuit. How magical? Within half an hour it turned every electrical system—all the wiring in the vehicle!—into toast.

Avoiding Motor Oil Mishaps

You already know what happens if you neglect the oil in the engine. It thins and loses its lubricating and cleaning qualities. But there are other ways of abusing your engine when it comes to oil. Fixable goofs? Yes, but better and easier to be avoided than fixed.

Too Much Oil in the Crankcase

So you've changed your own oil. Admiring your work, you draw out the oil dipstick to enjoy the look of the good clean oil clinging to it. At first you can't believe your eyes. You wipe the stick clean, plunge it back down its tube and pull it out again. There is too much oil in the crankcase. You pull out the owner's manual and confirm your suspicions. Your car takes only four quarts, not five.

You've got a pair of choices. The best choice is to slide back under the car with a drain pan, loosen (but don't remove) the plug in the oil pan, and let a quart of oil drizzle out. Tighten the plug, end of story. Easy fix.

Or, knowing that the extra oil will only make the crankshaft work harder and cause gas mileage to dwindle for only as long as the overfill condition exists, you can ignore the problem and drive on. Easier fix. But that extra oil will be beaten by the crankshaft, sort of like an egg beater beating an egg. The oil will thin because of the extra air mixing with it—a kind of motor oil meringue.

When many imports indicate a need to add motor oil, the required addition will be somewhat less than the one quart that domestic car dipsticks indicate. If by no other means, learn by trial and error what amount your import requires when the oil dipstick reads "add." But if you accidentally overfill by half a quart, don't worry.

Way, Way Too Much Oil in the Crankcase

Well-meaning people can overdo anything. As frequently as someone has their car towed to a shop because the car's out of oil (no one ever told them a car needed oil), someone attempting good car care will arrive with the engine nearly inoperable because they have filled the crankcase with oil—filled it all the way up to the top, with gallons of it. After all, their logic goes, you fill up a gas tank to the top, and by comparison, the crankcase looks empty.

Quick, the crankcase is full. The pistons must pump. Where does the oil go, and how can you tell that's where it went? You already know. Assuming the engine would still run, the oil slips past the pistons every time they slide downward in the cylinder. And oily smoke will billow from the exhaust, so long as the engine fights to keep running.

The Wrong Fluid in the Crankcase

Transmission fluid bottles look a lot like motor oil bottles. And often, transmission fluid and motor oil are sold in parts stores side by side. It could be an easy mistake to pick up a quart or more of transmission fluid along with the oil you want to purchase. So what do you do if one of the quarts you added during the oil change is transmission fluid?

Crawl back underneath and drain out all the oil from the oil pan and start over. That is the best thing to do. Period.

ALERT!

Some people use four quarts of motor oil and one quart of transmission fluid during each oil change. This is a mistake because transmission fluid is thinner and won't offer the same protective lubricating qualities between hot moving engine parts. And the higher RPM and hotter-running smaller engines of today make this practice of dubious value.

Evading Common Mistakes with Tires

Mistakes with tires are easily made, because tires are simply those black round objects rolling around beneath one or two tons of automobile.

Buying Tires in the Wrong Size

Some people think that if a tire fits on the wheel, it is the right size for the car. The optimal size tire for your car is the size of tire that came on it new—see Chapter 4.

Keeping Silent about Fix-a-Flat

Those cans of pressurized sealant that can pump up a tire and get you safely to the tire shop are great. Keep a can in the garage and a can in your car. They're quick, convenient, and there's no mess. But most people fill their flat tire with the stuff and forget about it if the tire doesn't go flat again.

Forgetting about it is the problem. If the tire develops another leak and you take it in, by forgetting to tell the mechanic that you've used the flat fixer in a can, you put the mechanic in harm's way because the product is flammable. The cans come with a brightly colored sticker to attach to the tire. Use the sticker to warn your mechanic.

Chapter 18

Steering Clear of Amateur No-No's

If you think pulling out the oil dipstick is a major feat of car maintenance, you can probably skip this chapter. But if you'd rather sever an artery than spend an extra buck on a mechanic, maybe you'd better read on. This chapter is all about absolute no-no's—repairs you should not try in your own garage.

The Transmission

To begin with, you won't have the proper tools for this job. To do a transmission repair properly requires certain specialized tools that have no other purpose than to work on transmissions. If you take good care of your car, changing transmission fluid and the transmission filter at the proper intervals, a transmission job may become necessary only once in 100,000 miles. Perhaps many tens of thousands of miles more will go by without a transmission problem. A properly cared for transmission may last the life of the car itself.

Rebuilding a Transmission Requires a Case Holder

A case holder sets the transmission on end and holds it in a position so that it can be worked on. If you're reading between the lines, you've also just realized that to work on the transmission, it must be removed from the car. To do so will require lifting the car high enough to be able to get under the thing.

ALERT!

> A transmission will weigh between 175 to 250 pounds. Even with a big strong buddy, that's a lot of weight to be holding over your head while someone makes certain every bolt is unfastened.

After the transmission is placed in the case holder, there are spring-loaded clutch packs in the transmission that require a special tool to relieve the pressure so you can get them apart to work on the clutch they contain. Still ready to tackle one? Read on.

A Transmission Must Be Specially Cleaned

If you've successfully broken down the transmission and repaired and replaced the necessary parts, it is extremely important to make certain that every part is thoroughly clean. It has got to be absolutely spotless. That will require a pressure cleaner or a heat cleaner.

Okay, okay. So you are really one of those stubborn (and maybe mechanically gifted) types. If the need for special tools, tools not found around the home garage, doesn't deter you, maybe this will. Forget the dozens and dozens of parts. Let's just look at cost. A case holder costs in the neighborhood of $200, the clutch pack, $150, and the heated pressure washer, around $1,000.

Add up the cost of those three special tools alone–forget about all the hours of labor, never mind the cost of replacement parts–and the cost is roughly equal to the total cost of hiring a trained mechanic to do the whole job for you, parts included. And a transmission shop will guarantee its work. Still thinking about it? Forgettaboutit.

FACT

The environment of the garage in which a transmission is being serviced must be very clean. Most people's garages simply won't do. One little piece of dirt tucked away in a newly repaired transmission can keep it from shifting into the proper gear or keep it stuck in one gear. Were that to happen, whose piece of dirt would you rather it be, yours or the transmission shop's?

The ABS System

The antilock braking system (ABS) is another absolute no-no. The hydraulic part of the system–the fluid and pressure that connect the brake pedal to the brake pad to the disk, the mechanical apparatus that actually stops the car–is virtually identical to a standard brake system. What makes the system different is a sensor that tells a computer when the wheels have stopped turning.

How the ABS Works

Suppose a car with an ABS system begins to slide on a slick road after the brakes have been applied. As soon as a slide begins, the wheel in a slide stops turning. The ABS system identifies the wheel that is no longer rolling–the wheel that the brake has locked. It activates control valves that release the brake from that wheel. Do you recall what you've been taught to do with old-style brakes if the car starts to skid? You pump the brakes, release and pump, release and pump. The idea is to keep traction under all four wheels and maintain control. ABS does that for you, only it releases and pumps the brakes much more rapidly and effectively than your brain and your foot can.

If the only problem with the brakes is worn brake pads or brake shoes, with the proper care, those can be replaced in the garage at home.

> The backyard mechanic is better off avoiding an attempt to deal with an actual ABS problem. Because the ABS allows the driver to mash more firmly on the brake pedal without loss of control due to skidding, attempting to set up the system yourself could yield unpleasant results in a braking emergency.

What ABS Work Will Require

If the ABS signal lights on the dash, it is signaling a problem other than worn brake pads. The first thing a mechanic will need is a diagnostic tool that he or she attaches to the assembly line data link, or the ABS diagnostic connector from which the mechanic will get the codes. These codes tell the technician what is wrong and where to begin to look for the problem. Actually, a do-it-yourselfer can purchase such a tool at some auto parts stores for around $150. The problem with the tool is that it only "suggests" where to search for trouble. A home mechanic can waste a lot of time trying to narrow down the actual problem area and can wind up replacing parts that don't need to be replaced. It is quite possible for you to spend more money troubleshooting the ABS than by going straight to a good auto repair or brake shop and having the problem diagnosed correctly the first time.

Repair shops have better diagnostic equipment than the typical car enthusiast will purchase for home use. The diagnostic tool a good repair shop uses costs a couple of thousand dollars, and it has the capacity to search through all the various electrical components and zero in (most of the time) on the problem.

FACT

Unlike the ABS, replacing brake pads and shoes isn't a complete no-no, but you'd better have a manual. And how much is your time worth? If greenbacks are scarce, it may be worth all the time it takes. But if you don't do it right, you'll wind up replacing more parts.

Fuel Injectors

In today's cars, the fuel-injection system has replaced the carburetor as the means by which fuel is put into the cylinders for detonation. A determined home mechanic can remove and clean or replace fuel injectors. Many auto parts stores have equipment that allows someone to drop off their car's injector unit for cleaning, pay for the procedure, and replace the unit on their car in the garage at home. And all that's required for this whole process is a good set of basic hand tools.

So why shouldn't you do this job at home? It is very easy to pinch off a wire when replacing the unit. Doing so may have no immediate effect. But eventually a short will result, and you are likely to be paying a good mechanic for his or her time to track down the problem you have no idea that you created.

The second and more likely problem associated with working with your car's fuel injectors is fire. Here is the typical scenario. You've hooked up a droplight under the hood to get a better look at the injector job you are so confident that you can do. Among the various wires and tubes you have unhooked or are unhooking is the fuel line. If the slightest amount of fuel spews on the light, the bulb will pop, and the spark of the bulb . . . well, you get the picture. Feeding the initial flame is fuel spurting under pressure. Break out the weenies. Or the fire extinguisher.

How likely is such an occurrence? Ask any experienced mechanic, and if he hasn't caused such a fire himself, or seen one of his cohorts get one started, he's probably fibbing. In other words, you could do this job, but plan on a full day, and be prepared just in case.

A Cracked Head

This is one of those jobs that, with a good manual, a good set of hand tools, a torque wrench, and a fuel line tool, you can probably do yourself. But there are some significant warnings. You might consider doing this job if you are long on time and short on cash. But if you break bolts off—a very good possibility—can you get them out? If you misplace a part or several small bolts or nuts and can't find the right size to replace them, there's the towing bill on top of your mechanic's to consider. And the mechanic's bill will be larger than it otherwise would have been, because it will take extra time to figure out which of the parts you have lost.

The Electrical System

So many cars today are equipped with electric mirrors, heated seats, automatically adjusting driver's seats, remote openers for the doors and the trunk . . . you get the picture. Add the computer that monitors the automobile's crucial systems to the list of gadgetry, and all the electrical circuits form an extremely complex interconnected system. That's the key word to this caveat: interconnected.

In this chapter of tasks not to try at home, the focus is on the big picture, the system as a whole. If something quits working, check the fuses first. They are easy to find, easy to replace, and cheap (see Chapter 6). If your trunk lid quits popping open at the push of a button, or all the power windows suddenly cease going up and down, then a fuse may have gone bad. That's a good place to start. But if that new fuse burns out quickly—in a day, a week, or a month—there is another problem with the electrical system. Don't make the problem much worse by being too smart.

Someone with just a little too much knowledge will try to wire across the fuse. And it will work—for about half an hour. Then it will blow other circuits, maybe even the onboard computer. Then your trusty mechanic will have to go on a hunting expedition, tracking down all the damaged wires, at your expense.

If a fuse blows quickly twice, it's the system, not the circuit, that needs checking.

The home mechanic could use a short tester (buy one for $40 to $100), but you have to be careful. You have to know what you are doing or you may overload the circuit you are testing. Here's a typical goof. A car buff has a circuit problem and begins testing on his own. He accidentally overloads a circuit he is testing, in this case, the car's air-bag system. Suddenly, the effort to save money is going to cost even bigger bucks, because the air bags have deployed.

Muffler Replacement

Mufflers are inexpensive to purchase. And replacing the worn-out one is a straightforward proposition: Cut out the old muffler, attach the new. But replacing an old muffler is always more difficult than it ought to be. If that isn't one of Murphy's Laws, it should be.

To begin with, there is the problem of elevating the car high enough to be able to work comfortably beneath it. But for now we'll assume that you have the equipment necessary to alleviate that difficulty.

The Time Factor

After tens of thousands of miles and several years of water and road salts, the muffler of your car will be attached beneath your car by clamps, mounting brackets, and bolts that are most likely rusted completely through. If you have time to kill, no problem. You can pass the hours working to unlock the rusted parts to your heart's content.

Once you have freed the muffler from its rusted brackets, the muffler must be freed from the rest of the exhaust system. And the muffler will be rusted onto the pipes into which it fits. More time. With a chisel, patience, a mashed finger, and some angry language, the muffler will come loose.

The Fit Factor

The force involved in getting the old muffler free will probably bend the end of the pipe with which the muffler is designed to mate. To fit the damaged end of the exhaust pipe with the new muffler will require a splice of extra pipe. That means that the easiest and least effective home remedy will have to be attempted: clamping the new muffler and the exhaust pipe together. It will work, for a while. But exhaust heat and vibration guarantee that the fix is temporary. The only effective way to bond the splice with the exhaust pipe and the muffler is to weld them together.

Given the specialty shops and the well-equipped repair shops that span the continent and compete for your business, this just isn't a project worth trying at home. A muffler installation at home can easily become a full day's job with six trips to the parts store.

Just because a certain part like a muffler is cheap to buy doesn't mean that the process of home installation is easy enough to justify doing it yourself. Sometimes you will wind up with a more expensive project in time and in money by attempting a task that your home garage is not equipped to handle.

Body Work

Body work requires specialized training and a number of special tools. Obviously, it takes some skill to repair or replace a damaged part of the auto body, match the contours of the original part replaced, and make the color and thickness of the paint consistent with the rest of the car. But there is an even more important reason not to attempt body work on one of today's cars: safety.

Most cars built today are of unibody construction. The frame and the body of the car are not separate units bolted or welded together. The frame and the body are one. Often, that means that damage to the car's appearance is also damage to the car's structure.

A "fender bender," for example, may have caused more than cosmetic damage. Behind and beneath the fender, the wheel well may also have been damaged. With unibody construction, the wheel well will have constant pressure on it. Accelerating, stopping, cornering: The performance of the car depends upon its secure structure.

It's possible that if you have an artist's eye, a rubber mallet, and a large amount of automobile body putty, you can craft a repaired part to look on the surface as it once did. But appearance is no guarantee of your car's safe performance when faced with an extreme driving emergency.

FACT

Among the tools a body shop uses are Mig Welders, Tig Welders, acetylene torches, special hammers, dollies (a tool for pulling out dents), spray guns, and air compressors. A Mig Welder is a wire-feed welder with a constant feed of metal wire that is heated and melted to bond two pieces of metal together. A Tig Welder is similar, but it is for aluminum welding.

Axle Shafts

An axle shaft is an example of a part that's not too expensive, but the cost has absolutely nothing to do with the complexity of the job. A front-wheel-drive car has a pair of front drive shafts. Over time, the likelihood of tearing the boot (the protective covering) on the joint of the axle shaft increases. With every turn of the axle, the torn boot covering the now-underprotected joint allows the grease that protects the joint to be thrown out and permits moisture and debris to enter. The axle joint begins to wear.

You can go to a parts store and buy an axle (well under $100). Like the muffler, the part itself doesn't look too intimidating. But also like the muffler, similar problems may come up if you undertake the job yourself.

Apart from having the right tools and following the correct procedure from a good manual, there are the problems of rust and old parts being stuck together. It is possible in attempting to separate the parts by force to get them wedged tighter together.

If time is what you have and even small amounts of cash are in very short supply . . . well, don't even try it then. A good mechanic won't spend more than two hours on the job, probably a good bit less. The job is just too inexpensive to risk botching it at home.

Emergency or Hand Brake Cables

Replacing a brake cable is another of those simple jobs with an inexpensive part that looks easy enough to work with but is probably best left to the professional. If you trust your competency as a home mechanic and have successfully installed brake shoes before, you can probably tackle the job. The big problem you are likely to run into is the cable adjustment.

The key to the installation of the brake cable is to make certain the cable is tight enough without causing the rear brakes to drag. The brake must be tight enough to be able to stop the car in an emergency, yet open freely enough not to grab at the wheel when the car is in motion.

If the brake is adjusted too tightly, travel around thirty miles and you will probably have burned the brake shoes, worn the brake drums, and destroyed wheel cylinders. You will have raised your repair costs and diminished your safety all at the same time.

CHAPTER 19

Making Maintenance Manageable

Proper maintenance increases the useful life of your automobile and reduces repair bills along the way. But the maintenance schedule given in your owner's manual may seem ridiculously pie-in-the-sky. So while this chapter recommends that you always follow the maintenance schedule in the owner's manual, you can develop a more realistic maintenance schedule here.

Basic Oil Maintenance

As a result of the meticulous makeup of an owner's manual ("do this at 5,000, and this at 15,000, and this at 25,000"), people who purchase their new car vowing to love, honor, and cherish until separated by engine failure wind up ignoring much of the maintenance listed, deceiving themselves into believing that by religiously changing their oil they are treating their cars well. There is a bit of truth to that.

Oil is the most abused fluid of the car. It is subjected to extreme heat and continuous contamination both from the engine and from the dirt in the air. The temperature of the engine crankcase that the oil lubricates will rise above 200 degrees Fahrenheit. By-products of the fuel burning in the cylinders contribute to the oil's eventual breakdown. Oil is constantly under pressure, putting more wear on the additives.

Check the Oil Level When You Get Gas

Get in this habit each time you fill up your car: Turn off your car. Start pumping fuel, grab a paper towel, pull out the dipstick, wipe it clean, reinsert it, pull it out, and read it. Close the hood of your car, and still you'll be standing around waiting to finish fueling, one minute in the middle of waiting well spent.

> While you're under the hood during the fill-up, make it a habit to give the various parts under the hood a quick glance. Listen for any hissing noises. And stick your nose close enough to notice any unfamiliar smells. This habit just might save you a long wait on the side of an unfamiliar road.

Change Oil Every 3,000 Miles

This is numero uno on the car maintenance list. Yes, manuals in the glove boxes of new, very fuel-efficient models do indicate an oil change every 7,500, and some say you can go even farther between oil changes. More fuel-efficient models do have fewer fuel by-products entering the crankcase, which means the oil will stay cleaner longer. But take a poll of mechanics and see what they think. Most will affirm the concept of more miles and less dirt in the oil in fuel-efficient cars, but most wouldn't want to treat their mom's car that way.

Plan on an oil change every 3,000 or three months, whichever comes first. This will ensure clean oil that is still doing its job of cleaning the engine, cooling its friction-prone metal parts, and keeping them slick as they move past each other. This 3,000-mile oil change is the basis for excellent car maintenance.

FACT

The entire basic maintenance schedule is designed around the 3,000-mile oil-change interval, because nothing is more important to your car's health than clean oil. Plan to keep up with oil maintenance, and all of the rest of the schedule will fall into place.

Basic Antifreeze/Coolant Maintenance

The cooling system of an automobile has numerous places where leaks can develop. Small leaks may be undetectable, happening only when the car is being driven. Large leaks can be disastrous. There are no guarantees that you can prevent all cooling system problems by a periodic check, but just like eating right and exercising, it improves the chances.

With Every Oil Check, Eyeball the Coolant Reservoir

Don't forget, with every fill-up you are already going to open the hood and check your oil. So take a five-second glance at the coolant reservoir. Will it tell you everything you need to know about your cooling system? No, but noticing the varying level of the coolant will tell you that the system is circulating the vital fluid. If you take off the reservoir cap for a closer inspection, you will surely notice unusual changes in coolant color or condition.

No liquid in the reservoir may indicate a small leak that you could not have noticed otherwise. If the reservoir is dry, replenish the reservoir with the right mixture (the owner's manual will tell you) and check the container daily for the next few days. Should the reservoir go dry again, you have a leak that needs attention. If you suspect a leak, don't wait for your next oil change to do what follows, do it now.

With Every Oil Change, Look in the Radiator

If everything seems to be fine with the cooling system, and the coolant reservoir level fluctuates but never remains dry for even a whole day, twist off the radiator cap or request that your mechanic do it when you change the oil, every 3,000 miles or every three months, whichever comes first.

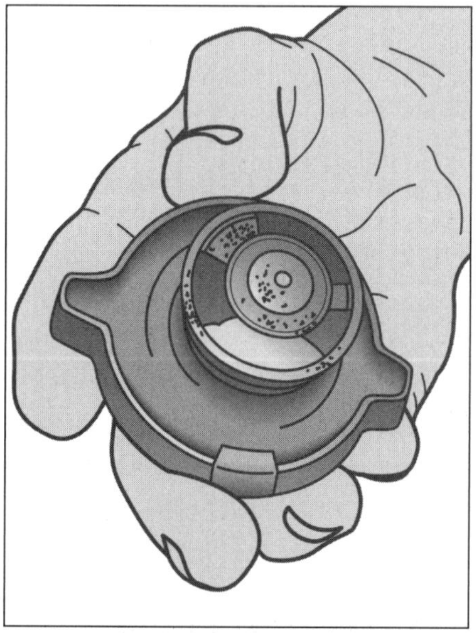

FIGURE 19-1: A worn radiator cap

Checking only the reservoir, that sight check conducted with every fill-up, can be deceptive. It is possible to have a full reservoir and still be losing coolant. If the radiator cap has grown weak, unable to contain the amount of pressure for which it was designed, coolant may be leaking from the system, but the system lacks the ability to draw from its reserve tank. Periodic checks of the radiator itself are a must. (See **FIGURE 19-1**.)

It is always safer to remove the cap when the engine is cool. That fluid is hotter than boiling water and under pressure when the engine is warm. Twisting open the cap just after an engine has been running can be dangerous. If removing the cap must be done while the engine is hot, place a handful of rags over the cap, press down on the cap to control the release of pressure, keep your face and body away from the mouth of the radiator, and twist it open slowly.

> Replacement radiator caps available at parts stores have a pressure relief valve built in. This allows you or your mechanic to more safely open the cap when the engine is hot. Just flip open the valve and all the pressure escapes in a few seconds.

At the first hiss, stop turning, keep downward force on the cap, wait for the hiss to stop, and twist slowly again; each time apply downward pressure and wait for the hiss to cease before proceeding. When there is no more hiss, take the cap off. Be careful. With all that heat, liquid may still surge upward and out of the radiator. This surging effect is more likely to happen if the radiator coolant has been allowed to drop too low. With the cap off, check the fluid level. If the fluid level is below the neck of the radiator, the car's cooling system has a leak.

FIGURE 19-2: Radiator neck

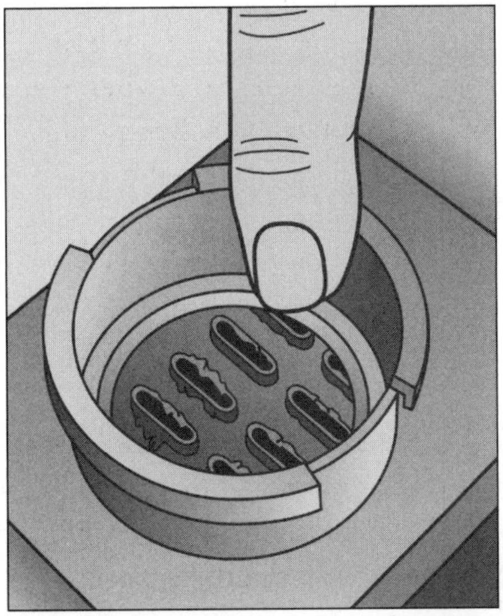

If you have never checked under the hood of a car until now, you may not know what the neck of the radiator is. Relax. The very top circle on which the radiator cap rests is the mouth of the radiator. The neck (see **FIGURE 19-2**) is that approximately half-inch circular extension between the mouth of the radiator and a second, slightly smaller circle, called the throat. The coolant should come to the top of the throat.

Basic Braking System Maintenance

There are a lot of components to the brake system. All of them are reliable most of the time. The quickest and easiest way to monitor the brake system's health is to keep an eye on the brake fluid.

Parts of the braking system are subject to corrosion. The main brake line, for example is made of steel. Improper maintenance, and sometimes even proper maintenance, allows for corrosion to wear at the line over a period of time, making a pinhole leak possible. Or the metal line moves beneath the car to where it rubs against the body of the car, and eventually a leak will develop. The rubber hydraulic hoses may develop cracks, permitting fluid to seep.

To check these parts of the system directly will require some very close inspection and more time. But a check of the brake fluid itself is a quick reliable indicator of the system's current health and safety. "Current" is the key word. At the moment of its checking, the brake fluid will help tell the status of the system, but it won't tell you that the old brake lines or the worn brake shoes are about to fail. But if monitored with each fill-up, adding another four or five seconds under the hood, you will be able to prevent many problems before they can occur.

Pay Attention to the Level of the Brake Fluid

There is a line on the translucent cylinder containing brake fluid indicating "full." Brake fluid will not evaporate. Therefore, any drop in the level of the brake fluid is a telltale sign of something going on with the system.

There are two reasons the brake-fluid level might drop. The first reason is a leak, and the longer you own your car, the more likely a leak will develop. The second reason for a drop in brake fluid is that the brake pads are wearing. Every time you apply the brakes and the pad squeezes down on the disk, the pad is wearing away minute amounts of itself. That means that with each braking application, a little more brake fluid is required to mash the brake with the identical effect.

Since you are going to be keeping up with basic maintenance from now on, you will probably know if the drop in fluid is from a leak or from normal wear of brake pads. How will you know? Because over time, as you rotate your tires, you are going to ask the technician to check the brake pads for wear and to look at your car's brake lines while the car is on the rack, checking for corrosion and leaks.

E ALERT!

If you own a car with drum brakes rather than disk brakes, the level of brake fluid in the master cylinder will not decrease as the brakes wear. Drum brakes are self-adjusting: The brakes adjust themselves so that no additional fluid is required to apply the same pressure to stop the car.

Pay Attention to the Brake Fluid's Color

Brake fluid darkens for two reasons: contamination and moisture. The chances are high that even dark brake fluid will stop your car with almost the same efficiency as fresh brake fluid, unless you are being extremely hard on the brakes. In that case, dark brake fluid may boil from the heat, and stopping will not be as swift: You will be mashing the brake pedal to the floor.

Moisture also leads to corrosion of some of the metallic parts, meaning there will be a more expensive repair job ahead once the brake calipers begin to stick.

When the brake fluid turns from clear to dark, change it. Don't rush. It isn't an emergency, but make sure you get it done.

Look at Battery Cables and Connections

Most batteries sold today are maintenance-free. They are designed to trap the moisture attempting to escape from the cells and return it. It works. On maintenance-free batteries, there is no reason to open the top and look into the cells, ever.

But they aren't maintenance-free on the outside. Every time the hood is open, look for corrosion at the connection points where terminals and cables come together. About the only drawback to the maintenance-free battery is that by capturing moisture and returning it to the cells where it belongs, more hydrogen gas escapes undiluted. Hydrogen gas is both explosive and corrosive. Look for white to whitish green deposits on the battery cables.

Corrosion is a more significant problem in today's automobiles than it was in the past. There are far more electrical systems on cars today. The computer makes many ongoing adjustments to the engine to keep it performing at an optimal level, adjustments that in the past required a variety of tools and a human hand. It used to be that corrosion would eventually prevent a car from getting enough electrical energy from the battery to start. That still happens, but a drop in voltage from the battery or from the alternator due to corrosion will also affect the computer's function and your automobile's performance.

Corrosion can also be an indicator of alternator or voltage regulator problems. If the battery is getting overcharged, corrosion will continue to reappear. Eradicate it. But get the alternator and regulator tested, too.

Note: You can draw a line right here in the chapter. Everything before this line can (and should) be checked with each fill-up. And with the exception of the rare to occasional need to remove the radiator cap, all of this fill-up maintenance can be done in fewer than five minutes a week. How much easier can car care get?

FACT

Just because a system or part needs less than weekly notice doesn't mean that a check of the system isn't important. It just means that from week to week, you are less likely to notice any changes. But these basic items simply need less frequent attention.

Power-Steering and Transmission Fluids

Unlike the level of brake fluid, there is no reason for either the power-steering fluid or the transmission fluid level to decrease under normal usage. When you check these fluid levels, which should be done each time you get your oil changed, check to see if either is lower than full. If you notice a drop in the fluid levels, there is a leak in the system. However, the probability is good with both of these systems that you won't have to worry about a leak for tens of thousands of miles. That's one reason these systems need no more frequent checking; unless, of course, you spot a drip on the driveway (see Chapter 8).

With the transmission, there is another good reason to check it at least every oil change, looking for changes in the color or smell of the fluid. Transmission fluid like the oil is working in extremes of heat and under pressure. If you are using your car to tow heavy loads, and in this case, towing means carrying heavy loads even in the trunk; or if you drive like a maniac, putting your transmission through its paces at every opportunity, your transmission fluid will—not may, will—break down and need to be replaced more frequently than normal. Ignoring the need to replace the fluid when the signs indicate the need is a sure way to a transmission replacement job. Enough said.

Basic Tire Maintenance

Tires received their own special treatment earlier in the book, but as a basic maintenance item, there are a few extra things to remember. Tire pressure will vary with temperature. Rotation is vital to long tire life and provides an extra measure of safety by putting the technician's eyes close to the brake system as well as to the tires on a regular interval.

Rotate Your Tires Every Two Oil Changes

The manual likely will say every 7,500 miles. That's fine—but hard to remember. The important thing to keep in mind is to rotate tires at regular intervals. Every other oil change makes convenient sense.

Besides, if you have ever watched an oil change, the technician raises the car, places a giant funnel beneath the oil pan to catch the used oil, removes the drain plug, and goes off to do other chores while the oil drains completely. It saves time to have your technician rotating tires while the oil drains. If this is the place where you purchased your tires, too, your mechanic will thank you for coupling these two projects. After all, your tire rotation is free, or dirt cheap, too inexpensive to generate a buck off the service.

If you are rotating four tires rather than five, have the mechanic check the pressure in the spare tire, too.

> Rotation is a must on every car for long tire life. But on front-wheel-drive cars, rotation is extra vital. Front-wheel-drive cars make double demands on front tires: pulling and steering. If you don't rotate, a car can easily wear out its front tires in 30,000 miles.

Check Your Tire Pressure Twice a Year

Check your tire pressure when the outside temperature gets hot, and be sure to check it again when the outside temperature gets cold. That may not be very specific, but the advice is specific enough. If you live in Atlanta, temperatures get plenty warm in April. If you live in Minneapolis, you can wait a couple of months.

Always check tire pressure when the tires are cold. Yes, you can drive a few miles without warming them up. Inflate the tires so that the pressure reading on the gauge corresponds with the printed tire specifications found either in the owner's manual or on the tire placard on the driver's side door jam (or on the door).

Tire pressure will expand some once the tires warm up. Don't "chase" the proper pressure. Tires will tolerate a variance without becoming overinflated. Just establish your "cold" pressure standard twice a year and don't worry about it.

ALERT!

Low tire pressure ruins tires and gas mileage. If a tire has lost pressure, have a technician look for a leak. If a leak cannot be found—no puncture in the tread, and the sidewall appears in good shape—check the tire again in a week or so.

Check Tread Depth When You Check Tire Pressure

You shouldn't need to check tread depth any more often than this. The technician who rotates your tires will notice wear patterns and tread depth, too. Checking it yourself is merely an extra level of safety. Besides, it is too easy and quick not to do. So grab a penny, and go stand President Lincoln on his head (see Chapter 4).

Check the Air Filter at Every Tire Rotation

The air filter does only one job: It filters the air going into the engine (see **FIGURE 19-3**). As the filter gets dirty, the engine loses air flow.

The engine has to pull harder to get the air it needs, and the car loses gas mileage.

The owner's manual will probably say to change your air filter every 20,000 miles. If you don't live in a dusty climate or a smoggy one, that interval will work. But if your area is suffering through a drought, if traffic is extremely heavy, or if you live near a densely industrialized area, you may need to change your car's air filter more frequently.

You can check the filter yourself, or have your mechanic do it for you. The air filter—usually white or light-cream colored when new—will look a bit dirty before it loses its efficiency. Pull it from its holder (called a breather housing). If you can tap it against a hard surface and it releases dust, it is dirty. Change it.

FIGURE 19-3: Car engine

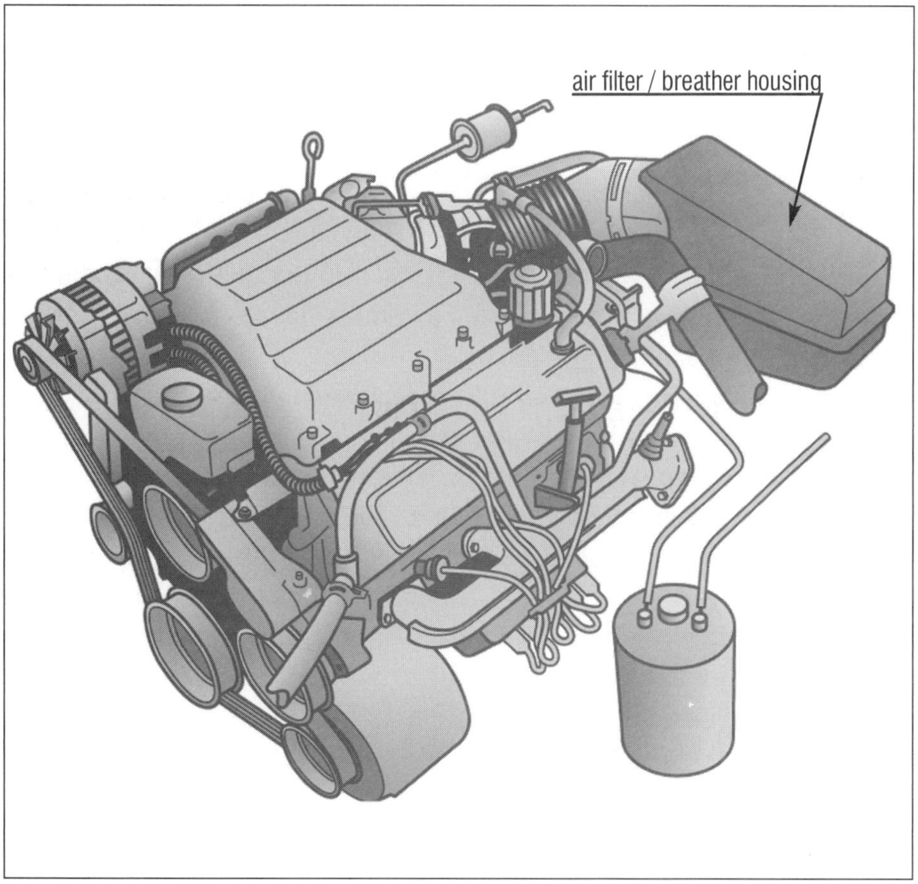

When you change the air filter, change the crankcase filter, too. They both do the same kinds of jobs, cleaning intake air. When you observe that the air filter is dirty, without taking time to check, you know the crankcase filter is dirty, too.

Change Transmission Fluid Every 50,000 Miles

An automobile's transmission is designed to last the life of the car. To prolong that life, change the fluid at 50,000 miles or at two years, whichever comes first.

"Whichever comes first" is a catch phrase we all know. The reason for it in this case is that once transmission fluid (or motor oil, for that matter) is assaulted by the heat and pressure of the system, it begins to break down. Be sure to change the transmission filter at the same time.

Change Brake Pads with Transmission Fluid Change

Will they need it? Maybe, maybe not. But chances are that if you have been rough on your car's transmission, the brakes have worked hard, too.

There is a no-brainer way to decide when to change brake pads. Most brake pads available for purchase today are designed with an audible warning device built in. The device is simple. It has a piece of sheet metal at the end of the pad. The metal extends one to two thirty-seconds from the brake pad backing. When the brake pad wears to within that one or two thirty-second distance from the backing, the protruding piece of metal squeaks or chirps its warning: The brake pad is still good for a few hundred miles, but get it replaced now. The noise it makes is similar to a fingernail on a chalkboard. It is the sound of that piece of metal scraping against the wheel rotor. When the device first starts contacting the rotor, you'll hear the noise while traveling down the road, even when the brakes are not deployed. Touch your brakes and the noise will go away. But within a few hundred miles, you'll begin to hear the screech or whistle every time you mash on the brake pedal. When you hear the noise, change the pads.

Three Additional Steps of Transmission Service

With each transmission service (every 50,000 miles), also do the following maintenance:

- Change the rear differential and transaxle lubricant. Have wheel bearings cleaned, repacked, and adjusted. Note that most front-wheel-drive cars use permanently sealed bearings, so wheel-bearing service on these vehicles is not required.
- Change the fuel filter.
- Change the fan belts, drive belts, accessory belts, and timing belts.

FACT

On most cars, a major tune-up is a more expensive tune-up than ever. But these days, cars are capable of going unbelievably long before requiring one—up to 100,000 miles—so the cost isn't too bad. And there's not a chance you can do a tune-up at home, not on late-model cars. At 100,000 miles, have the mechanic put in a new PCV (positive crankcase ventilation) valve, too. The valve removes fumes from the crankcase and eliminates crankcase pressure.

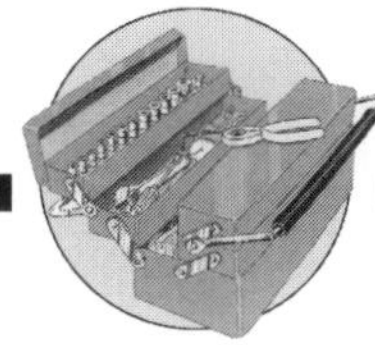

Chapter 20

Finding the Right Mechanic

Finding the right mechanic is a lot like finding the right family doctor: You want one who makes you feel confident, understands what you mean when you describe symptoms, asks the right questions, listens carefully, and respects you. Here is how you can find the right mechanic.

Finding the Right General Mechanic

Unless you have a major auto emergency requiring a specialist—the transmission has just fallen off your car and onto your driveway—finding the right general mechanic is always the place to begin.

Go to a mechanic's shop to have your oil changed. Instead of heading directly to a quick oil lube shop, make an appointment with a repair shop. And you probably will have to make an appointment with a mechanic as opposed to simply driving in and expecting instant lube service.

By going to a repair shop, you will have time to get a feel for the place, hear and observe how other customers are treated, and see how the mechanics go about their jobs. Are their respective service bays orderly? Do they call over another mechanic occasionally for a consultation or a helping hand? Is there a supervisor who checks periodically on the progress of particular jobs?

Do you notice any horsing around? An occasional playful moment is one thing, but if the atmosphere of workplace discipline doesn't return to the service bays quickly, it does give you cause to wonder about their efficiency and your precious time.

Once your car is in place for oil service, ask if you can go in and inspect under your car. Some repair shops have strict policies against letting customers into the work area, while others are more lenient. Neither approach is good or bad, but remember, you are looking for a shop that makes you feel comfortable.

FACT

If the repair shop lets you in to speak to the mechanic working on your car, carry out your task, thank the mechanic, and return to the waiting area. A good mechanic is proud of the work he or she does, but no mechanic likes a hovering car owner who questions every move and notices every slip of the wrench.

If the person at the customer-service desk informs you of a policy against allowing customers into the work area and then asks you if there is some particular concern you want checked out, you can always come up with the usual list: "Could you have the mechanic look for oil leaks, transmission leaks, and holes in the exhaust system? I don't think there are any, it's just that I'm in the habit of checking them out myself at each oil change." Then watch to see if your request is carried out.

Looking for Certificates of Certification—Not Great Coffee

It is true that a nice, comfortable waiting area can be an indication of a great repair shop, but the two do not necessarily go together. You are looking for the quality of the mechanics who will be working on your car, your pride and joy, not the great coffee or the magazine selection or even the comfort of the waiting area. However, most good shops will make certain that their waiting areas, no matter how modest, are reasonably clean. Do expect a certain amount of cleanliness to be a sign of respect and interest in customer satisfaction.

While you wait, look around for mechanics' certifications: current, up-to-date certificates. It's no longer a comfort to see that a mechanic earned a certain certification decades ago. Automotive technology has evolved at a very rapid rate, meaning that mechanics are required to study to keep up. Current certifications and mechanics who take pride in keeping up with automotive innovations through continuing education are keys to excellent service for your car.

Look for ASE certifications from the National Institute for Automotive Service Excellence. You'll want to look in two places, both fairly obvious. Look on the walls; any certificates on the walls will have the name of the mechanic and his particular certification. And look for shoulder patches; a mechanic qualified in a single specialty will wear this patch: ASE Certified Automobile Technician.

Some shops have their mechanics trained in specific specialties to fill a void in the shop's ability to serve its customers. But just because a mechanic is certified in a certain specialty doesn't make him a great mechanic. And some very good mechanics are not certified. Still, most shops insist on getting mechanics to attain certifications and retrain periodically.

> Shops aren't certified, mechanics are. A mechanic certified in brakes may not be the best choice to do a heating and air-conditioning job. However, a shop run by an ASE Certified Master Technician (a mechanic certified in all eight specialty categories) will usually do a good job no matter which technician works on your car.

Evaluating a Mechanic's Listening Skills

How a mechanic behaves when a customer is describing a car's symptoms is equivalent to a physician's bedside manner. Does the mechanic listen? And when the customer gets stuck, unable to employ the right automotive vocabulary to describe what the car is doing, does the mechanic ask questions that further the diagnostic process?

Some shops immediately want to run diagnostics tests on every automobile brought in to the shop. Sometimes that best suits the customer, making the client feel more secure about what work will be done as a result of the testing. But testing is an added expense. If a mechanic feels that testing is necessary, trust him or her. But be concerned if the shop runs diagnostics tests for nearly every problem, every time.

With the right combination of listening and leading questions, many mechanics often can guide you to help them diagnose a problem without the added expense of a test. After you have led a mechanic as far as you can with a description of the noise your car is making or the way the car "feels" when you accelerate or shift gears, a good mechanic will often surprise you with his questions. Sometimes it is almost as if the mechanic is reading your mind. That is a good sign that he's not only heard someone other than you describe similar symptoms, but that he listens carefully to his customers and has kept up with service bulletins on your make and model.

Estimating the Cost of Repairs

Any reliable repair shop will extend to its customers the courtesy of a written estimate in advance of work to be done. However, there are exceptions. If you have found a good repair shop and have established a good relationship of trust over time, a written estimate may not be necessary. In cities, the written estimate in advance of work may be required by the shop or the chain for its own protection against unscrupulous customers, but in small communities, where people know each other, neither party may consider it necessary after each has gotten to know the other.

Communication is the key. Expect a written estimate, or request one if you believe it is necessary. And never say to the repair shop manager—unless you absolutely mean it—"just fix whatever you find wrong." Unless you know each other well, such a blanket request will make the manager anxious, not knowing whether the shop has done too little or too much.

Considering Dealership, Independent, and Chain Repair Shops

Just as some fine mechanics are not certified (but most are) and some poor mechanics are certified (but most aren't), going to any particular type of repair shop is no guarantee that the work will be done to your satisfaction. People are often of divergent opinions on which type of repair shop will give them the best work for their dollar. Most opinions come from anecdotal evidence. You will hear how some people always go to a dealership for repair work and have never had any complaints, and you will hear about others who believe that the same shop cheated them, and they'll never take their car there again.

ALERT!

Most car repair jobs call for a general practitioner, but one who won't hesitate to send you to a specialist when your car needs it. After all, your mechanic wants your trust and your repeat business. When you need good advice on a specialist, ask your mechanic to suggest the best place to send your car.

Remember, you are looking for the right mechanic. At first glance, chain repair shops many seem mostly identical from one shop to the next, but every mechanic will be different in terms of experience, training, and personality. There are plenty of good mechanics out there working at all types of shops. All you want to do is find the right one, or the right shop, that best takes care of your needs.

Helping Your Mechanic Understand Your Problem

Once you have found the right shop and the right mechanic to help you keep your car operating as it should, do not assume that your task is over. The mechanic you have found (and appreciate) is not a mind reader. You'll need to work with your mechanic to keep your car in optimal working order.

How can you avoid shady mechanics?
Before your car needs major work, talk to friends, coworkers, and neighbors about their positive auto-repair experiences. If someone you trust has a regular mechanic, go there for an oil change or other maintenance, and be sure to mention why you chose that shop when you take your car in.

Learning the Jargon

Much of what you learn in this book will come in handy, but don't try to bluff the mechanic into believing that you know more than you really do. Either the bluff will work and you may never understand much of the shop talk your mechanic will use, or you'll quickly give yourself away, and the mechanic will be uncertain whether to talk down to you and maybe embarrass you, or keep up the charade, knowing that you don't understand what he's talking about.

Try to learn at least one new thing every time you take the car to the shop. Ask questions. Never be afraid to say, "I don't understand," or "Could you explain that again?" Once a thing is explained, restate it in your own words and ask the mechanic if you've got it right. You will learn more about your car, and your mechanic will appreciate the effort.

Describe Without Instructing

When mechanics "talk shop," they'll often tell stories about their worst customers. Like the customer who enters the repair shop, announces to the mechanic or the service manager that the front end wobbles, and then orders the shop to perform a front-end alignment. Such customers have a way of making it clear that they don't want a dialogue with a service technician; they already have the right answer, and no other service will be acceptable. Then when the alignment job doesn't fix the wobble, the customer returns and angrily speaks so that all in the waiting area can hear about what rip-off artists the shop has for mechanics, or what lousy technicians. If, from the beginning, the customer had simply described the problem, answered the service manager's questions, and worked with the shop as though a member of the team, the problem might have been solved. And by the way, wobbles don't come from alignment problems.

FACT

To do the best job on your car, mechanics need your help. Good descriptions of the problem and recollections of similar problems in the past with the same vehicle will help the mechanic eliminate some possible sources of a problem, and permit him to spend more time (and less of your money) targeting the most likely causes.

Dealing with Unresolved Problems

Here's another manner in which physicians and mechanics are alike: Never has one lived who fixed every problem correctly, certainly not the first time. Sometimes the reasons for a customer's unresolved car problem center on the customer, and sometimes the mechanic has just plain missed something.

When a problem isn't resolved, forcing you to return to the shop, speak discreetly to the mechanic or to the service manager. Anger and volume will not speed the resolution. The shop doesn't want your car staying around the shop any more than you do. When you speak, use words and a tone that says "we" have a problem. The shop will appreciate you not embarrassing its personnel by broadcasting its failure, and the use of "we" places the customer and the shop on the same team.

Reviewing the problem together, you may discover that:

A. Something was left out of your description of the problem.
B. Another problem you didn't notice previously with similar symptoms (noises, smoke, etc.) was discovered and remedied.
C. The problem corrected was more serious and the mechanic assumed without malicious intent that that was what you wanted to be fixed.
D. The mechanic truly goofed.

In most cases when you have allowed the repair shop to work with you to resolve a problem that wasn't fixed, the shop will do what it can to help you leave satisfied. It has no reason to want any other resolution of the situation. Repair shop personnel understand that when the customer is made happy by their extra efforts, they have a second chance at good word-of-mouth publicity.

If the repair is too expensive, ask about a less-expensive remedy, especially if you think you'll be selling your car soon. You can also get a second opinion at another shop, either by explaining your intentions to your mechanic and asking for the name of another reputable mechanic or by seeking out another mechanic on your own. You can also ask around the neighborhood for a good recommendation.

Developing a Strategy for Vacation Repairs

Put this on your list of life's unpleasant moments. En route to your vacation destination, your car quits. Now what? First, put the whole experience into perspective. It could be worse. If it were 150 years ago, it could have been the wheel falling off your prairie schooner out under the big Montana sky.

The American driver has resources at her disposal as never before: the cell phone and 911 service, state patrol vehicles constantly cruising, auto clubs with helpful numbers to call for roadside assistance, perhaps even towing services free or at reduced rates. Getting off the highway and to a repair shop may be a hassle and may be time-consuming, but it is not too difficult. But locating the right repair shop can be. Certainly you can be towed directly to the repair shop affiliated with the local towing service. But remember the pains you have already taken to find the right mechanic at home. Do you really want to be at some stranger's mercy, someone you will never see again who can treat you and charge you any way and any amount without much fear of repercussion?

The flip side, of course, is that the towing service may be connected with the finest repair shop in the Florida Panhandle or with the best independent mechanic in all of the wine country of California. But you can't possibly know that.

If you are a member of an auto club, you may find some help locating a repair shop through them. Or try the following resources:

- Ask the state patrol officer who stops when your car breaks down where the patrol gets its cars repaired.
- Ask the officer to contact the local sheriff's office or police station for a recommendation.
- Call the local branch of your auto insurance company.
- Contact the local chamber of commerce and ask the person on the other end of the line where she gets her car worked on. Ask if she'll contact the garage to tell them you are coming in. (This makes the repair shop personnel feel good that someone has recommended their services, and they'll be on their game to please both you and the person who thought so highly of them.)
- Call a large local church. Larger churches are apt to be staffed full-time. The church secretary may know of a good place, whereas the chamber of commerce may feel an obligation to be diplomatic and spread traveler misfortune around.

ALERT!

Never underestimate the power of a personal introduction. When a regular customer of a repair shop is willing to make the initial contact for you, the shop will extend to you the same courtesy it would extend to the regular customer.

Taking Care of Your Favorite Mechanic

If you live in a small community, you probably know your mechanic personally or know some of the members of the mechanic's family. If you live in a metro area, you probably won't know anything about him except that he works at the garage you patronize.

In a small town, the mechanic probably knows you, while in a city, the mechanic will get to know your car inside and out but may never be certain of your name. In either case, the same rules apply to cultivating or keeping a beneficial relationship.

Remembering to Say "Thank You"

Okay, so you're in the habit of saying "thanks" all the time. Fine. But when your mechanic has taken care of your car's problem and you truly feel grateful for the speed at which the problem was resolved or for the advice given or for the careful notice that prevented some larger problem, go back and thank your mechanic. Or if the repair shop usually keeps customers away from its mechanics—after all, time is money—pick a time when the shop seems busy to walk in and express your thanks in a conversational voice that other customers are sure to hear. Most of the time the only thing the shop hears after the money has changed hands is the complaint, hardly ever the good stuff.

If you live in a metro area, don't let more than a few days pass before returning. Bring your receipt, including the work done on your car. Stride up to the service desk, identifying yourself by name and by the car you had worked on, at the same time offering the receipt, and tell them how much you appreciate the service you received. Really, in a busy metro shop, the service manager and your mechanic are just as likely to remember the parts replaced on your car and the type of car worked on as they are to remember your face. Your name is a distant third. Even in a busy shop, sometimes you'll get to speak to the mechanic. The service manager may call him out of his service bay just so he can bask in the praise for a moment.

You've made the mechanic's day, you've made the service manager happy, and you've banked some goodwill.

FACT

Don't carry praise to excess, but always remember that people who do good things for you, even though they're paid to do them, deserve to be thanked. Going into the shop is a great way to show your appreciation. So is a short three-line note, identifying your car and the good work done. Notes like this are sometimes pinned to the wall for everyone to read.

Referring Friends to Your Repair Shop

If you are really sold on the place where you take your car for repairs, recommend it to your friends. If the need for repair is immediate and you've convinced your friend that the shop where you take your car is the best place in town, attach your name to the recommendation. Call the shop, identify yourself and the car you've had the shop work on, and tell them you are sending a friend to them. Describe the car, perhaps offering a clue as to what needs to be fixed.

The shop will appreciate the new business, and since you're a satisfied customer, they'll take pains to satisfy your friend.

Keeping the Relationship Beneficial

If you are the kind of person who keeps all your relationships in proper order, knowing where the boundaries are, always honoring them, skip this section. But if you have occasionally found yourself at fault for straining a relationship, check out the following suggestions.

- Refrain from borrowing tools from your mechanic: They're not cheap. A mechanic you've come to know and trust will have a tough time saying "no," so don't put the person who keeps your car's engine purring in that predicament.
- Keep good records of repair and service work: Keeping these records makes it easy for you to discuss a faulty repair or a replacement part that has failed while still under warranty.
- Work through complaints: Be objective. Listen as much as you speak. Give the shop a chance to please you and give them another chance to please you if the first attempt fails.

Perhaps the easiest place to store a particular car's repair and service records is in the glove box. Purchase a zippered pouch about the size of a number-ten envelope and make it a habit to stash every itemized list of the work done on your car, along with the receipt for payment, in that pouch.

APPENDIX A

Glossary of Automotive Terms

This appendix helps you communicate with other do-it-yourselfers and with your mechanic. Memorize these terms, and you'll sound like a car-fixing guru in no time!

A

accelerator: The gas pedal.

additive: Solution usually added to the gasoline or motor oil to improve certain characteristics of the original product, such as the antiknock qualities of gasoline or the lubrication capacity of the oil.

advance the timing: To alter the timing of the spark from the spark plug so that it occurs earlier in the firing stroke.

air cleaner: Device designed to remove dust and other contaminants from the air before it is drawn into the engine.

air filter: See *Air cleaner.*

air-fuel ratio: Mixture of air and gasoline that makes its way into the engine.

alternator: Device that produces AC (alternating current) and supplies the automobile with energy for its electrical systems while the engine is running. The current must be rectified (changed into DC) for use, but an alternator will generate more power than a DC-producing generator.

ammeter: Instrument used to measure electrical current in amperes.

ampere: Unit for measuring the level of current in a circuit.

antifreeze: (1) Another name for the coolant in the radiator. (2) The additive in the coolant that prevents its freezing in winter.

antiknock: Gasoline additives that improve the fuel's resistance to preignition detonation.

API: American Petroleum Institute. Symbol used on a can of motor oil in conjunction with the rating of that oil.

aspect ratio: Ratio between height and width of a tire. Higher-aspect ratio tires yield softer rides; tires with lower-aspect ratio are geared toward performance.

atomize: To break a liquid into minute particles. Fuel injectors atomize gasoline for more efficient burning.

automatic transmission: A transmission that shifts gears automatically based on speed, load, and other factors.

axle: Drives rear wheels.

B

backfire: Fuel explosion caused either by faulty timing or by the passage of unburned fuel into the exhaust system, where it explodes.

backup lights: White lights on the rear of a vehicle that come on when the transmission is put in reverse.

balance: Technique of evening out the weight of wheel and tire assembly for a smooth ride. Modern tires usually need balancing only twice, when purchased and at first tire rotation.

battery: Device that releases electrical energy on demand through a chemical reaction.

battery capacity: Determined by plate size and number, and the composition of the electrolyte, the rating of current output.

battery charging: Process of restoring electrical energy to the battery by reversing the chemical process that released the energy.

battery, maintenance-free: Practically every battery sold today. Designed to need no additional electrolyte during the battery's service life.

battery, reserve capacity rating: Measures the number of minutes a fully charged battery can discharge 25 amperes at 80 degrees Fahrenheit and maintain at least 10.5 volts (1.75 per cell).

battery shedding: Natural process of losing plate materials from the battery with discharge. Materials settle in the bottom of the battery case, and after several years of usage will short out the battery.

battery voltage: Number of battery cells times two. All car batteries today are 12 volt.

bearing: The contact surface of a moving part.

bearing clearance: Space between moving parts into which oil is forced for lubrication.

bleeding: Removing air from a closed system.

bleeding the brakes: Removing air from the brake system by opening bleeder screws found at each wheel cylinder.

block: As in engine block, the part of the engine that contains the cylinders.

blow-by: Escape of exhaust gases by the piston rings.

body putty: Material designed to smooth and fill out dented areas. Once hard, it is sanded to proper contour and painted.

brake backing plate: Rigid steel plate to which brake shoes are attached.

brake band: Band that encircles a brake drum, most often found on the parking brake in late-model cars.

brake (disk): Brake system employing a steel disk seated between a pair of brake shoes (pads). When the brakes are used, the shoes press in on either side of the steel disk.

brake (drum): Brake system employing cast-iron or aluminum housing that rotates around the brake shoes. When the brakes are used, the shoes rub against the inner surface of the drum.

brake fluid: The fluid used in hydraulic braking systems.

brake line: Steel tubing that delivers brake fluid under pressure from the master cylinder to the wheel cylinders.

brake lining: The material of the brake shoes that presses against the moving surface to slow and to stop.

brake (power): Brake system that uses vacuum pressure to reduce the force a driver must exert to stop the vehicle.

brake shoes: Part of the brake system to which the brake lining is attached.

butterfly valve: Used in carburetors, the device by which fuel was once injected into the cylinders of every engine, named because of its resemblance to a butterfly.

C

caliper (brake): Part of the braking system to which the shoes are attached and produces the pinching action on the disk.

cam: Teardrop-shaped parts of the camshaft that, when turned, raise valves, allowing fuel and air into the cylinder or exhaust gases out.

camshaft: Shaft with cam lobes that open the valves.

carbon: Black deposits found on plugs, in cylinders, under piston rings, and on valve heads that can cause predetonation.

carburetor: Forerunner of the fuel injector, used to mix fuel and air.

catalytic converter: Part of the exhaust system designed to reduce toxic emissions.

cell: Each separate 2-volt compartment in a battery containing positive and negative plates suspended in electrolyte.

charcoal canister: Emission-control device that stores gasoline vapors from the gas tank and releases them into the cylinders to be burned.

charge (A/C): A specific amount of refrigerant inserted into the air-conditioning system.

charge (battery): Passing electric current through the battery to restore it.

chassis: Every part of the car but the body and fenders, includes among other parts, the frame, engine, springs, and axles.

circuit: Resistance unit and wires that form a path for electrical current from the battery or alternator through an electrical part (horn, radio, etc.) and back to the source.

circuit breaker: Protective device in some circuits designed to break flow of excessive current.

clearance: Amount of space between two parts.

cold cranking rating: Measurement of the amperes that a battery can deliver for thirty seconds at 0 degrees Fahrenheit and maintain a minimum voltage of 7.2.

combustion: The process of burning the fuel and air mixture in a cylinder.

compression: Reducing the volume of the fuel and air mixture to increase the power of the burn (explosion).

compression check: Test run on the cylinders to determine the condition of valves, rings, and cylinders.

compression stroke: The upward movement of the piston through the cylinder to compress the fuel and air mixture.

compressor: Air-conditioning device that causes refrigerant to flow through the system.

condensation: Moisture deposited on a cool surface.

condenser: Air-conditioning device that cools refrigerant and turns it from a vapor to liquid.

coolant: Liquid in the cooling system.

cooling system: System that maintains engine temperature in optimal range and prevents overheating.

corrode: Dislodging of surface metal by chemical action.

crankcase: Part of the engine encasing the crankshaft.

crankshaft: Shaft running the length of the engine.

cylinder: A hole in the engine block that contains a piston.

cylinder head: Metal section bolted to the top of the block, often containing valves.

D

dash: Short for dashboard, part of the car's interior containing the instruments.

detergent: Additive to oil to improve certain characteristics.

detonation: Fuel burning (too) explosively.

diesel engine: Engine that uses diesel fuel instead of gasoline, and uses compression rather than spark to ignite fuel.

differential: Unit that drives both rear axles while allowing them to turn at different speeds in a turn.

dipstick: Metal rod that passes into an engine fluid requiring measurement.

drive train: All parts that generate power and transmit it to the wheels in the center of the tires.

E

EGR valve: Exhaust gas recirculation valve.

electrochemical: Chemical production of electricity; the method by which a car battery produces electricity.

electrolyte: Battery solution of water and sulfuric acid.

electronic fuel injection: Most common means of fuel control, involves injector, sensors, and onboard computer.

emissions: By-products of combustion, including water vapor, carbon monoxide, and nitrogen, among others.

engine mounts: Pads made of metal and rubber that hold the engine to the frame.

ethylene glycol: Chemical solution added to cooling system to protect against freezing.

evaporator: Part of the air-conditioning system where cooling takes place.

exhaust pipe: Pipe directing flow of exhaust gases from the engine to the muffler.

exhaust stroke: Upward movement of piston that expels burned gases from a cylinder.

exhaust valve: Valve that allows passage of exhaust gases out of a cylinder.

F

filter: Device designed to remove impurities from air, oil, water, or fuel.

flooding: Most commonly refers to condition in which excessive fuel has reached the cylinders.

four-stroke engine: Engine requiring four strokes, two complete cycles of the crankshaft, to fire a piston once.

four-wheel drive: Vehicle in which all four wheels provide power for motion.

fuel filter: Device that removes impurities from the fuel before fuel from the tank can enter the engine.

fuel pump: Device that draws gasoline from the tank and sends it to the fuel injectors.

fuel tank: Stores gasoline; formerly made of steel, now made of plastic.

fuse: Protects electrical circuits when current exceeds capacity by burning through.

fusible link: Special wire in a circuit that behaves in a manner similar to a fuse, but with a major difference: It permits temporary amounts of excessive current required of some circuits such as power windows without burning through.

G

gasket: Material that creates a seal between two (usually metal) parts.

gear ratio: Relationship between a pair of turning parts. A ratio of 2 to 1 means one gear must turn twice to cause the other gear to turn once.

ground: Terminal of the battery connected to the metal framework of the car. The negative terminal.

H

horsepower: Measurement of an engine's ability to do work. One horsepower equals 33,000 pounds lifted one foot in one minute.

hose clamps: Metal bands used to hold hoses to their fittings.

hoses: Rubber tubes for carrying fluids.

Hp: Abbreviation for horsepower.

hydraulic: Pertaining to a fluid in motion.

hydraulic brakes: Brakes operated by hydraulic pressure.

I

ignition: In a gasoline engine, firing the fuel by means of a spark.

ignition switch: Switch on the steering column that connects and disconnects power to the ignition and other electrical systems.

ignition timing: Relationship between the moment a plug fires and the position of the piston in the cylinder.

inhibitor: Refers to a type of additive in any engine fluid designed to prevent certain actions, such as rusting.

intake stroke: Piston downward motion that draws the fuel mixture into the cylinder.

intake valve: Valve through which fuel enters the cylinder.

internal combustion engine: Engine that converts heat energy into motion.

K

knocking: (1) Bearing noise created by worn or loose bearing. (2) Also a fuel condition created when gasoline in the cylinder ignites too quickly.

L

low brake pedal: Condition where brake pedal must be pressed too close to the floor before braking becomes effective.

lubrication: Reducing friction between parts by coating them with a lubricant such as motor oil.

M

main bearings: Bearings supporting the crankshaft.

master cylinder: Part of the brake system where pressure is generated.

muffler: Device through which exhaust gases are passed, muffling (quieting) the sound emanating from the running engine.

multiviscosity oil: Oil that meets SAE requirements for low and high temperature. The flow qualities vary according to engine temperature.

N

negative terminal: Battery terminal from which current flows. Designated by (–) and the color black.

O

octane: Measure of a gasoline's ability to resist detonation. The higher the octane, the greater the resistance to detonation.

odometer: Instrument that registers the number of miles traveled by a car.

oil filter: Filter that removes impurities from the oil before returning the oil to the engine.

oil pan: Bolted to the bottom of the crankcase, it collects oil when the engine is not operating.

oil pump: Pumps oil into the engine.

overdrive: Gear set with the capacity to turn the drive shaft faster than the transmission output shaft.

overhead camshaft: Camshaft mounted above the head.

P

pinging: Rattling sound occurring during acceleration when ignition timing is too far advanced for the octane of fuel being burned.

piston: Round plug attached to a rod that slides up and down in the cylinder.

port: Openings in cylinder head through which fuel and exhaust flow, controlled by opening and closing of valves.

positive terminal: Battery terminal to which current flows. Designated by (+) and by the color red.

power plant: Engine.

power steering: Hydraulic system that increases the driver's turning effort.

power-steering pump: Produces the pressure for the power-steering system.

power (firing) stroke: Downward movement of the piston resulting from fuel ignition and transmitting power.

preignition: Fuel igniting prematurely.

pressure cap: Radiator cap designed to hold a specific amount of pressure in the cooling system, allowing the coolant to run at a higher temperature without boiling.

propeller shaft: Shaft connecting the transmission output shaft to the differential pinion shaft.

purge: To bleed the system, usually to eliminate air from a hydraulic system or from the cooling system.

R

radiator: Removes heat from engine coolant. Heat from the coolant entering the radiator is conducted through fins by air forced through by the fan or by the forward movement of the car.

radiator cap: Pressure cap that fits on the radiator, allowing coolant to operate at a higher temperature without boiling.

reciprocating action: Back-and-forth piston action.

rectifier: Changes AC to DC.

regulator: Controls voltage and current output from the alternator.

resister: Lowers voltage in a circuit and decreases flow of current.

retard: To set ignition timing so that spark ignites fuel later in the cycle.

riding the clutch: Resting one's foot on the clutch pedal while driving a car equipped with a manual transmission. Will cause the clutch to wear out faster.

RPM: Revolutions per minute.

S

SAE: Society of Automotive Engineers.

seal: Device that prevents oil from leaking around a moving part.

serpentine belt: The main belt operating most pumps in late-model cars. Has largely, though not completely, replaced the V-belt.

shimmy: Front wheels shaking side to side.

sidewall: Side of the tire, between the tread and the bead.

sludge: Thick deposits in the engine made of oil and debris churned together by moving parts.

spark plug: Ignites gasoline by creating an electrical spark between two electrodes.

starter: Electric motor that cranks the engine.

stick shift: Manual transmission with gear shifter, the "stick" rising from the floor of the car.

T

tachometer: Gauge indicating engine speed in RPM.

tailpipe: End piece of the exhaust system running from the muffler to the rear of the car.

temperature gauge: Instrument on the dash indicating temperature of engine coolant.

thermostat: Controls flow of coolant relative to temperature.

timing: Coordination between the firing of the spark plug and the position of the piston on the compression stroke.

timing belt: Toothed belt used to rotate the camshaft.

timing chain: Drive chain used to rotate the camshaft.

timing gears: The gears attached to the camshaft and to the crankshaft.

tire inflation pressure: Recommended tire pressure indicated on sidewall.

tire rotation: Moving tires on the car to even out wear.

tire tread: Part of the tire that grips the road.

torque: Turning/twisting force the engine places on the driveline.

transmission: Makes changes between engine RPM and driving wheel RPM.

V

vacuum: Sealed space in which air pressure within is less than air pressure without.

valve: Device used to open and close an opening.

vapor: Gaseous state of a substance normally occurring as a liquid or a solid.

varnish: Hard coatings inside the engine caused by motor oil breakdown.

V-belt: V-shaped belt once commonly used to spin various pumps. Has largely though not completely been replaced by the serpentine belt.

viscosity: Measure of a liquid's (oil) ability to pour.

voltage: Difference in electrical potential between the two ends of a circuit.

W

water jacket: Hollow area around the engine through which coolant flows to control temperature.

water pump: Pump that circulates coolant through the cooling system.

Appendix B

Car-Care Charts

This appendix gives you a variety of different tables to help you keep track of maintenance jobs, troubleshoot, and decide whether doing your own maintenance for certain projects is worthwhile.

VEHICLE MAINTENANCE LIST

ENGINE	DATE 1	DATE 2	DATE 3	DATE 4
Engine oil filter				
Engine oil change				

TRANSMISSION	DATE 1	DATE 2	DATE 3	DATE 4
Transmission fluid change				
Transmission fluid filter				
Rear differential/transaxle lubricant change				

CHASSIS LUBRICATION	DATE 1	DATE 2	DATE 3	DATE 4
Fluid levels check				
Wheel bearings cleaning/repacking/adjustment				

TIRES	DATE 1	DATE 2	DATE 3	DATE 4
Tire condition, including spare				
Air pressure				
Tread depth				
Wheel balance and rotation				
Vehicle alignment				

ENGINE	DATE 1	DATE 2	DATE 3	DATE 4
Performance analysis				
Spark plugs				
Air filter				
Fuel filter				
PCV valve				
Crankcase filter				
Canister filter				
Emission control system				
Exhaust analysis				

VEHICLE MAINTENANCE LIST (continued)

BRAKES	DATE 1	DATE 2	DATE 3	DATE 4
Brake system inspection				
Brake-fluid level/condition				
Brake system flush/bleed/adjustment				
Parking brake adjustment				

COOLING SYSTEM	DATE 1	DATE 2	DATE 3	DATE 4
Level/condition				
Antifreeze protection				
Pressure test				
Radiator cap				
Hoses/clamps/thermostat				
Power flush and heater operation				
Drive belts				
Fan and accessory belts				
Camshaft/timing belt				
Belt tension/adjustment				

BATTERY	DATE 1	DATE 2	DATE 3	DATE 4
Electrolyte level/condition				
Connections/cables				
Battery protection treatment				

AIR CONDITIONER	DATE 1	DATE 2	DATE 3	DATE 4
Performance test				
Discharge/evacuate/recharge				
A/C filter/dryer				
Leak test				

VEHICLE MAINTENANCE LIST (continued)

STEERING/SUSPENSION	DATE 1	DATE 2	DATE 3	DATE 4
Inspection				

EXHAUST SYSTEM	DATE 1	DATE 2	DATE 3	DATE 4
Inspect				

LIGHTING/HORN	DATE 1	DATE 2	DATE 3	DATE 4
Lamp/bulbs				
Main headlamps				
Horn operation				

WINDSHIELD	DATE 1	DATE 2	DATE 3	DATE 4
Washer level/operation				
Wiper refill/blades				
Glass				

STATE INSPECTION	DATE 1	DATE 2	DATE 3	DATE 4
Safety				
Exhaust emission				
Vehicle registration				

EASY VEHICLES FOR SELF-SERVICE OIL CHANGES

Automobile Make	Reason Changing Oil Is Easy
Cadillac Sedan DeVille	Filter location
Chevrolet Lumina	Filter location
Chevrolet S-10 Blazer	Filter located next to air filter
Dodge Intrepid	Filter location
Dodge Pickup	Filter location
Ford Pickup	Filter location
Ford Taurus	Filter location
Nissan Maxima	Filter location

DIFFICULT VEHICLES FOR SELF-SERVICE OIL CHANGES

Automobile Make	Reason Changing Oil Is Difficult
Buick Park Avenue	Certain year models have filter at rear of engine
Dodge Pickup (diesel)	Oil filter below intake
Jaguar	Filter location
Mercedes	Filter and drain plug
Nissan Pickup	Filter location
Olds Cutlass Ciera	Four-cycle models have filter in oil pan
Pontiac Grand Am	Four-cycle models have filter in oil pan

NOISE, WOBBLE, VIBRATION TROUBLESHOOTER

Type of Car	If Rear, Check:	If Front, Check:
Rear-Wheel-Drive Car		
	Tires	Tires
	Differential gear (and gear oil)	Brakes
	Brakes	Wheel bearings
	Drive shaft U-joint	
Front-Wheel-Drive Car		
	Tires	Tires
	Brakes	Wheel bearings
	Wheel bearings	C-V joint
Four-/All-Wheel Drive		
	Tires	Tires
	Brakes	Brakes
	Differential gear (and gear oil)	U-joint
	U-joint or C-V joint	C-V joint

AUTOMOBILE SMELLS TROUBLESHOOTING CHART

Smell Description	Probable Cause
Burning smell from under the hood (after driving the vehicle)	Oil leak from engine onto the exhaust system
Musty, stale odor from vents (when using A/C)	Mold and bacteria growth from evaporator core in heater box under the dash
Rotten egg/sulphur smell (when stopped at a traffic light)	Catalytic converter not functioning properly
Sweet smell inside the vehicle (floor may also be damp)	Heater core failure, leaking engine coolant inside vehicle

AUTOMOBILE SMOKE TROUBLESHOOTING CHART

Smoke Description/Location	Probable Cause
White, thick smoke from tailpipe	Engine is burning coolant from internal leak
Bluish white smoke from tailpipe	Engine is burning oil from piston rings or valve seals
Black smoke from tailpipe	Fuel system problem, too much fuel entering engine
After vehicle has warmed up, steam or smoke from under the hood	Coolant leak from the radiator or oil leak from the engine
After vehicle warms up, steam	Heater core has leak from defroster ducts, allowing hot coolant inside vehicle

Index

A

B

C

D

G

H

N

O

P

R

T

U

V

W